WITHDRAWN

P9-DOC-409

3 1611 00156 7939

THE WELFARE OF CHILDREN WITH MENTALLY ILL PARENTS

To the invisible children and their parents

MUSÉE DES BEAUX ARTS

About suffering they were never wrong,
The Old Masters: how well they understood
Its human position; how it takes place
While someone else is eating or opening a window or just
    walking dully along;
How, when the aged are reverently, passionately waiting
For the miraculous birth, there must always be
Children who did not specially want it to happen, skating
On a pond at the edge of the wood:
They never forgot
That even the dreadful martyrdom must run its course
Anyhow in a corner, in some untidy spot
Where dogs go on with their doggy life and the torturer's horse
Scratches its innocent behind on a tree.

In Brueghel's Icarus, for instance: how everything turns away
Quite leisurely from the disaster; the ploughman may
Have heard the splash, the forsaken cry,
But for him it was not an important failure; the sun shone
As it had to on the white legs disappearing into the green
Water; and the expensive delicate ship that must have seen
Something amazing, a boy falling out of the sky,
Had somewhere to get to and sailed calmly on.

(Reproduced from *Collected Poems* by W.H. Auden by
permission of the publishers, Faber & Faber Ltd.)

THE WELFARE OF CHILDREN WITH MENTALLY ILL PARENTS

Learning from Inter-Country Comparisons

Rachael Hetherington and Karen Baistow
Brunel University

Ilan Katz and Jeffrey Mesie
National Society for the Prevention of Cruelty to Children

and

Judith Trowell
Tavistock Clinic

JOHN WILEY & SONS, LTD

GOVERNORS STATE UNIVERSITY
UNIVERSITY PARK
IL 60466

Copyright © 2002 by John Wiley & Sons Ltd,
Baffins Lane, Chichester,
West Sussex PO19 1UD, England

National   01243 779777
International   (+44) 1243 779777
e-mail (for orders and customer service enquiries):
cs-books@wiley.co.uk
Visit our Home Page on http://www.wiley.co.uk
or http://www.wiley.com

All Rights Reserved. No part of this publication may be reproduced, stored in a
retrieval system, or transmitted, in any form or by any means, electronic, mechanical,
photocopying, recording, scanning or otherwise, except under the terms of the
Copyright, Designs and Patents Act 1988 or under the terms of a licence issued by the
Copyright Licensing Agency Ltd, 90 Tottenham Court Road, London W1P 0LP, UK,
without the permission in writing of the Publisher.

Other Wiley Editorial Offices

John Wiley & Sons, Inc., 605 Third Avenue,
New York, NY 10158–0012, USA

WILEY-VCH Verlag GmbH, Pappelallee 3,
D-69469 Weinheim, Germany

John Wiley & Sons Australia Ltd, 33 Park Road, Milton,
Queensland 4064, Australia

John Wiley & Sons (Asia) Pte Ltd, 2 Clementi Loop #02-01,
Jin Xing Distripark, Singapore 129809

John Wiley & Sons (Canada) Ltd, 22 Worcester Road,
Rexdale, Ontario M9W 1L1, Canada

RJ 507 .M44 W45 2002

The welfare of children wi
mentally ill parents

Library of Congress Cataloging-in-Publication Data
The welfare of children with mentally ill parents: learning from inter-country
comparisons/Rachael Hetherington ... [et al.].
        p. cm.
    Includes bibliographical references and index.
    ISBN 0-471-49724-X (cased)
        1. Children of the mentally ill—Cross-cultural studies. 2. Mental illness—Cross-cultural
studies. 3. Mentally ill—Family relationships—Cross-cultural studies. 4. Child
welfare—Cross-cultural studies. 5. Child protection. I. Hetherington, Rachael.

RJ507.M44 W45 2001
362.2' 0422—dc21

                                                                                2001045564

British Library Cataloguing in Publication Data

A catalogue record for this book is available from the British Library

ISBN 0-471-49724-X

Typeset in 10/12pt Palatino by Saxon Graphics Ltd, Derby
Printed and bound in Great Britain by Antony Rowe Ltd, Chippenham

This book is printed on acid-free paper responsibly manufactured from sustainable forestry,
in which at least two trees are planted for each one used for paper production.

CONTENTS

LIST OF FIGURES AND TABLES

FIGURES

TABLES

ABOUT THE AUTHORS

Karen Baistow lectures in psychology in the Department of Social Work, Brunel University. Her teaching and research interests lie in the field of child and family welfare. As a member of the Centre for Comparative Studies she has been engaged for a number of years in comparative European research on child protection practice and policy. Her publications in this field include journal articles and the jointly authored book *Positive Child Protection: a view from abroad*.

Rachael Hetherington is Director of the Centre for Comparative Social Work Studies in the Department of Social Work at Brunel University and co-editor of the journal *Social Work in Europe*. She trained as a social worker and worked in adult and child mental health settings. She taught on the social work CQSW and Diploma in Social Work courses at West London Institute and Brunel University. She has also worked as a Guardian ad Litem. Since 1990 she has been researching comparative European social work focusing on child protection and child welfare. Her publications include the jointly authored *Positive Child Protection: a view from abroad,* and *Protecting Children: messages from Europe* (Russell House Publishing, 1995 and 1997).

Ilan Katz is Head of Practice Development Unit NSPCC. He has worked as a social worker and manager in local authorities and voluntary agencies, mainly with children and disabled people. He is responsible for undertaking evaluative research and consultancy for the NSPCC and has managed a number of research/development projects for statutory and voluntary agencies. He has particular interests in children in the criminal justice system, and children and race, and family support. The subject of his PhD was racial identity. He has been involved with a number of research projects comparing child protection in the UK with other countries. He has published several books and articles including *The Development of Racial Identity in Children of Mixed Parentage—Mixed Metaphors* (Jessica Kingsley, 1996) and, with Amal Treacher, *The Dynamics of Adoption* (Jessica Kingsley, 2000).

Jeff Mesie is Operational Manager of the Practice Development Unit of the NSPCC. After completing his doctorate in public policy studies he trained and qualified as a health service manager and worked in both acute medical and mental health services. He subsequently worked in social services undertaking research and planning, first for mental health and then for children's services. In the NSPCC he has managed a range of research and consultancy projects for different agencies. He is increasingly interested in the measurement framework for performance management and to support this has qualified as a Chartered Management Accountant.

Judith Trowell is Consultant Child and Adolescent Psychiatrist, the Tavistock Clinic, Honorary Senior Lecturer, Royal Free and UCL Hospital Medical School, Vice-Chair Camden ACPC, Co-Chair Tavistock Legal Workshop and Expert Witness in cases relating to child care and parenting capacity. Her research includes outcome studies, service evaluation and mediation in public law cases. She is Founder and past Director of the Monroe Young Family Centre and organiser and tutor on MA and PhD in Child Protection and Family Support. She is a psychoanalyst and child analyst.

PREFACE

The welfare of children in families where there is a mentally ill parent is an issue of increasing concern to professionals in the field of child mental health, and much of the concern centres on the difficulties of co-ordinating the efforts of different agencies and services to support their families. It was in response to this concern that the authors of this book turned to cross-country comparison as a means of developing a new understanding of the problems that face professionals in the mental health and child welfare services.

The Centre for Comparative Social Work Studies at Brunel University had previously used European cross-country comparisons to study social work in child protection. The current project, called the Icarus project (for reasons that will be explained later), built on the work done with John Pitts and Andrew Cooper on child protection. It did not prove to be difficult to find professionals in social work and mental health services across Europe who were interested in joining the project, and none of the partners who joined the project at the initial stage dropped out. The members of the project were recruited in ten European countries (nine of which are members of the European Union) and Australia.

Finding funding was another matter. Support was provided by Directorate General XII of the European Commission for the data analysis, but most the work on the project in each country has been funded in the country concerned. The authors are very aware of the amount of work that was put into this project by mental health and child welfare professionals with many other calls on their time. The project would not have been possible without the commitment of agencies and academic institutions in Europe and Australia, and we are grateful to all the partners in the project who have given their time and persuaded their institutions to support their work.

Nothing would have been possible without the hard work and commitment of the research group members, Haris Assimopoulos, Lorna Bell, Arnold Böcker, Shane Butler, Christiane Deneke, Véronique Freund, Marie Gammeltoft, Geneviève Huon, Hanne Ingerslev, Yvonne Jonsson, Bernard Keutgens, Gloria Kirwan, Lene Lier, Gabriella Lucchitta, Anne Macloughlin, Marie-Paule Martin-Blachais, Roland Seligman, Rosemary Sheehan, Annemi Skerfving, Philip Smith, Lia Sparti and Vangelis Zacharias. We would also like to thank Julia Stroud for her help in devising the case vignette which was central to the research design and Andrea Warner for her support in the final stages.

The Department of Social Work, Brunel University, and the Practice Development Unit of the National Society for the Prevention of Cruelty to Children supported the project at all stages. We were able to consult the Kent User Forum during the process of writing the project research reports. Professor John Tsiantis and the Association for the Psychological Health of Children and Adolescents, Athens, were host to a meeting of the research partners in May 1998 at which the research instruments were agreed. The *Centre de Recherche Publique-Santé* of the Grand Duchy of Luxembourg supported and funded a workshop held in Luxembourg in March 1999, at which the research findings were finalised. The authors are indebted to all the participants in that workshop for discussions that stimulated the thinking behind this book.

Part I

INTRODUCTION: USING COMPARISON

This book demonstrates and embodies a particular way of developing ideas, which makes use of comparison as a means of reaching a new understanding of familiar material. It reflects the experience of the authors, who looked at alternative ways in which social welfare services are delivered in other countries and found that their understanding of their own system was profoundly altered. We hope to recreate that experience for our readers. The knowledge on which this experience rests is a knowledge of how the systems actually work on the ground and how they are experienced by the stakeholders—the professionals who operate them and the people who use them. The research methodology rests on the use of a common case story, a vignette which forms the focal point of the book.

It is interesting to learn about the social welfare services of another country, but we should ask ourselves, is it useful? We can point to some obvious ways in which it can be useful. If, for instance, a family in need of services moves from one country to another, what will their expectations be? Welfare professionals can only warn them in advance about differences—or help them to disentangle what is happening to them after they arrive—if they have some knowledge of the differences, or potential differences, between systems. Do other countries have ideas about specific services or ways of working that we could use? Almost certainly they do, but there may be obstacles to the introduction of these ideas in a different framework—they will only work if the potential problems of transplantation can be recognised.

So specific knowledge of the services and structures of other countries can be useful in direct, practical ways; but this usefulness has to be qualified. The knowledge will be useful *if* a process of comparison has taken place, which has led the worker to look closely at the ways in which the various systems are different or similar, and reflect on the possible reasons for these differences or similarities. The usefulness of the knowledge of another system is dependent on the process of comparing that system with one's own system. Comparison is not a question of building league tables and hierarchies, but of uncovering and discovering the ways in which systems and practice can differ, and trying to understand why. 'Why do they do it that way when we do it this way?' To profit from this experience an effort has to be made to stand in another pair of shoes and adopt a perspective that sees 'their' way as 'normal' and 'our' way as needing an explanation.

If this can be done, it is possible to develop new knowledge about our own systems and practices. While we can never fully enter the perspective of another culture, the process of attempting to adopt, temporarily, another way of understanding and conceptualising the major structures of our work— theories, systems, social relationships—leads to the discovery of new worlds.

This is a complex process, but it is not a linear process. This book need not, therefore, be read in a linear way (although it can be). Comparison is a circular process—a spiral staircase rather than an escalator. When you think you have found two things that are different, you look closer and find that certain aspects of them are similar. If you look again you may see further differences within the similarities. Behind every difference there is a similarity and behind every similarity there is a difference. We therefore suggest that the reader should feel free to dip and circle, and to facilitate this we give below an indication of what can be found, and where.

In Part I we explain the background to the research project and describe the methodology and process of the research. Information is presented about the structures of the mental health and child welfare systems of the research partners on a country by country basis. A summary of the different responses to the case vignette demonstrates how these structures operate on the ground. This information does not need to be tackled head on. It may be more useful to refer back to these descriptions of structures and practice as needed rather than read straight through them. Part I is mainly factual and reports on the research data.

The aim of Part II is to develop an understanding of the English response to the vignette by means of a comparative analysis of certain themes. The chapters compare the responses of the research participants and explore the implications. The themes that we have chosen consciously reflect an Anglo-centric perspective on the material. Project partners from other countries would have chosen other themes, or placed a different emphasis on what they elaborated. The themes we have chosen range over a wide academic territory, reflecting the fact that research in social work and social welfare, no less than the practice of social work, connects the micro and the macro. The activities of social workers on the one hand engage us with theories about the needs of individuals and, on the other, with theories about the relationship between the citizen, the state and the agents of the state.

Circular and reflective learning is built on the planned disruption of preconceptions. It uses the confusion that this may cause as a positive experience, a discomfort leading the person who experiences it to review, reflect and circle back on previous learning, and look at information again in the light of new ideas or from a different perspective. We expect the reader of the book to feel, at times, confused, as we have done. We hope that the reader will also find this experience of confusion and clarification stimulating, as we have done.

Part III considers the possible applications of the research findings within the English system and seeks to understand the particular difficulties that we experience.

Although this book ranges over a wide theoretical field, it is grounded in practice and in the very real problems that face families across Europe when parental mental health is at risk. Fundamental to the book is the case vignette, the fixed point to which all the work was anchored.* The vignette is the true introduction to our book; to be able to rewrite the vignette with a different ending is our aim.

THE VIGNETTE

Stage 1

Mary is a 27-year-old woman who is married to John. She has a 7-year-old daughter, Anna, from a previous relationship. She has not had any contact with Anna's father since shortly after Anna was born. One week ago she gave birth to a baby boy, Thomas. She was well during her pregnancy, which was planned, and worked until six months ago.

Four days ago Mary and Thomas came home from hospital, and John is now very anxious about her. Over the last two days she has seemed to be acting differently. She will not let anyone but herself touch the baby. She said to John, 'You are trying to poison him, like the nurses in the hospital'. Last night Mary sat up with Thomas all night, saying 'I must protect him'.

John decides that he has to seek help.

Stage 2

Three years later. Anna is now 10 and Thomas is 3. Mary is pregnant again and the baby is due in five months' time. John has lost his job, and has been unemployed for three months.

Anna's school is worried about Anna because she has begun soiling herself. She is becoming unpopular and shunned by the other children because of this and she is missing school. She has always been a quiet and rather solitary child, but there have not been any problems at school before.

Mary sees the head teacher who suggests that Mary and John should take Anna to see a child psychiatrist. Mary is unwilling to do so because of her own experience after Thomas was born. However, she says that she needs practical help herself because Thomas is very demanding and she gets very tired. She seems stressed and anxious, but she is certain that she will not become mentally ill after the birth of this baby.

---

* The case vignette is an invention. The persons and events described in it do not represent actual persons or events.

Stage 3

<u>Six months later.</u> Anna is 10½, Thomas is 3½ and the baby, Jane, is one month. Mary was in hospital for three days when the baby was born, and John looked after Anna and Thomas.

John has not found work. He has been alternately very withdrawn and quiet, then irritable when his family demands his attention. He is drinking excessively and they are short of money. Thomas is now attending nursery school; the staff there find him difficult to manage, violent towards other children and overactive.

At Anna's school, her teachers are increasingly worried about her. She is thin and unkempt, and for the last two weeks she has been falling asleep in class and seems to be desperately hungry. She is scavenging for food in the school and has stolen food from other children.

Two days ago John left home. Mary goes to the welfare services for help because she has no money. She is extremely anxious and says, 'I can't let them eat because he's trying to poison their food. They're only still here because I stay awake all night to keep them safe.'

Chapter 1

The Context and the Method

When a parent has severe or continuing mental health problems what happens to the family? Mental illness can involve loss of income, loss of social status, stigma and temporary or longer term incapacity. Its effects on the family are complex and carry different meanings for different family members, but it is likely to affect the functioning of the family as a whole and in relation to the outside world. The least powerful members of the family, the most dependent on the functioning of the family system, are the children. Whatever happens in the family affects the children, and when the family system is in difficulties children may be in need of support from outside.

Many families where there is a mentally ill parent will not need outside help except in relation to treatment for the illness. Because of their own strengths and through the strength and support of their wider family and community, as in the case of any other illness, outside help is not needed. We do not suggest that all families that have a mentally ill parent need outside support or any kind of professional intervention; but because of the continuing taboos around mental illness, mental ill health does bring with it problems that other people with ill health do not have to contend with. Its effect on the social, emotional and economic functioning of the family unit is different, and one common effect is to isolate the family from other support networks. If services are needed, mental illness in a parent is likely to involve the family in transactions with many services, some of them specialised. Specialised services may not themselves have understanding or experience of both mental illness and of families—they know about one or the other, but not both. In addition, there are likely to be complex professional and budgetary relationships between specialised agencies. Thus when a family with a mentally ill parent needs services, there are likely to be problems for the services in co-ordinating their responses and working coherently together.

In this situation it is very easy for the children to be overlooked. It is not that their needs are not seen as paramount, but that the adults (both family members and professionals) have difficulties in managing the situation, which obtrude on, and obscure, the child's experience. When we were looking for a name for the project that would have the same meaning in different European countries, we looked for something that would reflect the child's invisibility. We chose the name 'Icarus', basing this choice on a re-interpretation of the original myth. As an acronym, this can stand for 'Interventions for Children with Adult Relatives under Stress'. But Icarus, the child in the legend, represents the children whose lives and whose own anxi-eties are overshadowed by their parents' mental illness and who often take on great responsibilities to care for and protect their parents.

THE MYTH OF ICARUS RETOLD

Icarus was the son of Daedalus, a skilled craftsman and goldsmith. Daedalus had fled to Crete because he thought that he was being persecuted, and took Icarus with him. In Crete Daedalus began to see enemies all around him. He now saw his adversaries not as human, but as monstrous. He had delusions about the Minotaur, a creature from the depths of the earth, half man and half bull, who was pursuing him and would kill him. Icarus supported his father and helped him in his attempts to escape from his persecutor. Daedalus was convinced that he could fly, and Icarus had to help him to make the wings on which they would both escape. In trying to look after his father, Icarus had to accept his father's delusional system, and when Daedalus's delusional world was tested against external reality, Icarus fell to his death, and Daedalus was left to mourn.

The usual version of this myth pays little attention to the experience of Icarus and shows little sympathy for him. Indeed, Icarus is often blamed for the flight's failure. The needs of Icarus are overlooked, subordinated to those of his father. Auden's poem, quoted at the beginning of this book, reflects on just this casual acceptance by the adult world of the child's abnormal and frightening situation.

A NEW DEVELOPMENT

If we see the welfare of children with a mentally ill parent as an old problem, why should the question of services for these families be of particular concern at this time? If there have always been people with mental health problems who have had children, and there have always been children whose parents have had mental health problems, why should we now consider their experiences to be a matter for urgent inquiry?

In many respects, although this is an old situation, it is now a new problem. It arises from developments which in themselves are good, but which have consequences requiring new responses. The current situation is the 'unin-tended consequence' of improved practice. But improved practice is not expected to give rise to new problems, and a new problem arising out of improved practice may not be readily recognised. The developments that have led to this new problem are a combination of changes in public attitudes and changes in professional practice. These are not, of course, entirely separate categories; public attitudes influence the practice of professionals and their knowledge and practice has some impact on public attitudes.

The main changes in public attitude that have affected these families are a greater openness about mental illness accompanied by increased awareness of the civil liberties of people with mental illness.

One aspect of public attitudes to mental illness concerns the right to have children. It is not so long since people who were or had been mentally ill were very actively discouraged from having children. Sayce (1996, 2000) documents how the involuntary sterilisation of mentally ill patients took place in many parts of the world until the middle of the twentieth century and the discouragement of childbearing still continues to some extent. The fight for greater civil rights for people with mental illness has included a fight for the right to choose whether to have a child. To be effective, this in turn depends on the right to be given the support that the state gives to other people with disabilities. As the pressure to remain childless decreases, we should expect that there will be more families coping with this issue.

Changes in public attitude have been accompanied by changes in policy and professional practice. During the second half of the twentieth century, there was a global movement in the welfare field away from large-scale institutions. One aspect of this was the move to close large-scale psychiatric hospitals and, where possible, organise the care of the mentally ill either in general hospitals or in the community. The community care movement was part of, and contributed to, a climate of greater tolerance and greater respect for the civil rights of people with a mental illness. It may seem strange to claim this at a time when, in the British context, there is a considerable threat to tolerance and civil liberties for this group; but across Europe, over the last 50 years there has been progress, notably in Italy, where the development of the movement *Psichiatria Democratica* during the 1970s pioneered fundamental changes in the treatment of the mentally ill (Donnelly 1992; Goodwin 1997; Ramon 1996). Progress may be slow, but there is less secrecy about mental illness, and legislation in many countries has supported the civil rights and independent representation of people with mental health problems.

The history of the developments in mental health policies in the UK has been well charted from a variety of perspectives (Jones 1972, 1988; Foucault 1967; Goodwin 1997). The aspect that is relevant for us in this context is the development of care outside of institutions. Innovations that started in the 1940s with the development of social psychiatry in Scotland (Jones 1972) were encouraged by the 1959 Mental Health Act. In the 1960s the closed door of the psychiatric hospital was becoming a revolving door, and there were government reports advocating 'community care' (Ministry of Health 1962, 1963). In Britain, at that time, and in the context of a social welfare programme that accepted the legitimacy of state intervention, the phrase 'community care' was less ambiguous than it is now, and community care was understood to be care *in* the community (i.e. not in an institution) rather than care *by* the community (i.e. not by the state). Similar changes from institutional care to care outside of institutions have taken place across Europe. Goodwin (1997) tracks these developments and analyses the possible effect of changes in available medication and of the development of new psychotropic drugs on the process of the closure of large psychiatric hospitals. He concludes that there is no clear causal correlation between pharmacological developments and the move out of the old institutions. What he makes clear is that these moves happened across Europe at roughly the same period, in varying degrees according to the different pressures for change and the different resources available in different places.

At the same time, the general trend against institutionalisation affected the care of children. Across Europe there was pressure for the state care of children to move from large institutions to smaller ones or to foster homes (Colton and Hellinckx 1993; Madge 1994; Ruxton 1996). This was accompanied (or followed) by an increasing emphasis on maintaining children within the family, through support for their parents, through the encouragement of placement within the wider family, or, in the UK and other English-speaking countries, through the creation of a new family by adoption. The work of Bowlby (1969, 1973) on the importance of parent–child attachment and the potential long-term and deleterious effects of separating a child from its carers has been quoted to us by health and welfare professionals across Europe. Workers at the levels of both policy and practice have demonstrated that they are highly motivated to keep children in their families.

As a result of these changes there are likely to be more people in the community who are of parenting age and have some level of recurring or enduring mental ill health, which may or may not require hospital in-patient care. There will also be more active attempts to enable their children to remain in the family.

THE PRESENT SITUATION

Many children who have a mentally ill parent may not have serious problems. With a supportive family and friendship network, without the added problems of poverty, with a well-organised treatment regime and depending on the nature and progression of the parental illness, children may have lives no more disrupted than many of their peers. However, these children are vulnerable. Children with a mentally ill parent make up a considerable proportion of the children who come to the attention of social services departments, either as children in need of family support, children at risk or in danger, children in care, or 'parental' children, acting as carers to their parents. There are also a large number of children in these families who never come to the notice of services, and whose needs are not met.

The needs of these children are very complex, and depend on such factors as the nature and severity of the parental illness and the resources of the wider family as well as on the services provided for them. All children with a mentally ill parent are likely, at the very least, to experience disruption of their lives and anxieties about their own future mental health, and there are now a number of studies which demonstrate the association between parental mental illness and subsequent disturbances in the child (Ramsay *et al.*

1998; Henry and Kumar 1999). In the UK, the welfare of these families has been the subject of a number of recent publications (Sheppard 1994; Falkov 1996, 1998; Göpfert *et al.* 1996; Stroud 1997, 2000; Weir and Douglas 1999; Göpfert and Mahoney 2000; Reder *et al.* 2000) and conferences (Sieff Conference 1997; BASPCAN South East 1997; also Oslo [National Centre for Child and Adolescent Psychiatry] 1998; Stockholm 2000). It is an active area of concern for the Department of Health, which has recently published training material (Mayes *et al.* 1998; Falkov 1998).

There are no reliable national figures on the numbers of children affected in the UK, and the establishment of information internationally about the extent of the problem is fraught with difficulties over definitions. While it may be possible to suggest some indicative figures, these are a long way from giving statistically reliable data. For example, Bernard and Douglas (1999) illustrate the problem of arriving at an estimate of prevalence; all the figures refer to different individual authorities or trusts, and all are based on different groupings. However, taking two examples, a survey in Nottingham found that 25% of female patients in a psychiatric setting had children under 5; and in Kingston-on-Thames, 26% of children for whom there was an initial Child Protection Conference had a mentally ill parent. An NSPCC study undertaken in an inner London borough (Green *et al.* 1997) found similar proportions. Unless these figures are atypical and severely skewed, and there is no reason to suppose that this is the case, there are a considerable number of families involved. This is considered further in Chapter 12.

Thus there has been a major increase in the frequency, extent and complexity of the situations where the supporting services have to respond to diverse competing, and potentially conflicting, needs. This demands more and more highly developed co-operation and interdisciplinary understanding. The focus of this book is on the problems and challenges of inter-agency and inter-disciplinary co-operation. The changes in practice described above are Europe-wide, and each country has developed different ways of meeting the challenges to co-operation and liaison between agencies, depending on their existing patterns of care, on social and economic pressures, on cultural expectations relating to children, families and mental health and on expectations about the role of professionals in relation to the state and the family. Whatever the differences of approach, when we raised the problem as a possible research focus with professionals in other European countries, the response was always the same; that this was an increasing problem over which they had continuing and unresolved anxieties.

THE OBJECTIVES OF THE RESEARCH PROGRAMME

Cross-national research in the social sciences has a long history, and has been approached from many different directions, and with many different aims. Our objectives in using this means of research were four-fold. Firstly to discover how agencies co-operate in offering help for these families in other European countries. Secondly to discover more about the nature of the problems of this inter-agency co-operation. Thirdly to attempt to identify the lessons that could be learnt for our own services from these other examples. And fourthly to attempt to identify any reasons why we might have problems in this country in adapting alternative approaches.

Discovering how other health and welfare systems actually work is not straightforward. There are, potentially, differences in structures, systems, laws, professional task boundaries and professional cultures as well as resources, and any of these may lead to confusion and misapprehension in understanding the whole. However, globalisation as well as the greater closeness engendered by the European Union, mean that it is increasingly important that we do understand how other systems work, and how the different bits of a system relate to each other. It is also the first step towards beginning to be able to learn from each other and to build common goals. In our view it is not possible to gain an accurate picture of the operation of health and welfare systems from top-down descriptions of the structures. These are necessary, but have to be supplemented by descriptions of the work that takes place on the ground, which demonstrate how the systems and structures actually function.

As will be described below, the research was designed to focus on a specific situation which would demonstrate how the work of different services and agencies meshed together. This meshing together was of particular interest to us because failures in inter-agency co-operation and liaison had been identified so frequently in Britain as the cause of problems (Falkov 1996; Sieff Conference Report 1996; Reder and Duncan 1999; Reith 1998; Weir and Douglas 1999; Reder *et al*. 2000). It was also a concern for all our research partners. Cross-country comparisons provide an opportunity to compare the outcomes of different approaches. In the first place, we were saying: 'We share this problem, but we all tackle it differently, we have different resources, systems and structures. Does any one way seem to work better and if so, why?' What developed from this was the identification of the factors that seemed to facilitate a better outcome, and a clearer picture of the intrinsic aspects of the problem, the features that all systems shared, as opposed to the aspects of the problem as experienced in any one country which seemed to be related to the structures and systems of that particular country.

Identifying the factors that facilitated a better outcome was a step towards identifying the lessons that could be learnt for our own services. However, there are good reasons—historical, cultural and economic—why any system has grown up the way it has, and the soil may not suit ideas from a different climate. It is not enough to uproot the idea behind a successful structure or service, plant it again in a different context and expect it to flourish without further attention. If we understand enough about the wherefore of our own system, it may be possible to understand what can be transplanted without problems, and what will need careful acclimatisation or might fail to thrive. We use comparison to help to uncover the obstacles and barriers to the use in this country of ideas from elsewhere.

We therefore aim in this book, firstly, to set out the information that we have gathered on the different health and welfare systems of the participating countries, and the way in which the systems operate in relation to each other for the families with whom we are concerned. Secondly, to identify the intrinsic problems which services and agencies meet with in trying to provide a coherent response. Thirdly, to identify particular aspects of functioning or particular services which could be developed or changed to facilitate better outcomes. And, fourthly, to identify the underlying reasons for particular problems that there may be in England in implementing any of these changes.

Implicit in this approach is the assumption that the functioning of welfare regimes in any country is the outcome of the interplay between culture, the structures of government and the law, and professional ideologies, all of which carry the influences of historical experiences and geographical realities (see Figure 1.1). For a fuller discussion of this see Cooper *et al.* (1992), Hetherington and Smith (1995) and Hetherington *et al.* (1997).

Because of these interrelationships, an investigation of any one aspect of the system is bound to give an incomplete explanation of how it functions. For example, an analysis of the legal restrictions on compulsory hospitalisation of people with a mental illness does not explain what could happen to the family in the vignette in all countries, although it seems to do so for some. An understanding of the relationship between the individual and the state may help us to understand the attitude of the Scandinavian countries to mandatory reporting as compared to the German attitude, but this explanation does not prepare us for the fact that Sweden and Germany shared a very similar approach to supportive family intervention. In the same way, a shared ideology of the importance of the family and of attachment theory may not lead to the same outcome in different countries if the structures of services or, more importantly, the cultures of the family are different. In trying to understand how the relationship between structure, culture and ideology affects the functioning of the systems in England, Scotland and Northern Ireland, we will draw on comparisons between these countries and the others who took part in the research in a process of reflection on taken-for-granted aspects of the British welfare regime.

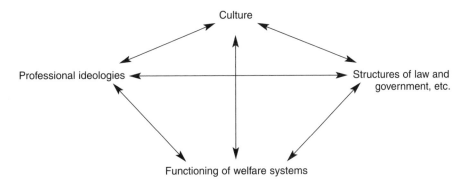

Figure 1.1 The interplay between structures, culture, professional ideologies and the functioning of welfare systems.

USING CROSS-COUNTRY COMPARISONS

As mentioned, cross-national research in the social sciences has a long history; but this history has not, on the whole, included social work. Research in the field of social policy and sociology has tended to be 'top-down', and has relied on comparisons of systems or of statistics generated by the systems. Looking back as well as forward, Øyen (1990: 1) wrote 'there is no reason to believe there exists an easy or straightforward entry into comparative social research'. Moreover, social work was described by Jones (1985) as 'a messy area for research' because of the great difficulty of finding any equivalence which could form the basis for a comparison. In a recent paper, Baistow (2000: 10) reviews 'the conceptual and practical problems' of achieving the aims of cross-national research, ranging from differences in historical experience to difficulties in finding funding. The methodology used in this research takes a 'bottom-up' rather than a 'top-down' approach and is qualitative rather than quantitative. However, the aim of the research is congruent with Øyen's definition of the aim of cross-national research as being 'to reduce unexplained variables and find patterns and relationships' (Øyen 1990: 3). It should be noted, however, that our expectation is that reducing unexplained variables is liable to lead to the exposure of further, underlying and still unexplained variables.

In this project and in previous projects (Cooper *et al.* 1992, 1995; Hetherington *et al.* 1997; Monkhouse and Hetherington 1997) we took as our point of equivalence the problem faced by the person or family for whom welfare services are being provided. We found that we could outline a social and human problem faced by a person or a family in such a way that it was accepted as real and current in all the countries with which we were working. This human situation is the basis of our work in cross-country comparisons.

We looked to Europe for our cross-country comparisons for a number of reasons. Across Europe, there are more ways of organising the delivery of welfare services than there are countries. The ways that welfare services are organised depend on many factors; for example, the nature of the constitutional and legal framework, the economic situation past and present, the history of welfare provision, the development of local government and the role of non-governmental structures. As these are different for each country, the welfare services will also have developed differently. Yet Europe provides a relatively homogeneous group of countries in terms of size, history, geography and socio-economic functioning. Within western Europe, social problems are similar and expectations are similar (not the same) though. Structures have developed differently, have various shared features. We can take advantage of this combination of common experience and different development. It enables us to study the effectiveness of different approaches by looking at some of the naturally occurring different systems across Europe to see what happens in them. To do this we need to look not just at how the system is said to work, but at how the system actually works; we need to look not only at the laws, regulations, services and government structures (though they are important), but at what happens on the ground.

To do this in terms of actual cases would be immensely complicated, indeed, virtually impossible. As soon as anyone comes into contact with a welfare system, the actualities of that system affect the way the situation develops. The initial problem may look the same, but as the context and dynamics of the case are determined by the resources and structures within which it takes place, developments are difficult to compare. This problem led to the development of a technique using an imaginary (but realistic) case situation as the starting point. A case vignette is written, describing a problematic situation which develops over time in three or four stages. The story is constructed episodically and is designed to elicit information about the possible responses of welfare services at each stage. This vignette is first checked with the researchers in the other countries taking part in the project to make sure that it is realistic for them. The vignette is then discussed with relevant professionals in each country—for example, social workers, residential carers, nurses, doctors, other health professionals—who are asked what, in their system and with their resources, would be likely to happen next. From their responses is built a grass-roots view of how their system could and would operate in the circumstances of the case.

We expected, because of the Europe-wide nature of the changes described earlier in this chapter, that the problem with which we were concerned would be recognised in other countries. This was borne out by the ease with which we recruited partners for our project. Of the initial approaches we made to contacts in mental health and child welfare services, only one did not result in a partnership being established. (The one country which did not join the project was already well in advance of others in developing relevant services.) The final group was larger than was originally projected because some partners asked for colleagues in other countries to be included, or heard about the project and were interested in joining it.

The Use of the Vignette Technique in Cross-National Research

Using case vignettes for the study of practice situations is common in professional education and training for welfare professions. As a research tool it has something in common with the case study approach and, as Yin points out, while this may not provide a basis for statistical generalisation, it does give a basis for analytical generalisation (Yin 1994). In the use of transcriptions of what people say about their system, it has common ground with ethnographic approaches (Atkinson 1992). In this project the case vignette is used to study the expectations of workers about their own and other services, and the concepts and values on which they expect to act. It is not a method which describes statistically what normally or 'on average' happens in a given situation; it describes what is possible within the parameters of the structures and culture of a particular place at a particular time.

The use of the vignette technique in cross-national research has been described and discussed in relation to a study using a sample of about 60 social workers in two countries, England and Sweden, in a cross-national comparison by Soydan and Stål (Soydan and Stål 1994; Weightman and Weightman 1995; Soydan 1996). This was a comparison of the responses of the individual social workers grouped nationally. The study yielded interesting information about the conceptualisations and responses of the research participants to the problem put before them (which involved child protection and attitudes towards race and parenting). There was no feed back to the participants of the views of their colleagues in the other country. The vignette was used to elicit information, but this information was not used reflexively to generate further information by asking participants to reflect on differences and similarities.

At about the same time the vignette technique was being used to study the group response of social workers in France and England (Cooper *et al.* 1992; Hetherington *et al.* 1997). In this study, groups of social workers in the two countries discussed the same case vignette. Their responses were video recorded and shown to the group in the other country, who then discussed the views of their foreign colleagues. The reflections of the participants on the approach and conceptualisation of the situation by workers in the other country formed part of the research data. The participants in this second, reflective, stage were asking not only 'why do they do it that way?', but 'why do we do it differently?'. They were questioning their taken-for-granted assumptions. This study was extended to include four further countries, and the methodology is described and discussed in Hetherington *et al.* (1997) and Cooper (2000). The methodology was reviewed by Mabbett and Bolderson (1999), who describe it as fulfilling 'the oft-cited purpose of comparative work of "holding up a mirror to one's own society" '. They add: 'Where the purpose of comparison is to learn lessons from other countries, … the interactive method used in this study clearly signals a big step forward' (Mabbett and Bolderson 1999: 53).

THE RESEARCH PROCESS

The Organisation and Co-ordination of the Icarus Project

The methodology bases itself on the use of the views of practitioners as the source of research information. The initial data provided by the practitioners on how they would respond to the situation is triangulated by information about the systems and structures of mental health and child welfare services in each country. The information about the systems is provided by the researchers in that country. This is a form of action research in that, by informing them of other systems, it presents the participating practitioners with choices, alternative perspectives and other ways of responding to their working dilemmas, and confronts them with the need to understand and justify (or criticise) their own practice.

The project partners in the Icarus research group were recruited by the Centre for Comparative Social Work Studies (CCSWS), Brunel University, who put forward the proposal and acted as co-ordinators. The research group was made up of the researchers from each country who agreed to undertake the work of the project in their country. Their work entailed, in each country, organising and leading the participating professional groups, recording and arranging for the transcription of the discussions and providing information on the structures of their own mental health and child welfare systems. Finally, at the end of the project, the research partners worked collectively, as a group, on the interpretation of the research findings.

The research group met three times. In June 1997 the group met to consider the project proposal and decide whether to participate. That meeting was attended by members from Denmark, France, Germany, Greece, Ireland, Italy, Luxembourg, Sweden and the UK (England and Northern Ireland), who all committed themselves to the project. The research group was also joined by researchers in Australia (who were unable to be present at that meeting) and later by researchers in Norway and Scotland. In May 1998 the group met in Athens, hosted by the Association for the Psychological Health of Children and Adolescents, to agree the research instruments and how they should be implemented. In March 1999, following the completion of the fieldwork, the research group met in Luxembourg for a workshop (funded by the Grand Duchy of Luxembourg) which was also attended by delegates from the professional groups who had participated in the research. The research group members from Australia, Norway and Scotland were also able to attend this workshop, so the discussions at this meeting were fully representative of the project membership. At this workshop, the collated findings of the research were discussed; there was clarification and correction of information about services and structures. Working in small groups and in plenary sessions, the research group defined the factors which had emerged from the research as being the most important in promoting effective help for the families with whom we were concerned.

The Research Design

Two groups of professional workers (for example, social workers, nurses, psychiatrists, psychologists) were recruited in each country. One group was recruited from the adult mental health field, the other from child welfare/protection. In two countries (Ireland and England) separate groups of child mental health professionals were also recruited. In England, groups were recruited in three locations in order to check on the reliability of group responses in representing a generalisable response. It was obviously important that the groups should as far as possible be recruited in similar ways, and that there should be a common style for the facilitation of the discussions. The researchers were therefore given a protocol for the recruitment of the groups. It was not possible to specify in detail the membership of the groups because we knew that there were different boundaries between tasks and different professions involved in different countries. The protocol therefore asked the researchers to select the groups from the professionals who worked in child welfare/child protection, and in community mental health, in their locality.

The optimum size for the groups was six to eight (although there was some variation, a few groups being considerably larger), and they agreed to meet three times. The introduction that the researchers gave to the group members was standardised, as was the group work approach that was employed. In introducing the group task, the researchers made it clear that the aim of the research was not to create hierarchies of good practice, but to understand the different ways in which a similar situation was treated in different countries. It was explained that at the first meeting they would be asked for their views on an unfolding case situation. As the same vignette was used in all countries, comparable data would be generated on the services that would be available and the approaches of the workers. At the next meeting, the group would be told the response to the case in one of the other countries.

Because of the time constraints on the professional groups it was only possible for the participants to be informed about and reflect on the data from one other country. At the second meeting, the groups were told about the response of the paired country and asked for their reflections on what was the same, different, interesting, or unexpected in the response of the country with which they were paired. We looked for a way of pairing countries that would be neutral and would not distort the comparison by introducing Anglo-centric preconceptions about like/unlike, or create any hierarchies of size or socio-economic development. We therefore paired countries by population density, as being relevant to service delivery and in other respects neutral, with no implications about similarities or dissimilarities of resources or structures (see Table 1.1).

Table 1.1   The countries paired for feedback

Denmark	Northern Ireland
Sweden	Ireland
France	Greece
England & Wales, Australia*	Germany
Norway	Scotland
Luxembourg	Italy

* Australia was paired with Germany for practical
  reasons rather than on the basis of population density.

The data from these two meetings formed the topic of the Luxembourg workshop, and was recorded in the interim research report.

At a third meeting, the groups were shown the interim research report summarising the responses of the groups in different countries, and asked for their reflections on these. In many cases the child welfare and adult mental health groups met together on this occasion. They frequently asked for further opportunities to meet and looked for ways of carrying forward some of the ideas that they had developed in their own locality. The research process is outlined in Figure 1.2.

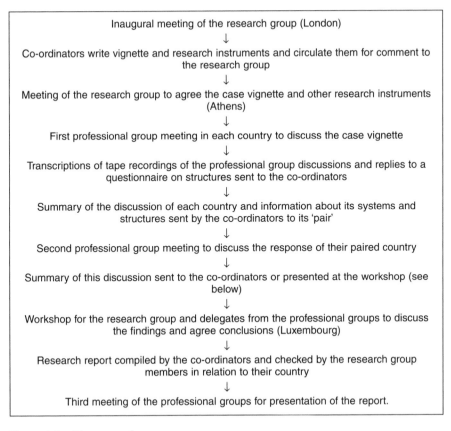

Figure 1.2   The research process.

When the group members were recruited they were assured of confidentiality, in that they would not be individually identified. The groups were also informed about what would happen to the data: a report would be published by the CCSWS and we would hope to find a publisher for a book.

In the UK, a group of service users was asked for their views and reflections on the responses to the case study from other countries, and for their comments on the different ways of working that were demonstrated. It was not possible to develop this aspect of the research as intended owing to the lack of funding.

The Research Data

The research process created two main data sets. The first set consisted of documents recording the discussions of the professional teams. The first meetings were tape recorded, transcribed and translated into English. The second meetings were recorded and summarised by the researchers in each country. (The discussions at the third meetings did not form part of the research data.) This process produced very rich and extensive data. There were at least two groups in each country, and a total of 13 countries (England, Northern Ireland and Scotland were treated as separate countries). As Ireland and England also had separate child mental health groups, this gave 32 sets of transcripts for the first meetings. Not all countries provided written summaries of the second meetings, but all reported orally to the Luxembourg workshop.

The second set consisted of the information about the systems and structures of the services concerned in different countries. This information was necessary for the understanding of the responses of the professionals. In the course of discussion with their peers, professional workers took for granted a whole range of knowledge about structures, laws, systems and the nature of resources. The researchers had to understand this background in order not to misinterpret the discussion group transcripts. For example, one of the Italian groups commented on the relationship between Thomas (age 3) and his mother, basing their interpretation on the expectation that he was attending nursery school, but without mentioning that fact because it was for them obvious. Their interpretation would have been misunderstood without this background knowledge. An understanding of the structural background also had to be provided for the groups of professionals at their second meetings when they were discussing another country's response. The information about structures and systems given by the researchers for each country provided a framework for looking at cross-country comparisons, a check on unrecognised assumptions about the systems of other countries and a source of information about many aspects of child welfare and mental health systems.

The transcripts of the group discussions provided an account for each country of the likely outcome at each stage of the vignette, taking into account the possible variables such as the seriousness of the mother's mental illness and the amount of help available from family and neighbours. In conjunction with the information about laws, systems and resources, this gave us a picture of the likely experience of the family in the different locations. A description of the structures of each country is given in Chapters 2 and 3. The transcripts also provided the basis for an analysis of the themes that came up in discussions. We looked for themes in two ways; firstly we looked for common themes that came up in all or many countries, such as discussions over hospitalisation and whether it should take place, or the difficulties of engaging with a parent who is scared of involvement with the services or anxieties about the children. Secondly we looked for idiosyncratic themes, themes that ran through or dominated the discussions of one or both groups within a country. For example, the French groups both had extended discussions about the task boundaries between psychiatrists and social workers—a topic which came up in other groups, but only briefly. These idiosyncratic themes might often be touched on in other groups, but did not dominate or permeate their discussions.

Both the factual and the thematic analyses provided the basis for our comparisons and for issues that we explore in Part II.

THE SHORTCOMINGS AND DANGERS OF THE METHODOLOGY

Non-equivalence

There are many problems in comparative methodology, some of them common to all approaches, and some of them particular to the vignette technique and the way in which we use it. Fundamentally there is the problem of what Øyen (1990: 5) describes as 'the non-equivalence of concepts, a multitude of unknown variables interacting in an unknown context and influencing the research question in unknown ways'. It is very difficult to find true equivalents, either in concepts or facts. It is, for example, unrealistic to attempt to compare outcomes of French and English child care policy by comparing figures on children in public care; the figures cover different categories, with different age boundaries and describe the result of widely different policies and different institutions. Neither the statistical basis nor the conceptual basis for comparison is there. As Hantrais and Mangen (1996) describe, both quantitative and qualitative approaches have problems. While statistics cannot be relied on to count the same things, qualitative approaches such as case studies and maps of service systems have problems over differences in language and the conceptualisations that lie behind language.

Language and Concepts

Our study did not use quantitative material, but had all the problems of qualitative approaches, in that language and conceptualisation of problems was central. There cannot be a complete answer to this. Both language and concepts differ between countries and there can be false similarities; things appear equivalent that are not. This may indeed reveal the core matter with which the research is concerned; for example, 'education' and *'éducation'* sound as though they are the same, but the meaning of *éducation* is far wider than the meaning of 'education'. *'Éducation'* is an inclusive word which covers up-bringing, social and emotional learning as well as academic learning, while 'education' is usually restricted to academic learning. Understanding this difference was fundamental to understanding the French approach to the social work task. It was important to be aware of the potential ambiguities and uncertainties of language and conceptualisations at every stage of the work. This was demonstrated by our difficulties in collecting information on the background to mental health and child welfare systems of the research countries. We ran into many problems of definition. Answers to a questionnaire were not enough; the English researchers inevitably drew up an Anglo-centric questionnaire which did not match the circumstances of other countries. What mattered was to be aware of this so that the reply to the questionnaire could become a starting point and not a finishing point in the data collection. The reply to the questionnaire was the basis for developing an understanding and was not enough on its own, nor could it ever be enough on its own. There was a process both for the English researchers who compiled the questionnaire and for the researchers from other countries through which we began to learn about difference and the possible range of differences through our questions and misunderstandings. This is not a process that has a finishing post. There will always be points that need further discussion, new differences and similarities to be explored and uncovered. However, the process itself is important. It helps to deepen understanding and to emphasise the fact that all descriptions and conceptualisations contain the possibility of different interpretations.

Language differences exist at different levels. Most of the countries that we worked with were not Anglophone. Altogether seven other languages were involved. Because of this we did not take understanding for granted and we became more aware of the risk that we might make unwarranted assumptions about equivalence within a language group, for example, between Australian-English and English-English. We used translators and the knowledge of other languages available within the group, but it was very important to allow time for discussing and resolving uncertainties in understanding. We widened our knowledge of difference by discovering the variations in the underlying meaning of words which might appear to translate easily. Language differences at all levels are an intrinsic part of cross-country research (even if the languages purport to be the same); but they are also the subject of study, not just the tools. For example, 'risk' is a word that can be translated, but it is also a concept, and the different conceptualisations of risk are one of the themes that we found to be important, even if the translation of the word was not a problem. Exploring words and meaning, and using the transcriptions as a source to give context to the way in which words were used, gave us a point of entry to understanding different conceptualisations of social institutions.

Differences in language in qualitative cross-country research are therefore both a problem and an opportunity—something to be grasped, not merely 'solved'.

Definitions

One major problem of definition was 'mental illness'. In the first place, what should we include in the UK context and, in the second place, would there be equivalence in other countries? The vignette describes a situation where a mother has a serious, possibly psychotic mental illness, and the father may be developing an alcohol problem. The material relating to the vignette is therefore relevant specifically to diagnosed psychiatric illness and alcohol abuse, but we also discuss inter-agency work in more general terms going beyond the parameters of the vignette situation. We did not wish to limit the discussions but we did wish to focus on the area where mental health services, child welfare and primary care overlap. We therefore used as our definition for the UK, diagnosed psychiatric illness, including dual diagnosis, but we did not focus on substance abuse and addiction. There are differences in the use of diagnostic categories between countries, as is discussed further in Chapter 8. Personality disorder in particular is included as a psychiatric diagnosis in some countries but not in all. The definition of 'personality disorder' (and now 'dangerous severe personality disorder') has been an issue in the UK for many years. The position outlined in the recent government white paper, *Reforming the Mental Health Act* (Department of Health 2001) post-dates our research; at the time the field-work was taking place the debate had not reached its present stage. The question of the diagnostic category of personality disorder is of particular importance in the UK because UK mental health law connects diagnosis and the power to use compulsion, and gives the medical profession much greater power, with less outside scrutiny (from legal or elected representatives) than other European countries. The definition is also important in the context of this research, because 'personality disorder' is a label frequently attached to parents where there are child protection issues. These differences of definition emphasise the importance of relating comparison of functioning to a shared situation or case. This reliance on one case situation as the fulcrum of the research does, however, unavoidably limit the breadth of applicability of the findings.

The Nature of the Group

A specific problem for our use of the vignette in combination with group discussion is that the groups may not be representative. Firstly, they only represent one location in their country and cannot be said to represent the country as a whole. Secondly, their response as a group may not represent the norm for that location, and the discussions and conclusions of the group may be skewed by the presence of a dominating or 'atypical' group member.

Throughout the book we refer to the groups as representing their country. In fact this is purely a convenience. It is a shorthand for saying 'this group represents a response that is possible within the laws of their country, the local regional and central government system, and the resources and culture of their locality'. We could have named the towns concerned but did not do so for two reasons: (1) we wished to provide some level of anonymity for the participants; and (2) it would create a spurious appearance of exactitude. When, for example, we give Italy as a heading, it has to be remembered that Italy is strongly regionalised and that the economic and social circumstances of northern and southern Italy differ greatly. What we are describing under the heading of 'Italy' is how the laws and structures of Italy can be used within the constraints of cultural expectations and local finances. Australia, Germany and Italy are probably the most regionalised of the participating countries, but the principle would hold good for smaller countries such as Luxembourg and Northern Ireland. We are never saying 'this is how it always works in Italy', or even 'this is how it always works in north east Italy', but say 'this is how, within the structures and culture of Italy, it *can* work'.

It is possible that the groups may not represent comparable professions. This a particular dilemma in comparative research because (as explained above) we could not be specific about the membership of the groups in different countries. The professions involved in the work and the boundaries between professions vary between countries. The same problem is described by Laot in a study of European doctoral programmes in social work. There, when selecting the programmes to study, the researchers decided not to provide their own definition of social work but to ask what the definition of social work was for the initiators of the different programmes.

> 'Ultimately this position proved significant on several accounts. Firstly it forced us to discard preconceived ideas and to keep an open mind regarding all the information we received. This prevented us from rejecting out of hand some programmes which turned out to be very worthwhile. Secondly, and as a direct result, it helped us to obtain an understanding of the extent of the subtlety of the subject and its complexities, which a more focused approach would not have allowed.' (Laot 2000: 2)

In the same way, the definition, and therefore the choice, of participants in each country had to be left to the research partners in that country. A genuine equivalence depends on the shared understanding within the research group of the aims and objectives of the research, which will enable them to recruit participants whose experience is relevant to these aims. We are confident from the experience of working together for two years that all the research partners did share the same objectives. However, it continues to be important to be aware of the make-up of each group, because this provides information about the way in which services are organised and about the assumptions on which the system is based. A list of the professions represented in each of the groups is given in the Appendix on page 223.

In the first research project in which this technique was used (Cooper *et al.* 1992), two groups were set up in each country in order to test the reliability of group responses in being country-specific. It was found that, although each group had its individual character, the responses from the two French groups were very clearly distinguishable from the responses of the English groups in ways which reflected the differences of culture, structure and ideology. In the second project (Hetherington *et al.* 1997), each of the other countries was paired with a different English group, so that there were in all seven English groups who responded to the same case vignette. The responses of all the English groups were very similar (in spite of differences in the make-up of the groups), and showed specifically English preoccupations. The discussions of these different groups elicited very similar comments from the other countries, which gave us confidence that group responses would not be heavily skewed or idiosyncratic. This supposition was reinforced in the current research. We had recruited groups in three different southern England locations, and found that, although their responses were affected by local factors, and although the groups had different personalities, they shared the same preoccupations and were giving very similar responses within similar structures, service requirements and resources.

Although it is clearly possible that a group could be unrepresentative either in personnel or in personalities, it is probable that these groups reflect the limitations, opportunities and characteristics of their setting and location. It also seems unlikely that a highly uncharacteristic group response would not be noticed and identified by the members of the research team.

In this chapter our aim has been to explain why, at the outset, we thought that the problem of co-operation for these families is important. We have explained why we chose to use cross-country comparison as a means of exploring the problem and we have described how the project was carried out. In the next chapters we present information about the systems and the structures of the countries in which the project took place.

Chapter 2

The Systems of the Partner Countries: Introduction and the Scandinavian Law Countries

THE COUNTRIES AND HOW THEY ARE CATEGORISED

The countries that took part were (from north to south) Norway, Sweden, Scotland, Northern Ireland, Denmark, Ireland, England, Germany, France, Luxembourg, Italy, Greece and Australia (Victoria). The original focus was on member states of the European Union, but that seemed to be no reason to exclude Norway and Australia, and there turned out to be particular advantages in the inclusion of those two countries. It must be emphasised that we do not consider that our study provides a statement that is necessarily valid for the whole of any of these countries. We only provide information about how the systems work in a particular area of any country, and an example of how the structures are likely to be used. In writing about the research we use the names of countries rather than towns or districts partly to provide more anonymity (which mattered to some, though not all of our participants) and because many factors of culture, law and government were national rather than purely local phenomena.

The process of comparing things, of sorting out the differences and similarities, tends to lead to categorisation. There is a considerable literature on the possible ways of grouping welfare systems and countries relative to their welfare systems (e.g. Esping-Andersen 1990, 1999; Castles 1993; Sainsbury 1996), and this will be discussed in more detail in Chapter 9. The categorisation that we use at this point was described by Therborn (1993: 246) as 'the legal families of nations'. Writing about the rights of children, Therborn describes the major division of 'legal families' as being between the Anglo-American Common Law tradition and the Continental European Civil Law tradition. Of our partner countries, Australia, Ireland, Northern Ireland and England fall into the former group. The Continental European Civil Law tradition is further subdivided into Nordic, Germanic and Romanistic. Denmark, Norway and Sweden fall into the Nordic group, while Germany and Greece (although Greece is also affected by Orthodox ecclesiastical law) are in the Germanic category. France, Italy, Luxembourg and Scotland are Romanistic.

In the following descriptions of systems and structures, we grouped together the Scandinavian countries which share a Nordic legal system. We refer to them as Scandinavian rather than Nordic because Finland was not included. These countries showed many similarities across a range of matters although there were also important differences between them. They shared a low use of non-governmental organisations, a state-centred delivery of health and welfare services, a high level of intervention, a similar approach to the mandatory reporting of child abuse and somewhat similar child protection decision-making systems.

The countries in the Romanistic and Germanic legal families we refer to collectively as the continental group, and in these two 'legal families' the differences between the health and welfare systems of the countries are more marked and the pattern less clear. Some aspects of the welfare regime structures cut across the 'legal families' grouping. For example, the principle of subsidiarity is highly important in the structure of the German legal system (Schäfer 1995; Smith 1995), but it is also important in Luxembourg, which is in the Romanistic legal group. On the other hand, France and Italy, which Esping-Andersen (1990) categorised with Germany, stand out as having very different levels of statism from Germany, and as they are in many respects similar to each other, this supports the 'legal family' categorisation. While France and Italy share with both Germany and Luxembourg some aspects of an insurance-based health system, there is the important difference that in France and Italy mental health services are not insurance based, and that the mental health, child welfare and maternal and child health services, although supported by non-governmental organisations (NGOs), are very largely delivered by government agencies. In Greece the approach to intervention and the flexibility in promoting the use of community strengths and resources are comparable to Italy, and there is little similarity to the German pattern in spite of the shared Germanic legal tradition. With the exception of Scotland, we have therefore grouped the countries in the Romanistic and Germanic Law traditions together.

With the exception of Scotland, the English-speaking groups in our study were clearly part of the Anglo-American Common Law tradition. Although they differed in many important respects, all these countries, including Scotland, were linked by a non-interventionist approach to welfare, and (with the exception of Scotland) an adversarial approach to child protection. We placed Scotland in the English-speaking group in spite of its different legal structure because of the similarities in local government structures, health service and laws. Although Scotland has a different child welfare system from the rest of the UK, and in Ireland subsidiarity is an important concept, these countries had more in common with each other than with any of the countries in the Continental European Civil Law tradition.

One factor in the differences of structures and services is, of course, the economic situation. These countries have very different levels of economic activity; they also, proportionately, put very different levels of resource into their health and child welfare systems; both choice and necessity are involved in the levels of service provided.

SIMILARITIES IN STRUCTURES AND SERVICES

Trying to trace patterns of similarity and difference between the systems and structures of European mental health and child welfare services produces a cat's cradle of interconnecting, criss-crossing links and divergences. Writing in the 1930s, the Czech novelist Karel Capek describes, in *The War with the Newts*, the (fictional) response of different European countries to a common problem.

> 'In short, every State met the Newt problem in its own and separate way; but the sum total of official regulations by which the public duties of the Newts were defined and the animal liberty of the Newts was suitably restricted, was everywhere much the same.' (Capek 1937, reprinted 1998: 221)

Sixty years later, the responses of a range of European countries to the challenge of providing health and welfare services for the mentally ill and for children shows the same mixture of difference of route and similarity of objective. In order to diminish repetition, we describe the aspects of the structures and systems, or of the service provisions, that are similar across all or almost all the countries in question, before giving a country by country account of the structures and service provisions that would be experienced by someone seeking help.

DEFINITIONS

Many of the terms used to describe services and structures have very specific meanings in one country and quite general ones in another. An example would be the English use of 'looked after' and 'accommodated' as terms for children in out-of-home placements. We have aimed to use general descriptive terms that are as far as possible independent of national systems and culture, and we outline these below.

'Primary Care Services' are the non-specialist health services, usually the general practitioner (a generalist doctor, *médecin traitant, medico di base*) and a public health nurse. Sometimes the child health nurse (e.g. the health visitor in the UK, a nurse with special qualifications in maternal and child health) is located in the primary health care service. Child health nurses may alternatively be located with the community paediatrician in local government services (as in France, where they are part of a multidisciplinary child welfare team with social workers), or as part of the school medical service.

An important aspect of primary health care service is that it is a universal service, used by all citizens, without stigma.

'Adult Mental Health Services' include psychiatric hospital services, out-patient (ambulant) services, day hospitals, private psychiatrists and multi-disciplinary teams working in the community (outside of the hospitals). 'Community Mental Health Team' (CMHT) is only used with reference to UK services.

'Child Welfare' is used as a general description of the services that focus on the child or the child in the family, including child and family sections of social services, non-governmental organisations, community paediatric health services and child protection, but not child and adolescent mental health.

'Child Mental Health Services' or 'Child Psychiatric Services' include in-patient and out-patient child and adolescent psychiatry and mental health care, child and family guidance clinics and school psychological services. 'Child and Adolescent Mental Health' (CAMH) services refers to UK services.

COMMON STRUCTURES

A framework of services for primary care, maternity and child health exists in all the countries studied. There is usually (but not in all countries) a community based general practitioner or family doctor, who acts as the standard entry point to the health care system. The maternity and obstetric services have a follow-up midwifery service, which is usually still involved between 5 and 14 days after childbirth. If there is a community maternal and child health service with child health nurses, this is notified and follows on from the midwifery service. This service continues to be involved with the family until the youngest child is of school age. Exceptions to this pattern are Germany and Luxembourg, where there is no state community maternal and child health service, and where the insurance system facilitates direct self-referral to specialists.

There are both hospital and community mental health services in all the countries in some form. In-patient and out-patient treatment were usually available in wards attached to a general hospital and the run down of large psychiatric hospitals was either in progress or nearing completion. Mother and baby units existed in some countries, but were always in short supply. The role, staffing and powers of community mental health services showed considerable differences. Emergency mental health care could be accessed in a variety of ways, but medical referral was needed in many countries. Italy was the country most open to self-referral for people with mental health problems. Medical and psychiatric reports were needed for compulsory hospitalisation, but there were important differences in the requirements for application for an order, in the grounds for an order and in whom, outside the medical profession, should be involved or informed.

Child and adolescent mental health services were variously located, and their availability was also varied. There was some level of service everywhere, but in some countries it was a very restricted resource. Additional information about the development of child and adolescent mental health services is given in Chapter 11.

Child welfare services for families in difficulties similarly existed every-where in outline, but varied greatly between different countries as to where they were located and how much was provided. Some services were avail-able through social services departments in all countries, but the importance of the role of non-governmental organisations varied a great deal. Although all the countries had a structure for the protection of abused children and the means to assume responsibility for abandoned children and children in danger, there were important differences in the grounds for intervention and in the structure and functioning of the judicial and other systems which were involved in taking responsibility for children against their parents' wishes or in their parents' absence. In all the countries except England and Northern Ireland, juvenile offending was included in the same system as child protection.

SOURCES OF INFORMATION

Much of the published information about the health and welfare systems of European countries is scattered through a range of comparative and single country descriptions related to different aspects of the systems and services. There are also some European-wide studies. Looking first at the publica-tions with a social work rather than social policy slant, the widest-ranging information on the structures for service delivery is given by Munday (1994) who describes the organisation of social services in the (then) 12 member states of the EU. Ruxton (1996) gives a range of information relevant to chil-dren, including the legal context, family policy, child care, health and educa-tion, for the present 15 EU member states. Colton and Hellinckx (1993) and Madge (1994) cover residential and foster care provision in Europe and more widely. Pringle (1998) covers European countries (including eastern Europe) thematically, looking at financial support, parental leave arrange-ments, day care provision, and social care provision. Hetherington *et al.* (1997) look at child protection processes in six European countries, giving an outline of the relevant structures for each country. Gilbert (1997) collects accounts, written in the countries concerned, of child protection and child welfare in seven European countries and North America (those relevant to this project are England, Sweden, Denmark and Germany). Goodwin (1997), in an analysis of mental health policy in western Europe and North America, includes a range of information on the mental health systems of EU countries. Ramon (1996) looks at concepts and developments in European mental health in a more general way, although with some comparative elements, and gives little information on the different systems, except in relation to Italy. Whitney *et al.* (1994) compare the compulsory hospitalisation procedures of four European countries (England, Germany, Italy and Spain).

There is a range of publications relevant to families in the social policy field. Millar and Warman (1996) give a summary of family policy in Europe, and the research report on which this is based provides detailed information on a country by country basis. More recently (in a rapidly changing field) Hantrais (1999) summarised the current state of research in family policy. Bradshaw *et al.* (1993) studied child support packages in western Europe (though there have been a number of changes and developments since that time). Hantrais and Letablier (1996) assemble chapters on a range of aspects of family policy, some of which are comparative across a range of countries, while others are more narrowly focused. Social policy studies on health services tend to be focused on health services as a whole, and mental health services do not receive separate treatment.

The descriptions of the structures and services given below are based mainly on the responses of the project partners to the questionnaires, which were part of the initial data gathering of the research. Other sources will be referenced where they have contributed to the information presented. The account of each system tracks the story of the case vignette, looking at the structures as they are encountered. As the vignette starts with a mental health problem, the descriptions start with the ways of approaching mental health services. This is followed by the information on family support services, which is relevant to Stages 1 and 2, and on child-orientated services relevant to all stages. By child-orientated services we mean services specifically for children, such as school-based services and child mental health services as well as community-based services such as clubs. Child placement services relevant to Stage 3 are then briefly described. Finally, the ways in which mental health and child welfare services can link together, either through underlying structures, through formal systems or through local and informal initiative, are noted. Additional information on the use of compulsion for hospitalisation and for child protection is given in Chapter 4. The sequencing of countries used in this chapter and Chapter 3 is maintained in subsequent chapters.

THE SCANDINAVIAN COUNTRIES

There are many similarities between these countries. They all provide services on the basis of citizenship entitlement to state provision, and combine high levels of taxation with high levels of service. They all have very few non-governmental organisations (NGOs). Health services and child welfare services are financed out of taxation, but there is considerable local autonomy over the organisation and extent of service provision. There is quite a high rate of psychiatric hospital admission and in the past there has been (though this has changed) a high rate of compulsory child placement. In all three countries professionals have a mandatory duty to report both child abuse and anxiety about possible abuse, while all citizens have a duty to report child abuse. The Nordic legal system is reflected in the law relating to state intervention in child protection, which is markedly different from both the continental and the English-speaking models.

Denmark

Entry to the mental health system

The point of entry to the medical system is the generalist doctor, who is the usual route for referral to specialist medical care. It is expected that everyone will have a generalist doctor, so a person wanting help with mental ill health would be likely to contact the doctor first. Self-referral to the psychiatric department of the local general hospital would also be a possibility. In the case of a puerperal illness, the family might contact the maternity ward, but would probably then be referred to the generalist doctor. Another alternative would be the health visitor service, which would have been informed of the birth of a child by the maternity ward. This service usually makes at least five home visits during the first year of life and is part of the social welfare office.

The mental health services are run by the area health board. There is some shortage of beds, and care in the community is increasing. Community psychiatric centres are multidisciplinary, staffed by workers (nurses, social workers, psychologists and psychiatrists) from the hospital mental health services, and there are also social centres staffed by health visitors, nurses and social pedagogues which cover the same geographical areas as the psychiatric centres.

In Copenhagen there is a specialist maternity service for mothers with mental health problems (Lier *et al.* 1995; Lier 1997). The aim of the service is to give prenatal and postnatal support to mothers in helping them to relearn mothering and accept support. It is a preventive intervention. The service has specialist midwives and health visitors to give extra support to the mothers. There is a regular monthly interdisciplinary meeting of midwives, child psychiatrists and psychiatrists. Midwives and health visitors are the main sources of referrals.

Family support

The first place a family in difficulties would look for help would be the local offices of the social services department of the commune. The communes (local authorities) provide a full range of social services, including specialist teams for children and families. The children and families teams work closely with the health visiting service which is part of the same organisation. These teams are multidisciplinary, and include psychologists, fostering officers, social workers and health visitors, and there are regular weekly team meetings. The commune also runs community family centres which are open to referrals from the social services and to self-referrals, giving an alternative initial point of contact.

The Social Welfare Act of 1992 states that:

> 'The local authority *may offer* single persons and families free day-to-day guidance and *is obliged* through fieldwork to direct such efforts to all persons who can be considered to be in need thereof.' (S. 28)

and

> 'The local authority *supervises* the living conditions of children and adolescents under the age of 18 years, and *it is an obligation* for the authority to offer parents guidance when a child or adolescent has problems with its surroundings or in other ways is living under unsatisfactory conditions.' (S. 32)
>
> (Bering Pruzan 1997: 130–131; italics added)

There is a duty for all citizens, and an obligation for professionals, to notify the local authority of child abuse or neglect, and for professionals to notify suspected child abuse or neglect. The local authority must then investigate, and offer the appropriate services.

Child-orientated services

There is a school health system with a school nurse, and a school psychological service, which can provide an assessment and educational support. The head teacher, as a professional, has an obligation to report neglect or the possibility of neglect to the local authority.

Child mental health services are provided through child and family guidance clinics and the school psychological service. There is also an in-patient service for adolescents (aged 14–18).

Out-of-home care

If the recommendation is for an out-of-home placement, and the parent/s do not agree, the case must be decided by the Child and Adolescent Committee of the locally elected authority (described in Chapter 4). Placements made on an order from the Child and Adolescent Committee have to be reviewed annually by the Committee. There is a high level of foster care provision and an extensive use of placements within the family system. Fostering services and residential care are part of the local authority social service. For any out-of-home placement, with or without parental agreement, a plan is required which includes provisions for family support and a statement of the aims of the placement.

Links between mental health and child welfare

The generalist practitioner was a possible link between systems, but was seldom referred to. The presence of the health visitors in the same location as social workers, and the sharing of regular team meetings with social workers, was the most important and most consistent link, connecting a universal service and a selective service. In Copenhagen, for mentally ill mothers with infants, the specialist unit described above provided an integrated service between midwifery, child psychiatry and the health visiting service. While there are no formal systems to link mental health to child welfare services, mandatory reporting increases the likelihood that concerns about children will lead to inter-agency communication.

Norway

Services are highly decentralised, and are the responsibility of locally elected authorities. There are therefore considerable differences in organisation between regions, but the legislation, guidelines and supervision of implementation are national.

Entry to the mental health system

The usual entry to the medical system is through the generalist medical practitioner (except for children—see below). There are three elements of mental health care: psychiatric hospital care, which is part of the general hospital system, providing emergency, intermediate and rehabilitation care; district psychiatric centres (DPS); and private psychiatric and psychological services. The DPS are being developed and provide care in the community. They offer both in-patient and out-patient treatment and day care and have direct and well-maintained links to municipal health and social services.

Family support

The general support and primary health prevention work for children is done by the health stations run by the local authorities. Almost all parents use the services of the health stations, which are open during normal office hours and provide pregnancy care and supervision, and courses for expectant parents. The health nurse visits all infants in their homes once within the first two weeks, thereafter the parents (mothers) come with the child to the health station approximately once a month for advice, infant and child medical and developmental support, and counselling. From the child's eighth month the mother and child visit the health station every two months until the child is 17 months old. Thereafter the mother and child visit the health station when the child is 2 years and 4 years old. From the age of 5 the health stations only support children with special needs. Parents may, if they prefer, use a medical practitioner instead of the health station, but must then inform the health station of their intentions. The health stations also run kindergartens, after-school centres and youth clubs.

   Help is provided for families in difficulties and children at risk by the social services. There is a Child Protection Agency (CPA) in each local authority which works closely with the social services and health stations, and may be under the same organisational umbrella as either of them. The CPA works with children and families where the child is in need of a child protection measure, which can be a supportive measure for the child in the family or an out-of-home placement. Before an order is made, the CPA undertakes an investigation. Nearly four times as many children receive supportive measures as out-of-home placements. Most supportive measures are for contact persons or contact families (support for the child or family by a voluntary worker), the funding of leisure activities, payment for a kindergarten place or family guidance. There is mandatory reporting of child abuse and neglect to the CPA for public employees such as social workers and teachers, and there is also mandatory reporting for professionals with professional codes of confidentiality, such as doctors and psychologists.

Child-orientated services

The health nurses of the health stations have clinics at schools. In addition to having an open door to the children they do vaccinations, and talk with groups and individuals. There are teachers with a special responsibility for a child's social well-being, and school psychological services, but these are mainly for scholastic problems. They can refer children to the child mental health services. The child and adolescent mental health services are part of the health service and are well resourced. They are regulated in the same way as other mental health services.

Out-of-home care

An out-of-home placement may be made by the CPA with the parents' agreement. If the parents do not agree the CPA applies for an order to the County Social Welfare Board (CSWB) and carries out their decisions. The CSWB is an administrative body at county level, and is the decision-making body for compulsory orders, both out-of-home placement and supervision.

Links between mental health and child welfare services

The location of services varies in different districts, but the health stations provide a flexible multidisciplinary core. The fact that the health stations as well as the social services are run by the local authorities facilitates contacts between them. Health visitors provide an active link into the school system, and there are also teachers with a special responsibility for the children's social well-being. There are new initiatives to develop awareness of possible parental mental health problems among nursery school staff, so schools play a significant part in connecting welfare services for children and health services. As in Denmark, mandatory reporting of concern about child abuse increases communication between agencies where children are involved.

Sweden

The professionals in the discussion groups were drawn from the local authority services of an area of Stockholm which has high levels of poverty and many immigrant groups. Some aspects of services may be specific to that district. Social and health services are run by the municipalities which have powers of taxation and, within the framework of the relevant national laws, have considerable freedom of decision-making in the way that services are provided (Hessle and Vinnerljung 1999).

Entry to the mental health system

The front line of the health service is the 'house doctor', who is employed by the district health authority and works in the local medical centre. The house doctor would be the first person to turn to over mental health anxieties, but he or she is not really a 'family' doctor, as children are more frequently cared for by the local paediatrician. Patients can, and often do, refer themselves to the mental health services. The local Child Health Care Unit (BVC), which provides health care during the pre-school years, takes over child health care from the maternity services within a few days of the new baby returning home.

The house doctor could refer a person with a mental illness to either the mental health team of the county medical services, which provide acute care and hospital services, or the community-based services, which since 1995 have had responsibility for the care of those who are no longer acutely ill. A large psychiatric hospital has been closed, and the development of community-based alternatives aims to 'normalise' the care of people with mental health problems.

Family support

Families in difficulties can go for help to the child and family team of the social services of the municipality. The 1980 Social Services Act states that the social welfare board of the municipality:

> '(1) shall endeavour to ensure that children and young people grow up in good and secure conditions, (2) act in close co-operation with families to promote the comprehensive personal development and the favourable physical and social development of children and young persons, and (3) ensure that children and young persons in danger of developing in an undesirable direction receive the protection and support they need, and, if in their own best interests so demand, are cared for and brought up away from their own homes.' (Olsson Hort 1997: 109)

Thus the child and family team is able to undertake family support as well as child protection work. In the research district, if intensive support were needed, it would be provided by the family team from the Community Resources Unit.

Child-orientated services

If a child were having problems at school, this would come to the attention of the school health service. Although their main work is in health promotion, prevention and consultation, they make assessments and can refer children in need of help to the house doctor or the child mental health service.

In the research district, there is a support group for children with a mentally ill parent, run by a community social work agency as part of a project set up by the Department of Research and Development, Psychiatry,

West Stockholm District Health Authority (Skerfving 1999). This project has also initiated a counselling service, which is offered at the hospital for the children of psychiatric in-patients.

Child and adolescent out-patient mental health services in Stockholm are attached to the services for people with learning difficulties, although they have a separate administration. In-patient services are part of the same system as adult in-patient services, and, in some regions, all child and adult mental health services are part of the same organisation. Social services can refer children to the child mental health services, or to child psychiatrists working privately. In some areas the municipality also provides a child guidance clinic.

Out-of-home care

The social workers of the municipal services work mainly with families on a voluntary basis. If they consider that a child needs to be removed from home and the parents do not agree, an application has to be made by the social welfare board of the municipality to the county administrative court. The application will be based on an inquiry by the social workers. There is mandatory reporting of child abuse; all citizens have a duty to report abuse or neglect. The relevant professionals are required to report abuse or neglect, and also have a duty to report anxiety about possible abuse or neglect.

Links between mental health and child welfare services

Acute mental health services are run by the regions but long-term mental health care and child health services are run by the municipalities, which facilitates contact. There are no formal links between services, but there is an expectation that services will work together. Co-operation is not complicated. There are a few joint ventures for children with mentally ill parents which demonstrate links between services, for example the local groups for children run by adult mental health and social services in co-operation. Mandatory reporting of concern about child abuse increases contacts between agencies where there is parental mental illness.

Chapter 3

The Systems of the Partner Countries: the Continental Countries and the English-Speaking Countries

THE CONTINENTAL COUNTRIES

In this group, we look first at the Romanistic legal group, France, Italy and Luxembourg, and then at the Germanic legal group, Germany and Greece.

France

Entry to the mental health system

Physical medicine is provided through health insurance, so patients are free to refer themselves direct to a specialist, but it is common for families to have a *médecin traitant*, a general practitioner. Psychiatric and mental health services are state run and free at point of use and patients can be referred to the mental health services by other health professionals or they can refer themselves. The services are administered through a system of sectors which are mainly co-terminous with local government service boundaries. The large psychiatric hospitals have been progressively phased out, and most psychiatric care is provided in wards in general hospitals. There is a hospital-based community mental health service which has some offices outside the hospitals in local areas. This service employs nurses, psychiatrists, psychologists, rehabilitation social workers and *assistantes sociales* (social workers with a generic training).

Family support

Community maternal and child health services are part of the service of the local authority. The service of *Protection Maternelle et Infantile* (PMI) provides *puéricultrices* (the equivalent of the UK health visitor—a nurse with specialist training in child health) who work with families with children up to school age (six years). They are in a joint multidisciplinary team (*Circonscription d'Interventions Sanitaires et Sociales*—CISS) with generic social workers from the social services and the specialist child and families service, *Aide Sociale à l'Enfance* (ASE).

The local authority provides a patch-based social work service; the social worker (*assistante sociale du secteur*) has a generic training and works with all the population of her specific area who need social services. Targeted child and family services are provided by the ASE, which provides workers with a specialist training in work with children and families (*éducateurs spécialisés*). This work can be formalised as an 'administrative' (i.e. not compulsory) order, called an AEMO (*Action Educatif en Milieu Ouvert*: order for support and supervision while a child remains within the family). The ASE is responsible for providing support for families in difficulties, but they only work with families on a voluntary basis.

If a worker within the social services considers that a child should be referred to the judge for children, the decision is taken by the ASE, which then makes the referral. Other services (hospitals, schools) can refer children to the judge themselves. The social work service for the judge for children (assessment, work with children and families in the community and some work with children in foster and residential care) is provided by the social work service of the Justice Department and by non-governmental agencies working under a contract agreed between the ASE, the court and the agency. The judge frequently uses a judicial AEMO (see above) as a way of providing family support.

Child-orientated services

There is a child and family mental health service, the *Centre Médico-Psycho-Pédagogique* (CMPP: centre for child mental health) which employs child psychiatrists, psychologists, child and family therapists and other specialists. There are also child and adolescent psychiatric services that are provided on a regional basis by the psychiatric services.

Non-governmental organisations (NGOs) operate a range of services for children such as groups and after-school clubs. Legislation relating to child welfare requires local authorities to ensure that there are designated 'prevention teams' which are expected to engage in primary prevention work through community strategies, including youth work. These teams may be run by NGOs.

Out-of-home care

The ASE is responsible for the provision of residential and foster placements. Residential services are frequently run by NGOs, which also run fostering agencies. Out-of-home placements can be made by the ASE with parental agreement. If parents do not agree, a court order is required from the judge for children.

In the region where the study took place, there is a specialist fostering service for children with mentally ill parents. Foster parents in this service have special training to enable them to support children and respond effectively to situations where the parent's illness leads to bizarre or unreliable behaviour. They take children to visit their parent in hospital and are prepared to offer a very flexible service of intermittent fostering, depending on the state of parental health.

For more detailed information on the French local authority social services and child welfare system, see Thévenet (1990), Renucci (1990), Hetherington *et al.* (1993) and Capul and Lemay (1993).

Links between mental health and child welfare services

The multidisciplinary team of the CISS creates a substantial link, firstly, because the health visitor (*puéricultrice*) is part of the same team as the social workers and, secondly, because the generic social worker (*assistante sociale du secteur*) is responsible for all people on her patch regardless of the nature of their social problems. Even if specialist social workers (or other professionals) are involved, the social worker still has a responsibility for all members of the family. Co-operation is also facilitated by the employment in community mental health teams of an *assistante sociale*, who has the same generic training as the *assistante sociale du secteur,* even though she is now working in a specialist role. Inter-agency meetings can be arranged as required but this is not part of a formal system. Boundaries between mental health sectors and local authority areas are often but not always co-terminous.

Italy

This account relates to a district in the north-east of Italy. The services are organised in different ways in the different regions of Italy, but the main health and child protection laws are national, though with some specific regional variations.

Entry to the mental health system

The family doctor (*medico di base*), who is generally the first person to have contact with someone with health problems, frequently has a lot of information about the patient's medical and social situation. The family doctor, therefore, is usually the filter and source of referral to other health or social services. The health services are organised and managed by the *Azienda per i Servizi Sanitari* (ASS) and deal with the health needs of the whole population. They are organised in multidisciplinary teams which comprise health professionals and, occasionally, social workers. Social workers are often included in the services for mental health, family consultation (*Consultorio Familiare*), drug or alcohol dependency, services for the handicapped and in the civic hospitals.

The Italian mental health service was radically altered in 1978, adopting the principle of normalisation (Donnelly 1992). In 1994 guidance was issued about the further closure of psychiatric hospitals. One aspect of the development of the mental health services has been the establishment of mental health centres (*Centro di Salute Mentale*—CSM) (Pino *et al.* 1993). The local CSM service is an active organisation reaching out to the community. It offers a range of out-patient services and treatments for mentally ill patients both medical and social, individual and group. It has some beds for emergency overnight use, but this is for respite and crisis response rather than acute mental illness. Beds in the local general hospital are available for the treatment of mental illness requiring hospital treatment. The CSM has taken trouble over publicising its role and over developing a good relationship with the *medico di base*. Self-referrals are accepted and are a common occurrence. Workers at the CSM expect to be involved in the community and they work to mobilise the resources of the community for their patients (Savio 1996).

Family support

The social and health services are organised separately, but both are involved in family support. The social services are organised and managed by the commune and concern themselves with all social problems, including those of children (Hetherington *et al.* 1997). They are mainly staffed by social workers (*assistanti sociali*) and also in some places by specialist social workers (*educatori* and *animatori*). Psychologists are sometimes employed for consultation on specific situations.

The *Consultorio Familiare* (CF) is part of the health service system, and at times works in collaboration with the local social services. The CF has a multidisciplinary team composed of social workers (*assistenti sociali*), psychologists, obstetricians, gynaecologists and health visitors. Its remit is to work on relationships with individuals, couples and families; to care for women's health and work on cancer prevention; to work with mother–child relationships in the first year of life, including support, information and preparation before and after childbirth; to provide information on contraception and abortion; and to promote health.

Responsibility for certain situations concerning the care and protection of children is divided between the local social services of the commune, the *Consultorio Familiare* and (if necessary) the NPI (child mental health service—see below). These situations are: child abuse, maltreatment or abandonment of children; requests to the tribunal (family court) for children to be placed out-of-home; and placement of the child with an alternative family for rehabilitation. Under the Civil Code, it is mandatory for anyone, but particularly for public officials, to report child abuse to the tribunal for children.

Child-orientated services

The child mental health service is provided by the service of *NeuroPsichiatria Infantile* (NPI), which is part of the health service system. They have working links with the local social services and the *Consultorio Familiare*. In the research district they had a strong systemic family theory orientation.

Out-of-home care

Residential and foster care services are mainly provided by non-governmental organisations paid for and accredited by the local authority. Foster care is an increasing but still scarce resource. Placements can be made with parental agreement by the local authority social services.

Links between mental health and child welfare services

The most important link between services is the multidisciplinary *Consultorio Familiare*, which employs both health visitors and social workers. The *medico di base* is also an important figure with links both to the CF and to the CSM.

Connections with the local authority social services are less effective. To improve co-operation and integration of services in such situations, regular meetings have recently been set up in the research district for the discussion of cases which involve several services. This has not been in place for long, but is regarded very positively by the workers concerned. Protocols for co-operation between health and social services are being developed currently, and are already beginning to facilitate co-operation.

The *medico di base* is often expected to take the role of co-ordinator, but in cases that involve many agencies this role is usually held by the *Distretto Sanitario* (district health service). The co-ordinator is then an employee nominated by the ASS and is given the mandate to manage the integration of health and social services. In the research district, there are professionals from both health and social services who are regarded as competent to co-ordinate complex interventions when several professionals or services are involved.

Luxembourg

This account relates to both Luxembourg city and the surrounding district. There are some differences in service provision, but many of the non-governmental organisations cover the whole area, and most of the costs of these services are refunded by social security. Families in difficulties are supported by a series of related services subsidised by the Ministry for the Family. The principle of subsidiarity (Schäfer 1995; Smith 1995) is very important in the structuring of service delivery in Luxembourg, and results in a wide range of organisations being involved in providing social welfare services.

Entry to the mental health system

There are extensive medical services based on an insurance-funded system. For gynaecological, paediatric or psychiatric care, a person can choose to go to a private specialist or to the hospital service. It is not obligatory to be referred by a generalist doctor, with the result that, while generalist doctors are available, a patient does not necessarily need to consult one.

A project to reform the psychiatric services was set up in 1992. Plans were made for the decentralisation of psychiatry, and for an increase in independent services for care and accommodation; for an increase in the services for support for mentally ill people in the community; for the development of crisis intervention services; and for the development of child and adolescent psychiatric services. These changes are happening slowly. At present there is a large psychiatric hospital and there are some psychiatric wards in general hospitals. There are two community mental health services for adults with separate day centres. The community mental health services are supported by the Ministry of Health on an annual contract basis, and are free except for fees for medical consultation, which can be reclaimed. Self-referral to mental health services is common. Most medical expenses can be refunded through social security.

Family support

In each region, there is a generalist social service, the *Centre-Médico-Sociale* (CMS), which provides school medical and child health consultations as well as a general social work service staffed by *assistantes sociales*. Some communes have developed their own social services. There are non-governmental services available for maternal and child health, which provide support for mothers with young children. Many services have been developed to respond to specific problems, such as a service for families with prematurely born children. The *Project d'Action en Milieu Ouvert* (PAMO: project for intervention in the home setting) works with families, with their agreement, to prevent the child being placed outside the family. ALUPSE (*Association Luxembourgeoise de Prévention des Sévices aux Enfants*: the Luxembourg Association for the Prevention of Child Abuse) works with cases of child abuse and child sexual abuse. The tribunal for children often turns to the *Service Central d'Assistance Sociale* (SCAS) for social work intervention. The SCAS undertakes assessments and works with children in their own homes. Almost 90% of placements are the result of a judicial order.

Child-orientated services

A child mental health out-patient service was set up in 1994 at the *Centre Hospitalier de Luxembourg*. A day centre was opened in this service at the beginning of 1999 to provide a diagnostic and treatment centre for children with complex problems. At present there are no in-patient facilities, and children who need this must be placed in other countries. The care of disturbed adolescents poses problems, as there are neither psychiatric beds nor out-patient care. There is a school psychological service (*Service de Psychologie et d'Orientation Scolaire*—SPOS) and a specialist service, the *Service de Guidance de l'Enfance*, which provides consultation regarding psychological, emotional and educational problems for children aged 4–15. This service offers thera-peutic and psychosocial help and psychological testing.

Out-of-home placement

Residential homes are mainly run by non-governmental organisations, paid for by the state. If a child is placed outside the home, parental authority is transferred to the person, family or organisation that has charge of the child's up-bringing.

Links between mental health and child welfare services

In 1998, as a direct result of the Icarus project, a project of collaborative work over difficult psychosocial case situations was set up which involves different health and social services in regular co-ordination meetings. There are many informal contacts between the professionals working in different teams, but as yet there are no multidisciplinary mental health teams. In a small and cohesive area, informal links are important and facilitate co-operation. The subsidiarity principle does not institutionalise inter-agency links, so a great deal depends on informal co-operation. The recently established child mental health service of the main hospital is beginning to develop a role as a central point for consul-tancy and inter-agency discussion in complex situations.

Germany

This account relates to a large urban local government area in north Germany. The individual regions (*Länder*: the largest local government units) determine mental health legislation, involving regional differences. Child welfare legislation is determined by the federal government. The principle of subsidiarity is very important in the structuring of service delivery in Germany, and results in a wide range of organisations being involved in providing social welfare services and in considerable local variation.

Entry to the mental health system

There is a statutory separation of institutional and ambulatory health care, which has resulted in the family doctor becoming an important and presti-gious figure in the health care system. However, health care is insurance based, and the patient has a free choice of which doctor to visit at any time. Thus the patient may choose to go directly to a specialist, rather than a general practitioner or family doctor. A patient seeking mental health care would be most likely to go to a family doctor or a psychiatrist, and less likely to go to the social services mental health team (see below).

There are state-run psychiatric hospital services, out-patient departments and sheltered living/occupational services. Community mental health services (*SozialPsychiatrische Dienst*—SPD) for adults are provided by the district authority. Day care services, as well as the many and various self-help/service user groups, are provided by NGOs.

Family support

The *Jugendamt* (child and youth social services) is the local government service for children and families (Wilford 1997). Under the *Kinderjugendhilfegesetz* 1990 (KJHG: Child and Youth Service Act) the *Jugendamt* has a duty to support families in caring for and bringing up their children, and it also works with the family court (see below). The general social service of the commune provides a service dealing mainly with financial and practical problems. A large proportion of social services for children and families is provided by NGOs. These services are partly funded by the charitable institutions that run them and partly by local government. Social services for children and families do not come under the health insurance funding and are usually free or make a nominal charge.

Among the services run by NGOs and paid for by the state are the services of *SozialPädagogische Familienhilfe* (SPFH). These are intensive family support services, staffed by trained workers, social pedagogues, whose training is equivalent to that of social workers. The SPFH is able to send a worker into a family for several hours a day several days a week, to provide a service where intervention at a practical level accompanies intervention on a social and psychological level. There was some debate as to how quickly this service could be mobilised, but there seemed to be agreement that it would not, in an emergency, take more than a few days.

There are also child-minding services, family support workers (home helps), parents' groups and carers' groups.

There is no state-run equivalent to the health visiting or community maternal and child health service, although there are sometimes services available under the medical insurance scheme. In the research district there is a service for mothers with small children (*Mütterberatung*) which offers advice and support on child care and health.

When a family is in need of help, in order to fulfil the spirit of the KJHG, the social services have to call an *Erziehungskonferenz* (help conference), a care plan discussion, attended by the social workers from the agencies concerned, the parents and the children (Schwabe 1999). This happens at an earlier stage than a child protection conference in the UK, and is triggered by need rather than risk.

Child-orientated services

There is a child and adolescent mental health service, which offers a special service for mentally ill parents and babies. There are also a variety of child and adolescent mental health services, which are part of the health insurance system. Both out-patient and residential/hospital services can be provided by independent professionals paid through health insurance. This generates a wide range of different child mental health facilities.

Schools have teachers with pastoral care responsibilities, and there is a school-based medical service. There is also an educational psychological service offering therapeutic work with children with emotional problems as well as psychological testing. This is part of the school system, and takes referrals from the school.

NGOs provide a wide range of services for children, such as clubs, street workers and counselling services. *Seelennot* is a local organisation for children with a mentally ill parent, which has recently set up a group for children and produces information leaflets for children and parents.

Out-of-home care

The *Jugendamt* has to assist the family court with all matters pertaining to a child's safety and welfare; this would include placement away from home or the removal of parental authority and appointment of a guardian. Under this act, in an emergency or if there is conflict, a child can be counselled without the knowledge of his parents if it is in his or her interest (KJHG 1990, para. 8, s. 3).

Residential and fostering services are run by NGOs and monitored by the *Jugendamt*. The research district has a service which provides support and training for foster carers and support for children in foster care.

Links between mental health and child welfare services

There are no formal links between services, and the subsidiarity principle results in a plethora of different agencies which might be involved. For children and families in difficulties, the social services is responsible for setting up a help conference (see above). This involves the family and professionals and can include any relatives or friends who might help. One function of the meeting is to co-ordinate efforts and to get agreement from the social services for funding for help from other agencies, so it takes place at an early stage in work with a family.

The lack of a general practitioner or a universal maternal and child health service increases the importance of good informal communication between agencies. There are no formal links between health and child welfare services.

Greece

The services and facilities referred to differ from one part of Greece to another, particularly between rural and urban areas. The problems created by the low population density of some areas were a factor in the discussions of the participants.

Entry to the mental health system

The health service is free at point of use and funded from taxation. Psychiatric hospital care and psychiatric services in general hospitals are run by the

Department of Mental Health of the Ministry of Health and Welfare. Community mental health care services are run by the local authorities, by NGOs and by organisations of occupational insurance. Mental health centres are being developed but there is a shortage of community mental health provision. The closure of the large psychiatric hospitals is planned and is beginning to take place, but progress is relatively slow (Assimopoulos 1998). There are 49 regional sectors for mental health, which support the provision of community mental health services by NGOs. The general practitioner was seldom mentioned and the gynaecologist was most often referred to as the first likely source of help. The gynaecologist would be most likely to refer a patient to a hospital-based psychiatrist. A patient could alternatively go to the social services, a psychiatrist in private practice or a general hospital with a psychiatric service.

Family support

The local social services for children are run through the regional offices of the Department of Child Protection which is part of the Ministry of Health and Welfare. Action to protect children can be taken by the social services offices of the Department of Child Protection. Children at risk are the responsibility of the judges of the juvenile court. NGOs are active in providing residential and foster care and some specialist day care. Local authorities run a basic social service department which provides some nurseries and runs summer camps.

Community maternal and child health services are run by the Ministry of Health and Welfare through regional offices, and are available in some areas. There are no organisational connections between the local authority services and services of the Ministry of Health and Welfare such as the community maternal and child health services. All the services suffer from low staffing and there is a shortage of day care provision for children.

Child-orientated services

Child mental health services are part of the mental health services of the Ministry of Health and Welfare. They are regulated by laws dealing with the mental health services. There are also some counselling and child mental health services that are provided by NGOs and local authorities.

In Thessaloniki, the child mental health department of the university hospital has set up a system of inter-agency co-operation for families in difficulties, which brings together workers from the social services, the child protection service and the NGOs at a conference convened by the child mental health service (Abatzoglou *et al.* 2000).

Out-of-home care

Residential and foster care services are provided by NGOs. Fostering services are often linked to residential homes and have developed in that context. Some fostering services are provided by the local authorities.

Links between mental health and child welfare services

There are few formal links between health and child welfare services. The child mental health department can provide such links (as described above) in Thessaloniki, but this depends greatly on individual initiative. Health-visiting services provide some links, but the action of social workers in mobilising support from the community and the interventions of local priest are the main co-ordinating forces.

THE ENGLISH-SPEAKING COUNTRIES

This group is made up of Australia, Ireland and three of the countries of the UK—England, Northern Ireland and Scotland.

Australia (Victoria)

This account relates to a region of Melbourne, Victoria. Each of the four regions of metropolitan Melbourne provides health, mental health and child welfare services, organised and funded by the Department of Human Services. Many services provided by the Department of Human Services are tendered out, which in certain respects is similar to the purchaser/provider split of the UK rather than the subsidiarity of Germany and Luxembourg.

Entry to the mental health system

General practitioners (GPs) provide a general medical service in the community, funded by Medicare, the Australian universal health insurance scheme. Health care insurance holders are refunded 85% of the costs of this service. Some GPs are located in community health centres, which provide a free multidisciplinary service with some home visiting. Community midwives provide an out-reach service in a few areas. There is a mental health crisis and assessment (CAT) team which is an emergency service working in the community. This team can work in crisis situations in the home for people with acute psychiatric illness as an alternative to hospital admission. The GP can refer patients direct to this team, or to the community mental health centre (see below) or to a hospital-based psychiatrist. Patients can also refer themselves.

There is a regional psychiatric hospital with a 15-bed intensive care unit, and an acute in-patient unit in the general hospital with 15 beds. This includes a six-bed mother and baby unit for mothers with psychiatric illness and their babies up to 12 months. There is a community mental health (CMH) centre and the mobile support and treatment (MST) team provides intensive outreach services for people with more severe mental illness.

Family support

Municipal councils provide a maternal and child health nurse service to support and monitor all new mothers and babies. Family support agencies provide a range of services for families in difficulties including home support, counselling, group work and practical help. These agencies are mainly church-based NGOs with state funding on a contractual basis. The child protection service is run by the Department of Human Services. The service has to respond to notifications of suspicions of child abuse and neglect, and intervene when harm has occurred or is likely to occur. Professionals in the health and welfare field have to notify the child protection service of suspicions of abuse.

Child-orientated services

The child and adolescent mental health service (CAMHS) is a regionally based service and has a multidisciplinary, family focused approach. It mainly provides an out-patient service, with some limited in-patient facilities. Fees for treatment by a private psychiatrist can be paid for from the medical insurance scheme, but this does not usually cover the full fee.

There are special interest groups in the community: these are self-help groups which have an interest in children with a mentally ill parent and offer support to them and their parents (Cowling 1999a).

Out-of-home care

Family support services frequently provide fostering and respite care services. Some also run group homes or residential care units. Most residential and foster care services are provided by NGOs.

Links between mental health and child welfare services

There is a formal protocol for communication between child welfare and mental health services, but problems in communication persist. The structure of services is quite fragmented, with GPs provided by Medicare, child health services run by the municipalities, child protection by the Department of Human Services and family support services provided by NGOs. The NGOs have, however, developed a range of services for families with a mentally ill parent (Cowling 1999b)

Ireland

The administration and delivery of health and social services in Ireland are devolved to eight health boards, each covering a specific geographical area; Dublin falls within the Eastern Health Board. The structures of the health boards are being reviewed, and there have been recent changes in the way that the Eastern Health Board delivers services, resulting in the creation of five programmes to oversee the delivery of all the board's services and duties. These are: (1) acute hospital services and the elderly services programme; (2) health promotion, mental health, addiction and social development programme; (3) child and families programme; (4) community care programme; and (5) services for persons with disabilities programme. This structure is specific to the Eastern Health Board.

Entry to the mental health system

The general practitioner (also known as the family doctor) works within the community care programme of the health board. A free medical service is available to those who qualify on the basis of a means test, and health services are funded from taxation as well as through various insurance schemes – private, occupational and state-run. The GP would be the person who was first approached, and direct self-referral to the local health centre or out-patient mental health service is not accepted, except in an acute state. Self-referral to the mental health services is therefore possible but not usual.

Large psychiatric hospitals have begun to close, and small units or units in general hospitals are being developed. Community resources are being developed on a 'sectorised' basis, aiming to provide a continuum of services in a particular area. Project participants referred to the possibility for a mother to be hospitalised with her baby, but there was some uncertainty as to how far this service was usually available.

Family support

The 1991 Child Care Act obliges the health and social services boards to promote the welfare of children living within their catchment areas. The boards are permitted to fund other agencies to assist in this, but they retain the ultimate responsibility for the health and welfare of children who are not receiving the care that they need.

The public health nurses (equivalent to a health visitor) and the public health doctors (community paediatricians) work in the community care programme and are based in the health centres. Family centres are run by health boards or by NGOs funded by health boards. The children and families social work teams of the health boards tend to work on a child protection basis, with the family support services (NGOs) and the public health nurses providing more preventive services. The health and social services boards are responsible for taking child protection cases to court.

Child-orientated services

Child mental health services in the Eastern Health Board have recently been transferred to the child and families programme. Thus, adult mental health and child mental health have been separated, at least from an administrative point of view, and child mental health is in the same programme as child protection services. The service is under-resourced and has six-month waiting lists. In some areas, self-referral is accepted, but elsewhere referrals have to be made by the GP.

After-school clubs are now being developed, but they are not usually funded by the health boards.

Out-of-home care

Residential children's homes are run by the health boards or by a variety of NGOs. Fostering services are run only by the health boards (except for some adoption agencies which run pre-adoption fostering services). There is a shortage of foster placements.

Links between mental health and child welfare services

The unifying effect of the Health and Social Services Boards is important. The Chief Executive Officer of the Board is responsible for both statutory mental health services and child welfare services, so that ultimately there is a single, responsible person. Even though services may be separately run, geographical closeness is still maintained in many places, and was felt to be very important in facilitating informal links. Problems may arise where the mental health services are provided by an NGO and, therefore, differently accountable.

The UK

There are important differences between the service structures of England, Northern Ireland and Scotland, and the Scottish legal system is fundamentally different from that of England and Northern Ireland. The three countries are therefore treated separately. We were unable to include Wales in this research for practical reasons, but note that they have the same legislation as England and the same local authority service structures. However, it is likely that with devolution differences will develop.

The UK health service is free at point of use. Hospital services (in-patient and out-patient) are organised on the basis of a split between purchasers of services (health authorities) and providers of services. This split was introduced during the 1990s in order to bring an 'internal market' into the provision of health care. Services are purchased by health authorities from National Health Service trusts and other independent non-profit making bodies which can be contracted to provide specific services. General practitioners are independent doctors working under contract to the health service to provide a service to patients who are registered with them. Shortly after the research took place, there was a change in the administrative system of the health service which increased the importance of locality based primary care groups (which include GPs, practice nurses and other medical auxiliaries) as the purchasers of health care.

England

This account relates to three boroughs in the south of England, two in London and one on the south coast. The National Health Service trusts in these boroughs have very varied catchment areas and cover different constituencies of patients. Child and adolescent mental health services are sometimes in the same trust as adult mental health, and sometimes quite independent. Community care teams (multidisciplinary mental health teams working with patients in the community) may be in different trusts from some of the psychiatric beds to which they relate. The boundaries of health trusts are not necessarily co-terminous with local authority boundaries. Social services are part of the elected local authority structure which is completely separate from the NHS trust system.

Entry to the mental health system

The most likely point of entry to the system is through the general practitioner, who can refer a patient either to a psychiatrist in the hospital service or to the community mental health service. Alternatively, he or she can arrange a visit to the patient at home, either from a mental health nurse, a social worker or a psychiatrist (or a joint visit).

In-patient services are provided by the health trusts, mainly in wards in general hospitals. There are a few specialist psychiatric hospitals, and some mother and baby units, though with a reduced number of beds. There is a general shortage of psychiatric beds. Community mental health services are provided through multidisciplinary teams run jointly by the health trusts and the local authorities. There is no set pattern of organisation.

Family support

The community maternal and child health service have fully qualified specialist nurses (health visitors). They provide a universal service, with some time (but very little) to provide extra support for parents in difficulties over child-rearing. They may be located in the primary health care team with the GP or may form part of the services of a health trust.

The local authorities provide the main social work service for children and families. The children and families teams of the local authority social services departments are orientated towards child protection. While they try to provide services for children 'in need', they are very limited in their resources. Some services are provided by NGOs, normally financed mainly by the local authority. NGOs provide some family support services, such as family centres, but in the recent past have increasingly been diverted towards services related to child protection. Most of the time of the children and families teams is taken up with child protection issues, sometimes in joint investigations with the police.

Child-orientated services

The local authority education departments run school psychological services. These mainly provide psychometric testing and assessments in relation to special school needs. In some places the school psychological service also provides other facilities; for example in one of the boroughs in the research, behavioural management training was provided. Child and adolescent mental health services are provided by health trusts, sometimes as part of a diversified trust, sometimes as a specialist mental health trust. Major hospitals are likely to provide a child psychiatric out-patient service; in-patient services and day hospitals are rare. The resources of the child mental health services are very restricted, and they frequently have waiting lists of six months.

Play therapy and a range of groups for children are provided at some family centres. There are also groups for young carers, which provide for the children of people with mental health problems as well as other disabilities.

The Sure Start programme is likely to increase services, but none of these services was operating at the time of the research.

Out-of-home care

Residential and fostering services are the responsibility of the local authority social services department. Residential homes are mainly run by NGOs and also by private organisations. Fostering services are run by both local authorities and NGOs. Foster carers are in short supply, but residential services are very restricted, and fostering is the majority option.

Links between mental health and child welfare services

The primary care services of GP and health visitors have the potential to create links between other services. Otherwise the structures of health and social services are very separate, with child welfare services isolated from other services, even within the local authority. The joint health and social services community mental health teams seem to have difficulty in maintaining links with child welfare, and tight budgetary constraints hinder co-operation.

Child protection conferences have some potential for encouraging co-operation between services and agencies, but as they are not called until there is a perceived risk of abuse, they are likely to be held too late for the development of preventive and supportive strategies.

Northern Ireland

This account relates to a relatively rural area of Northern Ireland. Northern Ireland has a service delivery structure of health and social services trusts, which locate social work services within the same structure as health services.

Entry to the mental health system

The most likely entry to the system would be through the general practitioner, who can refer a patient either to the acute/intake team or the continuing care team (see below). Self-referral is possible but not usual. The large long-stay psychiatric hospitals are being reduced, but still remain. There are mental health wards in general hospitals, mainly for patients with psychoneurotic illnesses. Multidisciplinary community-based teams are well developed. There are three levels within the adult mental health system. A community psychiatric nursing service is provided at the primary health care level; they deal with short-term therapeutic interventions (6–8 sessions on average). The secondary level is the acute/intake team which screens all new referrals and works intensively with individuals for 12–18 months. However, if it is assessed that the person is suffering from a major psychiatric disorder, he or she is referred to the third level—the continuing care team. Both the acute/intake and continuing care teams are multidisciplinary.

Family support

After the birth of a baby, the community midwife visits mother and baby at home for seven days. The midwife continues to visit after this according to need, until the baby is 28 days old. Thereafter the health visitor takes responsibility for monitoring the health of that child at agreed intervals until the child starts primary education.

The health and social services trusts fund most of the child welfare services, including child and family social work teams, family support services and family centres. They also support voluntary and local initiatives.

Child-orientated services

Child mental health services are also run by the health and social services trusts. They are a limited resource and there is a problem with waiting lists. In-patient units for children and adolescents are provided regionally (both units are located in Belfast), and these beds are accessed through the local child and adolescent mental health service. However, it is inevitable that, locally, young people are admitted to adult wards. There is a lot of unmet need as a result of trauma caused by the Northern Ireland troubles, and a small project is currently running in the research area focusing on this particular need. The large general hospital for the trust area has a child development clinic which works very closely with the child and adolescent mental health service.

Child protection guidelines draw attention to the needs of children with mentally ill parents and there are some support organisations for young carers. There are after-school clubs that are run by NGOs, private organisations and the community, and there is an education welfare service with social workers attached to schools.

Out-of-home care

The trusts fund residential childcare and fostering services. Residential services are run by NGOs and the trusts; fostering services are mainly run by the trusts. About three-quarters of children in out-of-home placements are fostered.

Links between mental health and child welfare services

The structure of the joint health and social services trusts fosters communication and co-operation between agencies, with co-terminous agency boundaries and the location of services near to each other. This enhances and promotes a good informal communication network, and flexibility in co-operation. As in England, the child protection conference has some potential for promoting co-operation, but is likely to take place too late to prevent problems from developing.

Scotland

Scotland has significant differences in legal and administrative structures from other parts of the UK. The most important of these relate to child protection.

Entry to the mental health system

General practitioners are self-employed but work under contract to the health trusts (see UK entry). They are the most likely way into the mental health system. The GP can make referrals to the hospital mental health services or to the community mental health services. Hospital mental health services are provided by the health trusts in the same way as other health services. Community mental health services are a shared responsibility between the trusts and the local authority. The local authority provides social services for people with mental health problems and works in multidisciplinary teams with the psychiatric hospital service. The health trusts and local authorities are encouraged to contract out the provision of services to independent and non-governmental organisations (NGOs). Psychiatric hospitals receive patients in emergencies or where there is compulsion.

Family support

Section 12 of the Social Services (Scotland) Act 1968 requires the social work departments 'to promote social welfare by making available advice, guidance and assistance on such a scale as may be appropriate for their area'. The local authority social services have specialist 'children and families' sections which provide child and family welfare services including advice, support and counselling, practical assistance including money, food vouchers and child protection (see below). They operate support services such as family centres. A range of services for families is also provided by NGOs.

Child protection services are provided in the first place by the local authority social service. If there are concerns about a family that cannot be resolved on a purely voluntary basis (because they are too serious, or because the parents do not agree), the social services must report this to the Reporter to the Children's Panel. The Reporter investigates, and if it is considered that the child may be in need of care or protection, the case is referred to the Children's Panel for a hearing. This system is explained further in Chapter 4.

Child-orientated services

Child mental health services are provided by the Health Care Trusts. There are also educational psychology services provided by the local authority education departments and school medical services employing nurses and paediatricians.

Out-of-home care

Residential care and fostering services are organised by the local authority social services departments.

Links between mental health and child welfare services

Scotland has the same separation between health and social services as England, and primary care has similarly the potential to promote co-operation and communication. The school has an important role through the school medical service and through social workers attached to the schools. In the district studied, regular meetings between schools and social workers laid the basis for future co-operation.

The reporting officer potentially has a role in liaison between services through his or her duty to investigate referred cases. However, like the child protection conference, this referral is likely to take place too late to be useful for preventive action.

Chapter 4

Compulsory Hospitalisation in Mental Health and State Intervention for Child Protection

Compulsory detention for patients with a mental illness and compulsory removal of children from parental care are two of the very few points at which the state intervenes to restrict a citizen's liberty when no criminal charge has been made or proven. The background information that we collected from the project partners gave us a picture of the wide differences between countries in their response to these situations. We were therefore interested to discover the grounds on which such interventions could be made, who was involved in the process, and whether these differences in structures appeared to be related to the responses of the professionals in our groups. In this chapter we give information for each country on the grounds and process, with an introductory analysis of the most noticeable differences.

THE GROUNDS FOR COMPULSORY HOSPITALISATION

The underlying rationale for many of the systems seemed to be that intervention could be considered if a person was a danger to him/herself or to others and that the person had a mental illness (but there were differences of emphasis in the wording of the regulations). Italy had the most 'health'-based and treatment-orientated regulations, requiring that 'the person has a severe mental illness such that urgent treatment is required; that this treatment is not accepted by the patient; and that his or her condition cannot be treated suitably outside of hospital'. Dangerousness was not mentioned. The most complex regulations were those of England and Northern Ireland, with three different levels of order possible. The treatment order, which is of the longest duration, includes a specification of the nature of the mental illness. The recently suggested reforms to the Mental Health Act (Department of Health 2001), particularly in relation to the compulsory detention of people with 'a dangerous severe personality disorder', will further complicate the situation.

There were wide differences in the regulations about the process of compulsion: who had to be informed and who had decision-making powers. The groups most likely to be involved were the mental health professionals (psychiatrists, psychiatric nurses and specialist social workers), local government elected members (including mayors and prefects) and the judiciary and/or public prosecutor. Table 4.1 gives the information for each country about the involvement of elected members and the courts in the procedures for compulsory admission to hospital.

Table 4.1   Procedures for compulsory hospitalisation. The involvement of the legal system or the administrative system in compulsory hospital admission and in appeals against compulsory admission (not including emergency powers)

Country	Admission			Appeals	
	Legal authority	Administrative authority	Neither	Appeal to judicial body	Appeal to administrative body
Denmark		X		X	X
Norway		X		X	X
Sweden		X		X	
France	X	X		X	X
Italy	X	X		X	
Luxembourg	X	X		X	X
Germany	X			X	
Greece	X			X	
Australia		X			X
Ireland			X	X	X
UK: England			X		X
N. Ireland			X		X
Scotland	X				X

Notes
Legal authority: the public prosecutor or the judge in the guardianship court.
Administrative authority: the mayor or an elected representative.
Neither: admission is decided within the hospital system without reference to a judicial or external administrative authority.
Appeal to judicial body: the courts or similar body chaired by a judge.
Appeal to administrative body: a body set up which may allow for legal representation and may include lawyers but does not include a judge acting in that capacity.

All the countries involved required two medical reports or applications (at least one from a psychiatrist) to initiate the process of compulsion. The role of specialist social workers in making applications was prominent in Ireland and the UK, but largely absent elsewhere. Psychiatric nurses had a role in Germany, where nursing reports could form part of the information required by the judge, but this was informal rather than a requisite. Sweden and Denmark used elected representatives at local government level to confirm orders. The continental European countries involved both the judiciary and the administrative sphere in the process of hospital admission. The decision had to be confirmed by the judge, and the administrative authority had to be informed, or might be part of the process of application. The English-speaking countries, except Scotland, relied on the health professionals and involved neither the judiciary nor elected members. When considering an appeal against an order, only England, Northern Ireland and Australia did not use the courts.

THE GROUNDS FOR JUDICIAL INTERVENTION TO PROTECT CHILDREN

The grounds are largely similar between countries, but vary in specificity. All countries except England and Northern Ireland have the same court system for children in need of care or protection and for children who have committed offences. England and Northern Ireland are the only countries to refer to the concept of the 'reasonable' parent ('the care given to the child or likely to be given to him if the order were not made, not being what it would be reasonable to expect a parent to give to him' (Children Act 1989, s. 31(2)(b)(i)). In relation to the situation in the vignette at Stages 1 and 3, there seemed to be general agreement that if the children were at risk, it would be possible to remove them, but not at Stage 2 on the information given. Only France debated the use of judicial powers at Stage 2, in order to put pressure on the family to accept help.

The Process of Intervention

Not all the countries in our study used a purely judicial body to make compulsory decisions about children. The Scandinavian countries had boards or courts which include a judge or a lawyer with competence to act as a judge, but which also included elected members. In Denmark and Norway the boards included co-opted members (with specialist knowledge, for example, child psychologists). In Norway the procedure of the board in relation to legal representation and hearing of evidence is more legalistic and more adversarial than in Denmark (Ingerslev 1999). The remaining countries all used some form of children's court. Apart from Australia, Ireland, England, and Northern Ireland these courts all used an inquisitorial rather than an adversarial approach.

There were considerable differences regarding who could introduce a child protection case to the decision-making system. Table 4.2 sets out the people who have access to the court or board to initiate a case. In the Scandinavian and the English-speaking countries, with the exception of Scotland, the initiative has to come from (or at least through) a social worker employed by the locality child protection agency. The continental European systems are open to a much wider range of applicant.

Table 4.2   Initiating child protection procedures. Professionals or others who can initiate proceedings for a child in need of care or protection to the court or social board (decision-making body with compulsory powers)

Country	Parent	Child	Other family	Social worker	Doctor/ nurse	Teacher	Other
Denmark				X			
Norway				X			
Sweden				X			
France	X	X	X	X	X	X	P.P. or judge
Italy	X		X	X	X	X	
Luxembourg	X	X	X	X	X	X	
Germany	X	X	X	X	X	X	Neighbours
Greece	X	X	X	X	X	X	
Australia				X			
Ireland				X			
UK: England				X			
N. Ireland				X			
Scotland							The Reporter

We give below a summary of the grounds for compulsion and the processes of compulsion country by country.

THE SCANDINAVIAN COUNTRIES

Denmark

Mental health

The grounds for compulsory hospitalisation   If the patient is mentally ill, or in an equivalent state, and it would be unjustifiable not to detain the patient for treatment because:

- expectations of restoration to health or an improvement in health would be worse
- the person is a threat to himself or others.

The process of compulsory hospitalisation   Compulsory admission to hospital for mental illness requires a certificate from a physician who is not a psychiatrist employed at the psychiatric hospital. The consultant physician on the psychiatric ward then decides whether the conditions for compulsory placement have been fulfilled. If the conditions are fulfilled, the patient must be detained. When the conditions are no longer satisfied, the detention must be terminated immediately. All compulsory admissions must be reported to the local authority. The patient must be offered a counsellor who advises him or her about hospitalisation and treatment, and helps the patient in relation to complaints.

The Patients' Complaints Board consists of the relevant chief administrative officer of the local authority and two members appointed by the Minister of Health on advice from the Danish Medical Association and the Federation of Disabled Persons Organisations. Appeals against compulsory detention can be made direct to the courts, with costs paid by the state. The hospital authority must bring the case before the court within five days of the complaint being lodged.

Child protection

The grounds for legal intervention   Cases are referred to the Board (see below) if placement away from home is needed for the child's welfare and the child's parent or guardian will not agree to this, or if an assessment of the need for such a placement is required. A deficit of parental care has to be 'proven' under strict conditions. There is mandatory reporting of child abuse or suspicion of abuse.

The process of legal intervention   Child protection cases are brought to the Board for Children and Young Persons. They can only be brought by social workers from the Social Services Department of the local authority. The Board is made up of three elected local government councillors, a judge and a psychologist or pedagogue. The Board can decide on compulsory assessment or placement away from home. Appeal can be made in the first place to the Social Complaint Board and finally to the County Court.

Norway

Mental health

The grounds for compulsory hospitalisation   Serious mental illness, normally interpreted as psychosis. It must also be shown that the patient is a danger to him/herself or to others, or that the patient will not recover without treatment in hospital; or that the patient will suffer harm.

The process of compulsory hospitalisation   An application may be made by the next of kin, or by a medical officer of health or someone with authority in the social service administration, or by a police officer. A medical doctor must give a clinical report and request admission for the patient. The senior psychiatrist at the hospital must give his consent to the admission and must certify in writing that the patient should be hospitalised. The report is sent to the Control Committee (see below). A patient can be detained for three weeks for observation (to be reduced to 10 days in a forthcoming Act), or for six months for treatment. This order can be renewed every six months. Appeal can be made to the Control Committee which is made up of four lay persons and one judge. If the appeal is rejected, the patient may appeal further to the courts.

Child protection

The grounds for legal intervention   The child protection services have a duty to investigate the living conditions of a child if there is reason to believe that there are circumstances which might require child protection measures. The investigation can take place with or without the consent of the parents. Administrative (i.e. with parental agreement) orders can be made for supportive measures carried out while the child is at home. The criteria for an administrative order are that the child is in need and the child's home circumstances make it necessary. There is mandatory reporting of child abuse or suspicion of abuse.

The process of legal intervention   If an intervention is required, and the parents do not give their consent, the child protection board requests an order from the County Social Welfare Board. The chair of the County Social Welfare Board is a lawyer with competence to act as a judge. A compulsory child protection order may be made by the County Social Welfare Board: (a) if the day-to-day care of the child is seriously deficient or if there are serious deficiencies in meeting the child's needs for personal contact and safety; (b) if the parents do not take the necessary steps to ensure that an ill, handicapped or especially vulnerable child receives the proper treatment or education; (c) if the child is battered or abused in the home; and (d) if there is an overwhelming probability that the health or development of the child will be seriously damaged because the parents are not able to take sufficient responsibility for the child. The County Social Welfare Board can make a supervision order or kindergarten placement order, take a child into custody, and make an order for placement for observation, assessment or short-term treatment of up to four weeks and long-term treatment for up to 12 months (renewable once) for children with behavioural problems. The Board can require medical examination and treatment if the child has a life-threatening illness, impose treatment on a child with special need for treatment and education, terminate parental contact, and give consent to adoption. The County Social Welfare Board is an administrative body, but the procedures are the same as a court, with evidence and legal representation.

All out-of-home placement orders have to be taken by the County Social Welfare Board, even if the parents consent. However, if the parents give their consent, they can also agree to a simplified decision-making process, also carried out by the Board at which there are no witnesses, no legal representation, no psychological experts and no formal hearings of the parties. In an emergency the child protection service may make a decision to place a child away from home with the parents' consent. The leader of the County Social Welfare Board must be informed of any decision within 48 hours, and has the power to annul that decision. A request for a care order must be made within six weeks.

Sweden

Mental health

The grounds for compulsory hospitalisation   The person must (a) suffer from a serious mental disturbance, (b) owing to his or her mental condition and personal circumstances, be in unavoidable need of care that cannot be fulfilled except by hospitalisation, and (c) refuse the care or, as a result of his or her mental condition, be obviously incapable of expressing a well-grounded decision.

The process of compulsory hospitalisation   The application for an order for compulsory hospitalisation has to be certified by two psychiatrists, and the decision has to be put before the county administrative court within two weeks. Care can be given as soon as the application for an order has been signed. A patient can be detained for six months, but this can be extended through an application for extension to the county administrative court. The patient can appeal to the administrative court of appeal, which must hear the appeal within two weeks. The members of the county administrative court are the chairman, who is a judge, and three elected jurymen. The members of the administrative court of appeal are three judges (one of them the chairman) and two elected jurymen.

Child protection

The grounds for legal intervention   Serious danger to a child's health and development because of parental abuse or neglect of the child's needs or because of the child's own behaviour, such as drug or alcohol abuse, delinquency, etc. There is mandatory reporting of child abuse or suspicion of abuse.

The process of legal intervention   Parents, children, other family members and professionals can go to the social services department for help, but only the social services committee can refer a case to the county administrative court. The court can make orders for compulsory care in residential or foster homes. Decisions about voluntary care are made by the local social welfare board. The county administrative court concerned with children is the same court as that concerned with compulsory hospitalisation.

THE CONTINENTAL COUNTRIES

France

Mental health

The grounds for compulsory hospitalisation   Compulsory hospitalisation can take place either on public order grounds (*Hospitalisation d'Office*—HO), or on health grounds (*Hospitalisation du Demande d'un Tiers*—HDT). The grounds for HO are that a person is creating a disturbance to public order and is endangering the safety of others. The grounds for HDT are that the patient's illness makes it impossible for him or her to consent to hospitalisation, and that he or she is in need of immediate care and surveillance of a kind only obtainable by admission to hospital.

The process of compulsory hospitalisation   For HO, an order can be made by the Prefect or, in an emergency, the Mayor, supported by one medical certificate. For HDT, an application must be made by the family or by another person who can act in the patient's interest, supported by two medical certificates. One must be from a doctor not working in the hospital. Within 24 hours a doctor working in the hospital must confirm or disconfirm the need for compulsory hospitalisation. The three certificates must then be sent to the Prefect of the *Département* and to the local authority commission (see below). Within three days of admission the Prefect has to inform the Public Procurator of the district where the patient has lived and the district where the hospital is located. After one month, an HO can be renewed by the Prefect for a further three months, and thereafter for six-monthly terms. An HDT has to be renewed after 15 days, and thereafter at monthly intervals. Orders can be renewed indefinitely. Appeal can be made in the first place to the local authority commission, the *Commission Départemental de l'Hospitalisation Psychiatrique*. This is made up of a psychiatrist and a judge from the local court, both appointed by the court of appeal, and two people, one a psychiatrist and one a member of an organisation representing the families of mentally ill people. The commission also has to review the renewal of all orders beyond three months. Appeal can also be made to the President of the *Tribunal de Grands Instances* (High Court).

Child protection

The grounds for legal intervention   That the health, safety or morality of a minor are in danger, or that the conditions of his or her up-bringing are seriously compromised. There is mandatory reporting of child abuse. In addition, the civil code requires all citizens to report ill treatment to the appropriate services or to the judicial system.

The process of legal intervention   Any citizen, therefore any family member and professionals such as doctors, nurses, social workers and teachers, can refer a situation to the public prosecutor. Referral to the judge for children can be made by the public prosecutor or by parents, the children themselves, or a person or service who has legal charge of the child. The judge can, in exceptional circumstances, refer to himself. Both child protection and juvenile justice cases come before the judge for children. Orders can be made for assessment and/or supervision at home or for placement away from home and the judge can refuse parental access to children placed away from home. Orders have to be reviewed every two years. Appeals against the judge's decision can be made to the High Court.

Italy

Mental health

The grounds for compulsory hospitalisation   The grounds for compulsion are that the person has a severe mental illness such that urgent treatment is required; that this treatment is not accepted by the patient; and that his or her condition cannot be treated suitably outside of hospital. Compulsion can only be used during acute manifestations of the illness.

The process of compulsory hospitalisation An application is made by a doctor which must be confirmed and validated by another doctor, usually a psychiatrist from the ASS *(Azienda per i Servizi Sanitari)*. The compulsory order *(Trattamento Sanitario Obbligatorio—TSO)* is arranged by the mayor of the local commune (who has a general responsibility to protect the health of the citizens of the commune), and the *Giudice Tutelare* (judge in the guardianship court), who is part of the normal judicial system of the Court of Justice, has to be informed within 48 hours of ratification. The judge must validate the TSO within four days of first admission. The order lasts for seven days but can be renewed for successive weeks as necessary. If an order is extended beyond seven days, the consultant psychiatrist of the ASS has to state the length of treatment required and the mayor must inform the judge of the expected duration of the order. Appeal can be made by the patient or any interested person to the local Tribunal, which must hear the appeal within 20 days. While on a TSO, the patient has the right to communicate with anyone he or she wishes.

Child protection

The grounds for legal intervention Permissible grounds are:

1. When a minor is abandoned or is being brought up in insalubrious or dangerous circumstances, or is being brought up by people who for reasons of negligence, immorality or ignorance are incapable of providing the minor with a proper up-bringing.
2. When a minor is mistreated within the family or by people concerned with his or her up-bringing, learning, care, medical supervision or guardianship.
3. When abusive methods of correcting or disciplining the minor are used.
4. Where the minor is exposed to violence or sexual abuse.

The process of legal intervention Social workers and other professionals who are concerned about a child must submit a written report to the public procurator for children *(Procuratore della Republica per i Minorenni)*. The procurator can take emergency action, or refer the case to the local children's court *(Tribunale per i Minorenni)*. The court comprises a president who is a magistrate, another magistrate and two honorary magistrates who have some specific competence in relation to children (child psychiatrists, pedagogues, social workers). The children's court can ask for further investigations, possibly by a social worker, or consult with the family during a formal hearing. When it has evaluated the situation, the court must make a statement. The children's court is responsible for children placed away from home, or under guardianship, and reviews placement orders. They may also in some situations work in co-operation with the *Giudice Tutelare*, the judge who is involved when there is no parent able to care for the child, when a minor needs an action authorised against parental wishes, or a minor's estate has to be administered.

Luxembourg

Mental health

The grounds for compulsory hospitalisation The primary aim of the Luxembourg mental health law is the well-being of the patient and not the protection of others to the detriment of the patient; however, a person can be compulsorily detained in hospital if serious psychiatric illness makes him or her dangerous to him/herself or to others. The treatment of the patient in hospital must, as far as possible, be aimed at his or her reintegration into society.

The process of compulsory hospitalisation An application can be made by a member of the family or other interested person, or by the mayor or the chief administrative officer to whom this responsibility is delegated by the state procurator, or by the judge of the guardianship court. A medical certificate is required stating that the patient is a danger to him/herself or to others, but should be signed by a doctor who is not the doctor at the hospital to which the patient is to be admitted. The director of the hospital has to register the application and the medical certificate and has to inform the *Commission de Surveillance* within 48 hours. After an observation period of 15 days the consultant psychiatrist treating the patient has to decide whether the order should be maintained. The *Commission de Surveillance* is independent of the hospital. Its members are a magistrate, a psychiatrist and a mental health social worker. After one year the commission reviews the order to see whether it is still necessary. If the order is continued, it has to be reviewed every two years. There is provision for appeal.

Child protection

The grounds for legal intervention The children's court (*tribunal de la jeunesse*) can make orders for the care, up-bringing and protection of all children. The judge can make an order if a child: habitually fails to attend school; is living a dissolute life; is involved in gambling, illegal dealing, or occupations that expose him or her to prostitution; is involved in begging, vagrancy or crime; or if his or her mental or physical health, education or social or moral development is compromised. If there are anxieties about the physical or mental state of a child, he or she can be placed for observation and medically examined. If it is then established on medical grounds that a child is unable to control his or her actions because of mental or physical problems, the court can make an order placing him or her in a special residential establishment, even abroad.

The process of legal intervention   The case is usually referred to the court by the *assistante sociale du secteur*, the generic social worker of the local social services department. Orders can be made for supervision or family support in the home or placement out-of-home. A child can be required to attend regularly a school or special school; to accomplish an educational or socially useful task suitable for his or her age and resources; or to submit to the educational and medical directives of a centre for educational development or mental health. Although there is no mandatory reporting, the civil code requires all citizens to report ill treatment to the appropriate services or to the judicial system.

Germany

Mental health

The grounds for compulsory hospitalisation   Mental health law in Germany is made at regional government level (the *Land*), not by federal government. The information here refers to the region in which the research took place. The grounds are that the person has a mental illness and is a danger to him/herself or to others, and this danger cannot be averted by any other means. Unwillingness to accept treatment does not of itself constitute grounds for compulsion.

The process of compulsory hospitalisation   Application for compulsory admission is made by the *Wirtschaft- und Ordnungsamt*, (a local authority service) activated by the investigating doctor. In an emergency a person can be detained for 24 hours on the request of the social psychiatric service or the police, but immediate application has to be made to the judge of the guardianship court for an order. If an order has not been made within 24 hours, the person cannot be detained, and a legal decision can only be considered after he or she has been released. A legal decision requires a report from the referring doctor and from the doctor at the institution which receives the patient. Nursing reports may be considered. An appeal against an order can be made to the judge, who will visit the patient in hospital. The patient can be assisted by a lawyer.

Child protection

The grounds for legal intervention   The civil code lays down that if the physical, mental or spiritual welfare of a child is endangered by misuse of parental care, by neglect of the child, through unavoidable incapacity of the parents or through the behaviour of a third party, then, if the parents are not willing or able to avert the danger, the family court should take the necessary measures to do so. The Youth Social Service (*Jugendamt*) has a duty to co-operate with the family courts in all measures concerning children and young people. It has to provide information and assessments and advise on plans to help the child. The *Jugendamt* can delegate or sub-contract work to other organisations, but remains responsible. It has a duty to refer to the court if it thinks that legal proceedings are necessary to protect a child.

The process of legal intervention   A child can be referred to the judge of the family court by parents, family members, neighbours or professionals. If there is acute danger to the child, there is mandatory reporting for social services professionals, but not for others. Juvenile offenders aged 14 and over are referred to separate youth courts. The judge can make orders for family support or supervision while at home, or for out-of-home placement. Orders have to be reviewed at least every two years.

Greece

Mental health

The grounds for compulsory hospitalisation   To forestall acts of violence directed towards the patients or third parties. The mentally ill patient must also be incapable of judging the best interests of his or her own health and either hospital treatment must be necessary for the patient's treatment, or lack of in-patient treatment must be exacerbating the patient's illness.

The process of compulsory hospitalisation   Applications can be made by the patient's family members, guardians or legal trustees. It can also be made *ex-officio* by the prosecutor of the Court of First Instance in the patient's place of residence. The application must be made to the public prosecutor and accompanied by full reports from two psychiatrists (or one psychiatrist and one doctor with relevant training). The public prosecutor orders the patient to be taken to a mental health unit, and the patient must, on arrival, be told of his or her rights, which include a right of recourse to the courts.

If the patient cannot be examined by psychiatrists, or if the public prosecutor has made an *ex-offico* application, the patient is taken to a state psychiatric hospital for an examination, which must take place within 48 hours. Within ten days the multi-member Court of First Instance decides whether the patient should be committed.

The maximum duration of compulsory hospitalisation is six months; exceptionally, the order can be extended on the approval of a committee of three psychiatrists, two appointed by the public prosecutor. Patients can appeal to the courts against an order, and the director of the unit where the patient is treated can also lodge an appeal. The appeal is heard by a three-member appeal court *in camera* within 15 days of its submission.

Child protection

The grounds for legal intervention   Both child protection and juvenile justice cases come before the juvenile court. The judge of the juvenile court is responsible for child protection (minors at risk). Court proceedings can result when children commit offences that are criminal if committed by adults, or if they commit offences applicable only to minors.

The process of legal intervention   Children are usually referred to the court by the police; they can also be referred by the parents or other family members, and by professionals (social workers, doctors, teachers). They cannot refer themselves.

THE ENGLISH-SPEAKING COUNTRIES

Australia (Victoria)

Mental health

The grounds for compulsory hospitalisation   The person must (a) appear to be mentally ill; (b) require immediate treatment and care which can only be obtained in an in-patient psychiatric service; (c) be detained for the person's health and safety or the health and safety of others; (d) have refused or is unable to consent to the treatment or care; (e) be unable to receive treatment or care in a manner less restrictive of the person's freedom of decision and action.

The process of compulsory hospitalisation   A 'request' form must be completed by an adult, and a 'recommendation' form must be completed by a medical practitioner to meet the criteria given above. The person can then be held for 72 hours. After completion of admission forms, an authorised psychiatrist must assess the person within 24 hours and determine whether the person is to be detained as an 'involuntary' patient. Continued detention of an 'involuntary' patient must be reviewed by the Mental Health Review Board after four to six weeks and thereafter at least every 12 months. Appeal can be made by any concerned person to the Mental Health Review Board. The Board is made up of a community representative, a lawyer and a psychiatrist and holds closed informal hearings. The patient is encouraged to attend any such hearing, together with an advocate, who may be a lawyer. The outcome of the hearing is provided in the form of a written decision.

Child protection

The grounds for legal intervention   If the child is abandoned, or its parents are dead and there is no other suitable carer; or if the child has suffered or is likely to suffer significant harm as a result of physical injury or sexual abuse, and the child's parents have not protected, or are not likely to protect the child; if the child has suffered, or is likely to suffer emotional or psychological harm of such a kind that his or her emotional or intellectual development is or is likely to be significantly damaged, and the child's parents have not protected, or are not likely to protect the child; if the child's physical development or health is or is likely to be significantly harmed and the child's parents have not provided, arranged or allowed the provision of basic care or effective medical, surgical or other remedial care, or are unlikely to do so.

The process of legal intervention   The child protection service has a duty to seek an order if any of the above circumstances pertain. The court may make child protection orders including supervision, custody and guardianship, and interim orders about placement. Child protection orders may last from three to 12 months. The Act obliges the court to review guardianship orders every 12 months. Parents, children and young people have the right to appeal against a child protection order.

Ireland

Mental health

The grounds for compulsory hospitalisation   There are two categories under which a person may be detained compulsorily in a psychiatric hospital: as a 'temporary patient' or as 'a person of unsound mind'. A 'temporary patient' can be detained if he or she is (a) suffering from a mental illness, (b) unsuitable for treatment as a voluntary patient or (c) an addict who is believed to need at least six months' preventive and curative treatment. To be detained as 'a person of unsound mind' the person must (a) require detention for care and protection and (b) be unlikely to recover within six months.

The process of compulsory hospitalisation   An application may be made by a spouse, relative, community welfare officer, the *Gardai* (Police) or any interested person. The application must be supported or recommended by the GP and accepted by the receiving psychiatrist of the hospital. A 'temporary patient' can be detained for up to six months and detention can be renewed every six months up to a maximum of two years. A 'person of unsound mind' may be detained indefinitely. Every mental hospital must have a Visiting Committee and they may hear the complaints of any patient. Each patient has the right to have a letter forwarded unopened to the following people: the Minister for Health, the President of the High Court, the Registrar of the Wards of Court, the Inspector of Mental Hospitals, the Visiting Committee.

Child protection

The grounds for legal intervention   Where there is a risk to the child's health and safety, for school non-attendance or for a criminal act (children aged 7 and over). Cases on all these grounds would be referred to the same court.

The process of legal intervention   Cases concerning child safety are brought to court by the Child Protection Services of the Health Board (which runs both child health and child protection services). The *Gardai* can make an application in an emergency. The social workers of the child protection service play a central role in court proceedings.

THE UK

England and Northern Ireland

Mental health

The grounds for compulsory hospitalisation

1. Admission for assessment (maximum duration England 28 days, Northern Ireland 14 days) requires that the patient is suffering from mental disorder of a nature which warrants the detention of the patient in hospital *and* that he or she ought to be so detained in the interests of his or her own health and safety or with a view to the protection of other persons.
2. Admission for treatment (duration up to six months, renewable for further periods of one year) requires that the patient is suffering from mental illness, severe mental impairment, psychopathic disorder or mental impairment and his or her mental disorder is of a nature or degree that makes hospital treatment appropriate; *and* that in the case of psychopathic disorder or mental impairment such treatment is likely to alleviate or prevent deterioration of his or her condition; *and* that it is necessary for his or her health and safety or for the protection of other persons that the patient should receive such treatment and it cannot be provided unless he or she is detained. In Northern Ireland 'personality disorder' is excluded.
3. Emergency application (maximum duration 72 hours): the grounds are as for admission for assessment, plus a statement that there is a need for urgency.

The process of compulsory hospitalisation   Applications may be made by the patient's close relative or by an Approved Social Worker (ASW: a social worker with a specific post-qualifying training).

1. Admission for assessment or for treatment: the application must be supported by the written recommendations of two registered medical practitioners. One must be a psychiatrist and one should, if possible, have previous knowledge of the patient (usually the GP).
2. Emergency admission: the application must be supported by one medical recommendation—if possible, from a doctor who knows the patient.

In England appeals can be made by the patient or his nearest relative to the area Mental Health Review Tribunal and, if no appeal has been made, the Mental Health Review Tribunal has to review all treatment orders at least every three years. The members of the Mental Health Review Tribunals are appointed by the Lord Chancellor and must include some members who have legal experience, some registered medical practitioners and some others with experience of administration or social services, or other relevant experience. In Northern Ireland appeals are made to the Mental Health Commission, which is appointed by the Department of Health.

Changes are likely to be introduced to the mental health legislation in relation to the compulsory detention of patients with a 'dangerous or severe personality disorder'. These had not been outlined at the time the research took place.

Scotland

Mental health

The grounds for compulsory hospitalisation   That the person is suffering from a mental disorder of such a nature and degree as to make hospital treatment appropriate; and that it is necessary for the health and safety of that person or the protection of others; and that the treatment should be given and that this cannot be done without compulsory admission or detention. These orders may be made for six months and can be renewed.

The grounds for an emergency order are that, for the health and safety of the person, treatment is a matter of urgency, and that to apply for an order as above would cause an unreasonable delay. These orders last for seven days but can be extended to 28 days.

The process of compulsory hospitalisation   Applications may be made by the patient's close relative or by a Mental Health Officer (MHO) with a specific post-qualifying training.

1. Admission for assessment or for treatment requires that the application must be supported by the written recommendations of two registered medical practitioners; one must be a psychiatrist, and one should if possible have previous knowledge of the patient (usually the GP). An application for compulsory admission or detention has to be made to the Sheriff.
2. Emergency admission requires that the application must be supported by one medical recommendation (usually the GP) and the Mental Welfare Commission must be informed.

Appeals, except for appeals against an emergency order, are made to the Mental Welfare Commission or to the Managers of the Hospital. The Mental Welfare Commission must include at least three women and at least three medical practitioners. It is chaired by a solicitor or an advocate. Only appeals against an emergency order can be made to the Sheriff.

England and Northern Ireland

Child protection

The grounds for legal intervention   That a child is suffering, or is likely to suffer, significant harm attributable to the care given to the child not being what it would be reasonable to expect a parent to give, or the child's being beyond parental control.

The process of legal intervention   An application for a court order is made to the court in England by the local authority (by the children and families section of the Social Services Department) or in Northern Ireland by the Health and Social Services Trust. The main orders that can be made are a care order (compulsory placement away from home) or a supervision order.

Orders last until the court alters or revokes them. The parents or the local authority can ask for an order to be altered or revoked. The parents and the child are separately represented in court by lawyers. The child is also represented by a Guardian ad Litem, an independent social worker appointed by the court to represent to the court the wishes and the best interests of the child.

Scotland

Child protection

The grounds for legal intervention   If there are major child protection concerns, or minor ones with which the family do not agree, the social work department must make a report to the Reporter to the Children's Panel (see below). The Children Act (Scotland) 1995 lists a range of grounds that can be considered by the Reporter as the basis of a referral to the Panel if he or she thinks that the child may be in need of care or protection. These grounds include juvenile crime. The decision whether to initiate legal intervention and refer the case to the Children's Panel lies with the Reporter.

The process of legal intervention   Each local authority has Reporters and a Children's Panel. The Children's Panel is made up of three lay members working on a voluntary basis. The Reporter investigates the grounds for the social work department's referrals and decides whether there are legal grounds to refer the case to the Children's Panel. The Panel holds a Children's Hearing, an informal meeting with quasi-legal powers at which the child, the parents, the Reporter and the social worker are present. If the parents agree with the report from the social work department, the Panel can make a plan for the care and protection of the children immediately. If they do not agree, the case is referred to the Sheriff's court, and the Sheriff will decide whether to accept the social work report. If it is accepted, the case is returned to the Panel for a plan to be made for the care and protection of the child. The Children's Panel then has the power to make compulsory orders.

COMMENTS

These differences in law and procedures for the use of compulsion in relation to hospitalisation of patients with a mental illness and the protection of children raise many questions. The English-speaking countries stand out as being those with least involvement of the judiciary in relation to compulsory hospitalisation and the heaviest use of the legal system in relation to child protection. A comparative project with a primary focus on the use of compulsion would be needed to investigate this paradox further. It seems likely that comparisons in these areas (and others), where the agents of the state use compulsion in the context of welfare, would throw light on the nature of state expectations in relation to social welfare and citizenship.

Segal (1989), comparing England and Wales, Italy and the USA, suggests that the use of dangerousness as a criterion for detention has the effect of emphasising individual rights and limiting compulsory admission, thus reducing demands on resources (as in England and Wales and the USA). Not using this criterion (as in Italy) reflects a 'needs-orientated' and paternalistic approach. Our study does not support this conclusion, as nations often categorised as 'paternalistic', such as France, use the 'dangerousness' criterion, and so does Germany. At the same time, the Italian and German participants were those least ready to hospitalise and use compulsion, although one country used the dangerousness criterion and the other did not. The research data suggest that there are differences in psychiatric practice and ideology which may reflect (or be reflected in) different regulations. (See Chapter 8 for further information on the different responses of England, Germany and Italy.) The Italian, French and German psychiatric services seemed to use a more psychodynamic approach than other countries. The difference that we observed is supported by studies reported by Van Os *et al.* (1994) who examined diagnostic decision-making in France and England, and this is discussed further in Chapter 7.

Another area that seems to show a difference in the use of diagnostic categories is in relation to personality disorder. Here it is a question not only of the naming of the mental state, but of expectations about treatability and the relationship between treatability and compulsion. As this was not an aspect of the situation in the case vignette, we do not have it in clear focus, but it is an aspect of the comparative legal position which will be of increasing interest with the changes that are likely to come in UK legislation.

Use of compulsion as discussed by our participants did not seem to be related in any observable way to legislation or to the processes of compulsion. It had an ambiguous relationship to resources. Countries with poor levels of family support (England and Greece) were more likely to use compulsion, but so also were countries with a high level of mental health hospital provision (Luxembourg and Sweden). The relationship was therefore not straightforward, but a matter of balance between availability and shortage in different sectors. One of the participants from Luxembourg thought that their readiness to use the hospital was taking the easiest way out (because beds were available). In Sweden where both hospital and family support were available, the decisions were based on a favourable evaluation of the effectiveness of hospital treatment. Italy with few family support resources was nevertheless very unwilling to hospitalise; and this was based on a very different attitude to the treatment of mental illness. There seemed to be a coincidence, and possibly a causal relationship, between the use of psychoanalytic theories in psychiatry and an unwillingness to hospitalise. However, resources remain important; England and Greece were short of mental hospital resources as well as family support, but, in a crisis, the beds became available although the family support did not.

In sum, it seems that the law is only one factor, and perhaps a secondary one, in the decisions of agents of the state to opt for compulsory powers to hospitalise the mentally ill or to remove children from their families.

Chapter 5

The Responses of the Partner Countries to the Vignette

In this chapter the responses of the groups in the 13 countries to the vignette are described. The preceding chapters have set out the structures within which the participants were operating; here we summarise their thoughts on what would be most likely to happen where they worked.

The responses of each country at each stage of the vignette provide the material on which later reflections are based, and to which the reader can refer. The countries are taken in the same order as in previous chapters. We therefore start with the Scandinavian countries, then the continental European countries and finally the English-speaking countries. The professions making up the groups in the 13 countries are listed in the Appendix.

Stage 1

Mary is a 27-year-old woman who is married to John. She has a 7-year-old daughter, Anna, from a previous relationship. She has not had any contact with Anna's father since shortly after Anna was born. One week ago she gave birth to a baby boy, Thomas. She was well during her pregnancy, which was planned, and worked until six months ago.

Four days ago Mary and Thomas came home from hospital, and John is now very anxious about her. Over the last two days she has seemed to be acting differently. She will not let anyone but herself touch the baby. She said to John, 'You are trying to poison him, like the nurses in the hospital'. Last night Mary sat up with Thomas all night, saying 'I must protect him'.

John decides that he has to seek help.

The common concerns were, firstly, seriousness of the mother's mental illness and her ability to care for the children and, secondly, the need to avoid separating the mother from the baby.

Denmark and **Sweden** both had similar concerns about the mother's mental state and that the mother would not accept voluntary hospitalisation. One of the Swedish professionals was particularly concerned about John, and thought that if he did not get support, there would be problems later. The groups in **Norway** were very focused on the family as a whole and the welfare of the family was the dominant concern. In all three countries there was an expectation that the mother would be hospitalised.

In **France** they wanted to find some way of keeping the mother and baby together, so they looked for ways to avoid hospitalising the mother. They were not sure that they would have grounds for compulsory admission. The child welfare group was more anxious about the children's emotional needs, and unsure whether the husband would be able to cope with looking after an infant. In **Italy** they were concerned not to pathologise or medicalise the mother's feelings. They wished to avoid hospitalisation, preferring to support the family so that she could remain at home. The Italians did not expect that the mother would be hospitalised, and did not feel that there were grounds for compulsion. They were concerned about the welfare of the children and were aware of taking risks, but thought that the long-term benefits of avoiding hospitalisation made this necessary. The groups in **Luxembourg** emphasised several times that this was a family problem and that concentration on any one member of the family would prevent work being done with the family as a whole. They expected that the mother would be hospitalised as hospital beds were available, and there was a risk that this would be taken as the easiest option.

In **Germany** there was emphasis on both the mother's mental health and the needs of the children. Compulsory admission to hospital was seen as being dependent on the mother's ability to feed and care for the children. The availability of the intensive family support service (the SPFH) meant that it might be possible to support the family so that the mother could stay at home. There were anxieties that the judge who had to consent to a compulsory hospitalisation order would consider that it would be more appropriate for the children to be taken into care so that the mother need not be hospitalised. There was a great deal of concern about Anna's emotional needs and suggestions about ways in which she could be helped. In **Greece** the main concern of both groups was the mother's mental state along with concern about the effect of separation between mother and baby on their mental health. They did not think that there was a formal support system that could prevent the mother's admission, but the child welfare group found it hard to believe that support from the community would not be forthcoming; such support might be organised by the local priest.

In **Australia** a significant theme in the children welfare group discussion was the importance of maintaining the integrity of the family unit. It was seen as important to provide services that were non-threatening, such as GP services and health visiting which could monitor the situation. By contrast, the adult mental health group focused on 'risk' and made little mention of the children's needs. It was considered probable that the mother would be hospitalised, possibly under compulsion. In **Ireland** the groups tried to look at the situation from a holistic, family perspective, feeling that focusing on the needs of the mother could be to the detriment of the children and the family unit. There was great reluctance to split the family up in any way and there was much caution expressed regarding compulsory admission, although there was anxiety about the way in which the situation might develop. Hospitalisation was expected because of the shortage of support services.

In **England**, care for the children was regarded by the mental health groups as a question for the children and families service and by the child welfare groups as a family responsibility. The child welfare groups thought that this case would probably not come to them because the expectation would be that the family would cope. The mental health groups felt that the children and families service would not be able to respond to a referral because it would not be seen as a priority. Because of concerns about the bonding between the mother and the baby if she had to be hospitalised, they all hoped for place in a mother and baby unit. In **Northern Ireland** the mental health of the mother was the main issue, but in both Northern Ireland and England there was a marked difference between the mental health and child welfare groups over assessment, with the mental health group rating the mother's illness as more serious at every stage. In **Scotland** the mother's mental health and the need for an assessment were the central concerns, but it was not clear what could be provided if the decision was made not to admit to hospital. Some of the responses to Stage 1 are summarised in Table 5.1.

Stage 2

<u>Three years later.</u> Anna is now 10 and Thomas is 3. Mary is pregnant again and the baby is due in five months' time. John has lost his job, and has been unemployed for three months.

Anna's school is worried about Anna because she has begun soiling herself. She is becoming unpopular and shunned by the other children because of this and she is missing school. She has always been a quiet and rather solitary child, but there have not been any problems at school before.

Mary sees the head teacher who suggests that Mary and John should take Anna to see a child psychiatrist. Mary is unwilling to do so because of her own experience after Thomas was born. However, she says that she needs practical help herself because Thomas is very demanding and she gets very tired. She seems stressed and anxious, but she is certain that she will not become mentally ill after the birth of this baby.

There was general agreement that Anna needed help and that the offer of practical help would be the best way of building a relationship with Mary that would allow other matters to be tackled.

In **Denmark** the main issue for the professionals was that the mother was thought not to understand the seriousness of Anna's problems and to be denying the risks to her own mental state. They were worried that the father was drinking and that the services had lost touch with the family and had not

Table 5.1 The responses of the partner countries to Stage 1 of the vignette

	Hospitalisation	Compulsion	Child welfare services	Family support services	Support for Anna	Support for father
Scandinavian countries						
Denmark	Very likely	Possible	Very likely	Very likely	Yes	Some
Norway	Likely	Possible	Very likely	Very likely	Yes	Yes
Sweden	Very likely	Likely	Very likely	Very likely	Yes	Yes
Continental countries						
France	Likely	Unlikely	Very likely	Very likely	Some	Some
Italy	Very unlikely	Very unlikely	Very unlikely	Very unlikely	Some	No
Luxembourg	Very likely	Very likely	Very likely	Very likely	Some	No
Germany	Possible	Unlikely	Very likely	Very likely	Yes	Yes
Greece	Unlikely	Possible	Very unlikely	Very unlikely	Some	No
English-speaking countries						
Australia	Very likely	Very likely	Very unlikely	Very unlikely	No	No
Ireland	Very likely	Very likely	Perhaps	Very unlikely	No	No
England	Likely	Likely	Very unlikely	Very unlikely	No	No
N. Ireland	Possible	Possible	Perhaps	Perhaps	No	No
Scotland	Very likely	Likely	Perhaps	Perhaps	Some	No

Notes

Hospitalisation and compulsion
There was a gradation of response to hospitalisation and compulsion. It was never the first assumption that Mary would be hospitalised. However in some countries it was more likely than not, whereas for others it was very unlikely.

Child welfare services and family support
These columns relate respectively to the involvement of general social services for children and families, and to specialist family support services run by NGOs or within social work departments.

Support for Anna and support for father
Where support was discussed but not clearly identified it is classed as 'some'. Support for Anna or father refers to support for them as individuals, and not to family support in general.

made plans before the birth of the new baby. In **Norway** they wished to involve the school more closely in the initial response to the situation, and thought that the school health service and the school psychological service should be involved, even if the latter then referred Anna to the child mental health service. One reason for wanting a referral to the school medical service was that Anna might have been sexually abused. They felt that practical assistance to the family, which was what the mother wanted, could be the key to gaining the co-operation of the family. They were keen to involve the mother in the process of intervention in the family, but not at the expense of any delay to the implementation of any decisions/plans for the family. In **Sweden** the priority was to enable Anna to receive help and to enable the mother to be in contact with the psychiatric system so that she could get help before the new baby was born. They had good family support resources to offer if Mary could be persuaded to accept them. There was concern for John and his need for support in finding employment. The possibility that Anna had been sexually abused was raised by the mental health group.

The **French** groups were anxious about Anna's mental state, and the possibility of sexual abuse was raised. The mental health group had a disagreement about the possibility of using the judge for children to compel a mother to accept psychiatric treatment for a child. The child welfare group discussed the possibility of using a formal 'supervision' order (AEMO, see Chapter 3) in order to make the parents realise that they had serious concerns about Anna. The child welfare group was particularly concerned to take action that would prevent problems when the third child was born, fearing that the mother would have another breakdown and that the father would fade out of the picture. In **Italy** they focused on the children's problems as an expression of the problems of the family, and were concerned to establish contact with the mother in order to work with the family as a whole. The child welfare group was particularly concerned that Anna should not be labelled as the family member with problems. The children's problems were seen in a systemic framework as an aspect of the problems of the family. The specific task identified was to reinforce the mother's competence as a parent and enable her to fulfil a parenting role and maintain the family as a unit. In **Luxembourg** the mother's request for practical help was seen as a way of making contact with her and establishing a relationship of trust that would enable her to look at other problems. A wide range of services was mentioned for different family members. Anna would be referred for therapy to the child mental health service and help was suggested for Thomas and the father.

In **Germany** there was an emphasis on obtaining the mother's co-operation and trust. They thought that the SPFH service could do this, though it would be difficult. They were anxious about the family and felt that they needed to be monitored very closely. They were concerned that the mother did not recognise Anna's need for help, and were afraid that she might not allow Thomas to go to a kindergarten. They felt strongly that Anna needed someone outside the family to support her, and that she should be referred to the school psychological service or other child mental health services. They wished to establish a support network for the family before the birth of the new baby. In **Greece** the group would have preferred the mother to have practical help at home with daily needs, but they thought that services did not exist to provide such help. They were concerned that, because of the lack of help on an everyday level, the possibilities for effective intervention were limited.

In **Australia** the groups wanted to provide practical help for the mother and to refer Anna to the child mental health services. They considered that if the mother did not accept one of these offers, the school should refer the family to the child protection service for support. They also felt that the mother should be encouraged to work with a family welfare agency rather than the mental health services, as this was more likely to be more acceptable to her. There was concern about the need for psychiatric intervention for the mother and for Anna, but no clear way of accessing these services. In **Ireland** the mental health group thought that referral of Anna to the child mental health service should be done by her GP, who would also be able to consider possible physical causes for her soiling. They were concerned about the likelihood of the mother developing a further illness at the birth of the new baby. The child welfare group felt that there was an opportunity for preventive work, but was doubtful if this would be given any priority because of resource shortages. As the child mental health service had a waiting list, Anna might need to be helped in some other way, perhaps by a school counsellor or a social worker.

In **England** the mental health groups said that they would not expect to be involved at this stage. The child welfare groups all thought that a 'needs assessment' should be made, and it was suggested that ideally a family support worker could monitor the family in a non-threatening way. However, the family's situation would not be seen as urgent and it would be unlikely that a family support worker would be allocated to spend much time on the case. Allocation to a social work student was mentioned as one possibility or referral to a family centre. An alternative, which might be acceptable to Mary, would be to arrange a paediatric appointment for Anna on the grounds that her soiling should be physically investigated. The groups discussed various possible reasons for her soiling, including sexual abuse. A referral to the child mental health service was a possibility, but there was pessimism about the length of the waiting list. The child and adolescent mental health group was not sure that there would be a referral to them and thought that a referral to the behavioural support programme in the school psychological service would be more likely. In **Northern Ireland** there was agreement that the best approach to the family would be through the primary care group. The GP would be able to make an appropriate referral for Anna and the public health nurse would be the best person to talk to her mother. The GP would be able to refer Anna to the child development clinic, which had access to a child psychiatrist. They felt that Anna needed someone to talk to and that she and her mother should be helped by the worker they liked best. In **Scotland** both groups suggested that the GP was the most important resource as he or she would know about the mother's previous illness and would be able to refer Anna for help either to the child mental health service or to a paediatrician. The health visitor would still be in contact with the family, and might be able to work with Mary to persuade her to accept a referral to the community mental health service. The school medical service and the school nurse were other important possible sources of help. The school nurse would talk to the health visitor, and thus involve the GP. Some schools have a multi-agency liaison group, and Anna's problems could be discussed at this group. The social work department would be able to provide some practical help if Mary would accept it. Some of the responses to Stage 2 are summarised in Table 5.2.

Stage 3

<u>Six months later</u>. Anna is 10½, Thomas is 3½ and the baby, Jane, is one month. Mary was in hospital for three days when the baby was born, and John looked after Anna and Thomas.

John has not found work. He has been alternately very withdrawn and quiet, then irritable when his family demands his attention. He is drinking excessively and they are short of money. Thomas is now attending nursery school; the staff there find him difficult to manage, violent towards other children and overactive.

At Anna's school, her teachers are increasingly worried about her. She is thin and unkempt, and for the last two weeks she has been falling asleep in class and seems to be desperately hungry. She is scavenging for food in the school and has stolen food from other children.

Two days ago John left home. Mary goes to the welfare services for help because she has no money. She is extremely anxious and says, 'I can't let them eat because he's trying to poison their food. They're only still here because I stay awake all night to keep them safe.'

In all countries it was expected that the mother would need to be hospitalised and that, unless the father could be contacted quickly, the children would be taken into care.

The groups in **Denmark** were concerned that the children would have too many changes and would be moved between placements. There was also concern that inter-agency collaboration might not work effectively. It was suggested that there might be a failure in referral to child welfare services because mental health workers or health visitors were unwilling to lose their 'alliance' with the family (and especially with the mother). In **Norway** it was suggested that measures would have been taken to prevent the situation deteriorating. For example, the mother would probably have been kept in hospital after childbirth, and as soon as Anna was found stealing food the school would have contacted the Child Protection Agency and the kindergarten. Emphasis was placed on finding the father to care for the children and help him to work through the issues. In **Sweden** the initial response was that it was quite impossible for the situation described to have taken place in their

Table 5.2 The responses of the partner countries to Stage 2 of the vignette

	Child welfare services	Family support services	Child mental health services	Adult mental health services	Support for father
Scandinavian countries					
Denmark	Very likely	Very likely	Likely	Likely	Discussed
Norway	Very likely*	Very likely	Likely	Very unlikely	Discussed
Sweden	Very likely*	Very likely	Likely	Likely	Specified
Continental countries					
France	Very likely	Very likely	Likely	Very unlikely	Not mentioned
Italy	Very likely	Perhaps	Likely	Possible	Specified
Luxembourg	Very likely	Very likely	Likely	Very unlikely	Not mentioned
Germany	Very likely	Very likely	Likely	Very unlikely	Specified
Greece	Very likely	Very unlikely	Possible	Possible	Discussed
English-speaking countries					
Australia	Very likely	Very likely	Unlikely	Very unlikely	Not mentioned
Ireland	Very likely	Perhaps	Unlikely	Possible	Not mentioned
England	Very likely	Perhaps	Unlikely	Very unlikely	Not mentioned
N. Ireland	Perhaps†	Perhaps	Possible	Possible	Not mentioned
Scotland	Very likely*	Very likely	Possible	Possible	Not mentioned

Notes

Child welfare services and family support services
These columns relate respectively to the involvement of general social services for children and families, and to specialist family support groups or services within social work departments.
'Perhaps' includes replies where the service was very limited and its availability doubted.
* Stressed the importance of the school and school medical services.
† Stressed the importance of the primary care services.

Child mental health services
All countries referred to these, but availability was very poor in some places.
Unlikely = pessimistic expectations, long waiting lists noted.
Possible = moderate expectation of available services.
Likely = high expectation of available services.

Adult mental health services
Adult mental health services were thought very unlikely to be involved in many countries, but in some it was considered possible. In a few it was considered likely, but nowhere very likely.

Support for father
The father's possible need for help was occasionally mentioned, sometimes specific suggestions were made.

country. The family would have been followed up after Stage 2, and in any case the children would have been having free school dinners, so they would not have been starving. Their dominant concern was the risk to the children. The child welfare group was concerned about the father and the need to give him help and get him back into the family. The mental health group discussed the conflict that there could be for mental health professionals between the requirement to report concerns about child neglect or abuse, and to maintain confidentiality and the confidence of an adult.

In **France** the groups were concerned about the danger to the children and thought that intervention was urgently required. They were concerned about the problems of maintaining the links between the mother and the children, especially the baby, if either the mother went into hospital or the children had to be placed. They were worried about the effect on the mother if the children were suddenly removed. They thought that hospitalisation was likely. In **Italy** it was seen as important to set up some system to protect the children. Home-based help was suggested with the ideal being for someone to live in the house to look after the children. It was acknowledged that if the mother did not co-operate and accept help, within a week at the most, compulsory hospitalisation might be necessary. This possibility caused real problems for the group—undermining the entire thrust of their approach. There was anxiety the children might be fostered permanently. They were very concerned about the children growing up without an attentive mother. In **Luxembourg** the possibility of finding a residential home which would accept the mother and the children was discussed, but it was thought that this was more likely to happen after she came out of hospital. Alternatively, when she left hospital she could be supported at home with a family aide and other social support. They too wanted someone to find the father to involve him in his responsibilities for the children and to see whether he needed help with his alcohol problem.

The groups in **Germany**, like the Swedes, thought that the story would not have developed like this. They thought that the support that they would have given at Stage 2 and the follow-up that would have been provided would have prevented Stage 3. They had a very clear focus on the needs of the children in their own right. They wanted to try to counteract the damage done by the children's experiences. They were also motivated by a wish to keep the family together, to draw the father back into the family and to support the mother. However, they saw the mother as needing hospital treatment, although it might have been possible to set up services to keep the children at home. The Greek groups, too, thought that the situation could not have reached this state in **Greece** because there would always be interventions from the community even if there was no wider family (which was thought to be highly unlikely). One of the participants commented that the story was obviously not written about Greece. However, they thought that if this situation had arisen, it was likely that the mother would be referred to a psychiatrist for urgent hospital admission. This might have been done in conjunction with work from other services to deal with the father's alcoholism. The children would be likely to be removed or placed in daily care and child psychiatry might have been offered. There was, however, uncertainty over whether the appropriate services would be found and how they would be co-ordinated.

In **Australia**, importance was placed on the co-ordination of services. The child welfare services described the problems that would be encountered in organising the provision of emergency care for the children if their mother was kept in hospital and their father could not be found. It would entail getting an interim care order, and finding emergency accommodation, which might be at a considerable distance. There was little discussion of hospitalisation, which seemed to be taken for granted. There was concern that some services for children and families such as this had been closed down. It was thought likely that the school and the nursery school would have reported their concerns to the child protection service already, and that they would be ready to co-operate in working with mental health services. All the groups in **Ireland** thought that there were grounds for the mother to be admitted to hospital for psychiatric care. The children might have been admitted to hospital to see if they needed medical attention. There was a suggestion that there would be a case conference to offer the family 'more concentrated support and education and advice', but only after the immediate situation had been dealt with. There were anxieties that it would be difficult to find foster care placements. The baby might be able to go into hospital with her mother, but it would be difficult to find someone to take the other two children and keep them together. The child mental health group emphasised the primary need for medical assessment for all the children. All the groups were very concerned about the father and thought that he needed help.

In **England** the biggest issue was the risk to the children. Compulsory powers would be used to ensure that the mother went into hospital, as she was mentally ill and a danger to the children. They expected the father and the wider family to look after the children. If there was any delay over the mother's hospitalisation, the children and family service would apply for an emergency order to care for the children (if there were no family members able to look after them immediately). They would have to try to find the father who would have parental responsibility for at least two of the children. The child welfare groups thought that there would not be a child protection conference as the situation was too urgent to wait for one, but a planning meeting would be called by the children and families team.

In **Northern Ireland** it was thought that the Health Visitor should have been visiting regularly and that matters should not have been allowed to get to the crisis stage. The school would have referred Anna for help, and they doubted whether this situation could have arisen. However, if it did arise, there would be either a case planning meeting or a child protection investigation. This would depend on the results of the mother's previous psychiatric assessment. The GP would be alerted and he could arrange for a visit by an approved social worker together with a psychiatrist. Any child protection investigation would run concurrently with a mental health assessment. In **Scotland** the mental health group considered that it was unlikely in their area that the family's problems would not have been recognised earlier, but thought that in an urban area it would be quite possible. Both groups had immediate concerns that the mother could harm herself or her children, but they were also worried about the short-term and long-term physical and emotional development of the children. They wanted a full physical and psychological assessment with the child mental health service or the educational psychology service involved if necessary. The children required some stability and the school would be an important provider of this, particularly if the children had to move from their home. The school and the nursery school were both seen as important in the co-ordination of help for the family. Some of the responses to Stage 3 are summarised in Table 5.3.

Table 5.3   The responses of the partner countries to Stage 3 of the vignette

	Hospitalisation	Compulsion	Family support services	Child mental health services
Scandinavian countries				
Denmark	Very likely	Very likely	Very likely	Planned
Norway	Likely	Possible	Perhaps	Planned
Sweden	Very likely	Very likely	Very likely	Planned
Continental countries				
France	Likely	Possible	Very likely	Planned
Italy	Possible	Possible	Very likely	Possible
Luxembourg	Very likely	Very likely	Very likely	Planned
Germany	Likely	Possible	Very likely	Planned
Greece	Very likely	Likely	Very unlikely	Possible
English-speaking countries				
Australia	Very likely	Very likely	Very likely	Planned
Ireland	Very likely	Very likely	Perhaps	Possible
England	Very likely	Very likely	Very unlikely	Not mentioned
N. Ireland	Very likely	Very likely	Very unlikely	Not mentioned
Scotland	Very likely	Very likely	Very unlikely	Possible*

Notes

Hospitalisation and compulsion
There was a gradation of response to hospitalisation and compulsion. It was usually assumed that Mary would now be hospitalised. While for most countries it was very likely for others it was still strongly resisted though possible.

Family support services
By this stage, child welfare services were involved in all countries, but not all had family support services that they could use, or thought appropriate. Some countries were very unlikely to use family support services at this stage, others might have only very limited services, some were very likely to use family support services.

Child mental health
In some countries, referral to child mental health services was part of the plan for the children. In others it was not mentioned, or mentioned but rather unlikely.
* School psychological service.

The tables that summarise the response show, perhaps more clearly than the detailed records, that the experience for a family could be substantially different in different countries. The participants in the research, when they heard about the responses of the country with which they were paired, tended to notice in the first place the similarities between their responses. It was on further reflection that they began to notice differences.

Chapter 6

Issues

THE SHARED ISSUES

Initial examination of the discussions held in each country suggested that a number of common themes were emerging, but that these issues were negotiated in different ways. Not all of these variations were reducible to straightforward differences in legal powers and processes. Rather they appear to have reflected a complex distillate of resource availability, professional culture and the national conceptualisation of the appropriate relationship between citizens, families and the state. We therefore focus in this chapter on the differing approaches to the issues that were important to all countries.

The vignette was designed to open up discussion on issues of inter-agency and interdisciplinary co-operation, the use of powers to compel in relation to mental illness (and, to a lesser extent, in child protection), and the focus by different agencies on the well-being of children. At the end of their discussions, the groups were also asked to consider what, if anything, would be different if the family came from an ethnic minority or were refugees. Further issues emerged from the analysis of the discussions. We survey below the discussions of the groups on the following issues in relation to this case:

- compulsory intervention
- the role of the extended family
- the use of official resources to support the family
- support for the father and the children
- work with the whole family
- responses to risk
- trust and co-operation between families and professionals
- inter-agency co-operation
- services for ethnic minorities or refugees.

Compulsory Intervention

Discussion about compulsion took two different forms. One was the possibility of compulsory psychiatric treatment for the mother at each stage. The other concerned the compulsory removal of children from their home, which was only envisaged as an alternative to hospitalisation of the mother. This section therefore focuses on compulsory psychiatric treatment or admission. For most of the countries concerned, the focus of psychiatric care quickly centred on the issue of admission to hospital, but attitudes to the use of or necessity for compulsion varied.

At Stage 1, the majority of countries suggested that hospital admission might be necessary if the mother refused support services or if she was very ill. The Scandinavian and the English-speaking countries suggested that this was a possibility if she refused to come into hospital on a voluntary basis (as was thought to be quite likely). In Luxembourg the child welfare group assumed that hospital admission would certainly take place. In France and Germany the issue of compulsory admission was placed more firmly in the context of trying other family support services first before considering admission.

For all the above countries the case for admission was based on the perceived level of risk to the children, and the outcome of any assessment of this risk. The German group suggested that action taken by service providers to protect the children could have ongoing effects and repercussions for the family. It was suggested that 'escalation in the mother's illness would create a situation where action had to be taken to protect the children. This might well exacerbate the mother's illness to the point where admission to hospital was necessary.'

The country that stood out over the use of hospital treatment was Italy, where both groups very actively wanted to prevent the mother from being hospitalised. They did not consider that compulsion was likely to be necessary. They realised that maintaining the mother at home with the support of the community entailed some risk, and accepted that a certain level of risk was necessary to achieve this goal. This emphasis on the maintenance of the family was a recurrent theme in the Italian contribution, but it was not their only reason for avoiding hospital treatment. They also thought that it would 'medicalise' Mary's attitude to her own illness, and that it would be better for her to be helped to understand the connections between her past experience and what was happening now.

At Stage 2, all the participants thought that there were no grounds for either compulsory admission to hospital or compulsory removal of the children. However, the fact that this was the second reported episode did increase the amount of emphasis that workers placed on psychiatric intervention in a number of countries, for example in Australia. Conversely, the English child welfare groups thought that mental health services might remain completely unaware of the situation.

At this stage the focus of psychiatric intervention was seen as preventive, and was couched largely as providing support to the family. However, German workers appeared to make a more explicit attempt to be ready for the worst. They commented that there were no grounds for placement for the children, but they wanted to arrange for increased support for the family after the birth, and to make contingency plans for the children in case the mother had a psychotic relapse.

At Stage 3 there was a split on the issue of compulsory intervention. This pattern was not readily predictable from previous responses. The Australian participants summed up a belief common to the majority of countries:

'There is now a clear need for assertive action on behalf of both adult psychiatric services and child protection services and child protection services. The latter are, however, involved as an adjunct to the mother's hospitalisation, which seems to be the deciding factor in the need for intervention.'

The pattern observed regarding hospitalisation was:

- *Expected*: Denmark, Sweden, Germany (child welfare), Greece (mental health), Luxembourg, Australia, Ireland, the United Kingdom.
- *Possible*: France, Germany (mental health), Greece (child welfare), Italy, Norway.

The expectation of hospitalisation was made most clearly in Sweden where the senior doctor said, 'it was not a question of where the mother would turn for help, but where she would be taken, with or without her own consent'.

In France, Germany and Norway there was uncertainty as to the legal position and the likely response of the authorities to a request in these circumstances. The German participants had a lengthy discussion on the role of the judge in accepting or rejecting an order for compulsory admission, which demonstrated the existence of checks on the powers of health and welfare services and reflected the power of the justice system to prevent unnecessary intervention and protect the rights of the individual. Greece and Italy wanted first to try to provide family support for a trial period, if they could find local resources. Although legal powers of compulsory admission to hospital and/or removal of children were similar in most countries (Italy being the main exception) there were differences in the way these powers would be used. The differences in practice appear to stem not so much from different legal systems as from differences in culture, in professional views about psychiatric illness and in attitudes towards the relationship between the state and the family. In Sweden, where, at Stage 3, all were convinced that the mother would need hospitalisation and that the children would be taken into care, workers were very clear about the authority of the state to intervene in family life.

Where mother and baby units were available, this greatly affected the planning of the professionals. If the separation of mother and baby could be avoided, one of the disadvantages of hospital treatment was removed and Mary's voluntary acceptance of hospital care was more likely. The possibility of admitting Mary to hospital with her baby was discussed in Norway, Sweden, Italy, Germany, Australia, Ireland, England, Northern Ireland and Scotland, but there was uncertainty in all these countries about the availability of this resource. There was an interesting discussion in Luxembourg on recent experience of having a baby cared for in the paediatric ward while its mother was in the psychiatric ward in the same hospital. This was possible, but set up many tensions between the nursing and medical teams, and needed very careful management. In Sweden it was commented that they had almost stopped placing babies with mothers because the severity of the illness of the other patients made it inappropriate, and they also now had fewer psychiatric beds. Ireland and the countries of the United Kingdom said that such provision was so scarce that it was unlikely to be available.

Italy and Greece both laid considerable emphasis on the role of the family, friends and other members of the community in supporting the family and helping to resolve the situation without compulsory intervention, and this is the next area to be examined.

The Role of the Extended Family

Most countries referred to support networks of family, friends and neighbours. However, some countries saw this as a preliminary level of support prior to any service involvement. State intervention would only take place once concerns reached a certain threshold. Others expected professionals to have a positive role in developing these networks as complementary or alternative to formal service interventions.

At Stage 1, the English child welfare groups gave an example of the former approach, focusing on thresholds. 'On the basis of what we've got, there's no reason for us to be involved at this point.' They expected the family to provide whatever support was needed. Only if the family could not help, and the children were assessed as being 'in need', would they offer what help they could. The Greek group not only discussed the need to check the potential for support and child care from the extended family—uncles, aunts and grandparents—they also expected to enlist the co-operation of other adults in the local area, such as people whom the children knew and trusted and who could help to support the mother.

Workers in Greece and England identified the lack of resources as one reason why they might be unable to provide services themselves at this point, and why family and social networks should be used instead. However, the Greeks expected to intervene actively to try to develop neighbourhood resources and ensure that such support existed.

There was not always agreement about the reliance to be placed on the family. For example, in France and Norway there was a discussion and some disagreement over the role and usefulness of the wider family. In Germany it was pointed out that Anna might need support from outside the family because the family would not necessarily be able to help her. In all except Italy, Greece and the English-speaking countries, it was assumed that the family would need support from formal services.

At Stage 2 there was little mention of using the extended family as a source of support. There was an implication that the mother would already have involved the family or the community if that were possible. There was much more reference to family again in Stage 3 when care of the children became an issue if the mother was hospitalised, and grandparents or relatives were being considered as temporary carers.

Thus most countries mentioned the role of the extended family or community in supporting the index family. The way in which professionals engaged these informal support networks highlighted a number of differences. There was a higher expectation of active professional involvement in investigating, setting up and supporting these networks in Italy, Germany, Greece, Ireland and Northern Ireland than elsewhere. However, the rationale was not the same for all. While the Irish referred to the importance of the subsidiarity principle of starting at the most local level, the Italians talked about the co-operative working relationships they had developed with the *medico di base* and saw work with the community as an important resource. For both Greece and Italy, there was an element of using the community as a substitute for other resources, but there was also an expectation that part of the role of the professional was to mobilise community resources.

The Use of Formal Resources to Support the Family

The alternative to informal intervention based on family and neighbourhood was to provide formal interventions. Intensive family support services were most extensively available in Norway, Sweden and Germany. Several countries had less intensive family support services such as family aides/family workers, who might be qualified (France) or unqualified (England). Not all countries felt that formal family support would be offered at Stage 1. As indicated above, this would be unlikely in Greece and England. In all countries visits from a social worker or a community nurse were suggested as an important form of family support, although it was often implied that this was combined with an assessment and monitoring role which, in the less well-resourced countries, would dominate. There was great variation in the time that the social worker or nurse might be able to give to this work, and in Greece and England shortage of professional time was felt most acutely.

Shortages of resources influenced the way that the professionals thought about their task. In Italy there was a clear preference for supporting the family at home as an alternative to hospital in-patient treatment: 'either there is compulsory hospitalisation, or there is support and observation'. They needed to see 'if she (the mother) can find a way of managing her children at home, above all if there is a network of support. Therefore we workers must contain our anxiety and accept the margin of risk'. In Italy and Greece, shortages of resources meant that family support services were seldom available but, as one of the Greek participants in the Luxembourg workshop said, 'lacking resources means that you have to be more inventive and imaginative'.

The route to family support varied. France, Ireland, Northern Ireland and Scotland all saw the GP or family doctor as providing the main access route not only to psychiatric services but also to other services, and in Germany the family doctor was able to initiate access to the SPFH service. In England, the children and families service of the local authority controlled access to family support services.

At Stage 2 formal family support was widely suggested because the offer of practical help was seen as a way of engaging Mary and gaining her trust.

There was a sharper focus on what such services were to achieve and many services were mentioned. The well-resourced countries could offer support more easily, but the support available was in reality very limited, particularly in the English-speaking countries and Greece. In England it was unlikely that a family support worker would be allocated, and the issue for the Australian and English social workers was whether they would be able to access any level of support. The services mentioned in Australia were in-home support, group work or possibly a parenting course, and both Australian and English child welfare workers suggested referral to a family centre. In Greece one of the participants referred to a service where a volunteer could visit the house to 'pay the bills, accompany the mother to the doctor, take the children to school, give her pills, and if she had a little time, would fix a small meal', but the availability of such services was doubtful. In Italy it was suggested that what was needed was someone who could help the mother in the home and, at the same time, help her to understand her daughter's problems. In Germany the SPFH service was seen as the key service if Mary could be persuaded to accept that, and realistic support services were also available in the Scandinavian countries (especially Norway and Sweden). Norwegian and Swedish workers proposed the use of a contact family—a volunteer family with whom the children could stay with for one, two or more weekends a month (for a description of this service see Andersson 1999).

For most countries, the role of family support at Stage 3 focused on supporting the family as a temporary measure during the mother's hospitalisation; some countries did not consider the use of family support. In France the *service des tutelles* (which deals with budgeting, benefits and the management of finances) would be brought in to make sure that rent and bills were dealt with and that the family home was maintained during the mother's hospitalisation. The German groups and Scandinavian groups took a long-term view. They were concerned about the help the children would need to counteract the damage caused by their experiences. and what would happen if the father did not return to the family. They were also concerned that, after leaving hospital, the mother should not be over-stretched by caring for the family on her own, and saw the whole family as being in need of long-term support. As a German participant put it, 'the mother shouldn't all of a sudden have to cope with everything, one should put in something to support her. Because she can't do everything herself, otherwise after a short time she will be overburdened again'. Denmark, Norway and Scotland also discussed the need for long-term support. The Italian child welfare group was the only group to face the possibility that the breakdown of the family might be irreversible, and that it might be better for the children if they were never returned to their parents. In Greece home care was seen as a desirable service response but an unlikely one given the lack of such facilities. Long-term support was least discussed in the English-speaking countries.

The German and Norwegian groups gave a great deal of attention to the psychological and emotional needs of the children and how they could be addressed, but elsewhere the practical issues of care arrangements for the children tended to dominate discussions. It was generally accepted that if the father or relatives could not be persuaded to provide care then a placement in a foster or children's home would have to be considered for the older children, even if a unit could be found to take the mother and baby together. Everywhere there were concerns about the problems of finding foster carers who might be able to accept the sibling group and who could cope with such disturbed children.

Supporting the family tended to be seen in terms of supporting Mary in her role as mother. It is interesting to note that it was only in the context of the mother being in hospital that the needs and strengths of other family members were vigorously addressed. In some countries the father appears as a subject of discussion for almost the first time at Stage 3 as his ability and suitability as a parent is assessed. The needs of the children come to the fore when there is likely to be no mother around to support them. Mary's separation from family members other than the baby was seen as less of an issue and was rarely addressed.

Support for the Father and the Children

Supporting the father

The father was seen as a potential care-giver, but little mention was made of his own needs, though his role as an income provider was an area of concern. In Denmark it was noted that he would have been able to use his wife's paid maternity leave, if she was in hospital. In Sweden one worker was concerned about the father from the outset, and correctly predicted later developments, saying, 'You should look after the new father—it's a new situation for him. He may disappear since he thinks there is something wrong with him too. Then she'll be alone with the two children—he may leave, you really must take care of the father too'. In Germany it was suggested at the start that the father needed someone he could trust and talk to so that he could cope with his wife's anxieties (one of the English groups was very struck by the fact that work mates were suggested by the Germans in this role). In France it was suggested that he could be supported by an *accompagnement éducatif* (programme of home support), to work with him to prepare for the children's return home.

In general, the main concern about the father was his unemployment and his possible alcoholism. In Greece the father's drinking habits were immediately interpreted as 'alcoholism' and it was implied that this needed to be addressed with the father away from the children. One of the Luxembourg groups was concerned that, as an all-women group, they might be failing to pay sufficient attention to the father's situation. They thought 'someone should try to find the father to involve him in his responsibilities for the children and to see whether he needed help with his alcohol problem'. In Ireland an alcohol project was suggested and money counselling to help him to cope with the reduced income of unemployment, while in Italy and Luxembourg it was suggested that he could be helped to find work. Only these three countries referred to the economic situation of the family as well as its social well-being.

In Sweden, although the possibility was implied at Stage 2 that John might be sexually abusing Anna, this was tentative and it was still suggested at Stage 3 that he could accompany the children if they could be placed in a residential family unit. Other countries also raised the possibility of sexual abuse. While they did not identify the possible abuser, it was clear from the context that they thought it likely to be John.

Support for the children

The focus of the intervention was generally very adult based and quickly focused on the mother, with other family members being less visible. For example, at Stage 1 in Germany the adult services group were concerned to support the mother outside of the psychiatric system and encourage her to regain her health, and the need for supportive services for her husband and child was a secondary issue. The Scandinavian countries, and particularly Norway, were more concerned about the children, and in the German child welfare team the level of concern about the children was very high throughout. They saw Anna as needing help in her own right and they were very concerned about her. Even at Stage 1 they had thought that she needed someone to whom she could talk, and that there was an urgent need for someone from outside to become involved with the family as there might be no family member who could help her—they would have their own preoccupations. Anna was said to need 'someone who focuses on the needs of the child, whom she trusts and with whom she could be open about her feelings'. Similarly the discussion of family life was much more focused on the need of the children as individuals. This contrasted with other countries where often little was said beyond keeping the family together and promoting bonding. The English child mental health group said that Anna needed a 'good granny', but could not see any possibility that a professional would be available to take on this task if no granny figure was available.

At Stage 2 all countries discussed the possibility of help for Anna from the child mental health service or school psychological service, but in Greece, Australia, Ireland and the UK there were problems of lengthy waiting lists, and it did not seem as though this help would have been available. As one of the English participants commented in the discussion on Stage 3, 'if she had been referred to the CAMH team at Stage 2, she might by now be near the top of the waiting list'. Some alternative or additional services were mentioned to help the children. In England the family centre would be able give support to the children as well as the mother. The Swedish mental health group suggested the use of a support group for children of mentally ill parents and said that someone from the adult mental health team would see her and talk to her about what had happened. In Greece it was also suggested that it would be necessary to explain to the child what had happened to her mother.

In countries which did not have widely available nursery schools, such as Germany and the UK, a playgroup or nursery placement for Thomas was suggested at Stage 2, but was mainly seen as a service to the parent rather than the child. Thomas was scarcely mentioned in the discussions of most of the groups. Generally in the countries of the UK, especially England, contact with the children was seen as a way of getting information with which to determine the risk or existence of possible child abuse.

Work with the Whole Family

At all stages the child welfare team in Italy showed a strong systemic family therapy bias, and the focus was thus on the family as a whole. At Stage 2 they thought that Anna should not be singled out as the member of the family to have psychiatric treatment because this accepted the definition that she was the problem. Instead therapeutic work needed to be done, initially with the mother. There should be a thorough assessment of this multi-problematic situation, with the aim of reinforcing the mother's competence and giving her the task of not giving up on the 10-year-old girl. There was criticism of the school for identifying the 10-year-old as the problem and removing responsibility from the family so that 'the poor child is shunted from the parents to the school, by the school to a professional … and nobody assumes responsibility for anything'. However, one of the participants identified a risk that a family orientation might have the effect of denying any direct services to the child at a time when she might need them. The Norwegian groups, who also had a systemic approach, were more interventionist, possibly because they had the resources.

The unity of the family was a recurrent theme even in those countries that were very interventionist. For these countries, maintaining the unity of the family was the rationale for their readiness to intervene. This was not necessarily accompanied by a 'whole family' approach to how interventions were planned or executed. A priority of keeping the family together was not necessarily related to a systemic approach.

The importance of bonding was heavily stressed. In all countries this was the dominant concern at Stage 1, and it recurred again at Stage 3. This was most clearly stated in the Australian comment that 'the emotional desire to keep a mother and baby together influences decision making'. However, the concept of bonding did not always lead to the same conclusions. In Norway, at Stage 1, one participant saw bonding as a powerful force to be taken into account in assessing risk: 'at this stage when the mother is bonding and is in a symbiotic relationship with the child, the emotions can quickly change to hostility. It could be dangerous to leave the mother and child alone together'.

At Stage 3 some countries had extensive discussions on the need to prepare for the re-establishment of the family when the mother left hospital. In this context a participant in the German child welfare team said, 'I would not send her straight away back to the family, even if the mother says that she is taking the tablets and feeling good. I would want to see that there was something on offer for the children. The mother too could not just be left'. They talked about the emotional stresses on Anna and the pressures she would have experienced in caring for her mother.

At Stage 3, when the family was likely to be separated through hospitalisation, the issue of keeping the family together was referred to everywhere. The desire to keep the family together generally meant the mother and children, but did include the father. Previous comments have indicated how the father was seen as a potential resource for the family, despite his problems. In Sweden this led to the conclusion that 'he might have been drinking for years, he had left his family and was probably not much to count on, but was still important for the children. A father with problems is better than no father at all'.

Day or residential mother and baby units or family units made it easier to keep families together, but participants in many countries were very uncertain whether there really were mother and baby placements available. Where there were no such units and no intensive family support services, keeping the family together was extremely difficult. In Sweden it was possible for parents to stay with their children in residential care, and parents usually preferred to do so. This provided an alternative strategy for keeping the family together, although it would not have been possible for such units to accept a severely mentally ill parent.

Responses to Risk

At Stage 1, risk to the baby was much talked about. The nature of this risk was generally unspecified, but focused on the baby's safety. This was mentioned explicitly by groups in Norway, Italy, Luxembourg, Australia and the countries in the UK, and was implied by the others.

At Stage 2 the most obvious difference between the various countries was shown by those that discussed the possibility of the child being sexually abused, against those that did not (see Table 6.1).

Table 6.1   Countries suggesting possible sexual abuse

Sexual abuse mentioned	Sexual abuse not mentioned
Norway	Denmark
Sweden	Italy
France	Germany
Luxembourg	Greece
Ireland	Australia
England	
Scotland	
Northern Ireland	

For the English, the possibility of sexual abuse entailed a different approach to assessment and potentially far greater involvement in the family because it could lead to a child protection investigation.

At Stage 3 there was a general escalation of concern about the welfare of the children and their degree of risk. At this stage, where the risks were felt to be strongest and most immediate, the groups showed less anxiety about risk because the decisions to be made were, for most countries, more obvious.

Either the children had to be removed from the mother or the mother had to be removed from the children. In either case if the father could not be found (and by then it was largely assumed that there was no wider family) the state would need to care for the children. This position was less obvious to the Italians who would still try to keep Mary out of hospital. In the Italian child welfare group, the possible long-term risks to the children were an important consideration. However, in many other countries this discussion was omitted with most of the time spent talking about the practical arrangements for dealing with the situation.

Trust and Co-operation between Families and Professionals

A common concern was the development of an effective relationship between workers and the family. However, this was pursued with varying degrees of enthusiasm and the strategies for doing so appeared to vary.

At Stage 1 it was suggested, not unreasonably, that the father would contact people or services he already knew. This led German and Australian workers to suggest that this first port of call might be the family doctor, GP or community health centre. In the words of the German group: 'a good deal would depend on the pre-existing relationship between the mother and the family doctor, and the mother's willingness to accept help'. In Italy it was felt that services could be best introduced by a family member or a supportive friend, so that 'the mother would need to be persuaded that she needed help, probably by someone she already knew. This might be better done by a relative from her family of origin, so this family needed to be contacted'. It was also possible that John might go to the CSM, as they thought that there was some confidence in the service locally.

At Stage 2 the establishment of a trusting relationship with Mary was central; the possibility of effective intervention seemed to depend on the quality of the family members' relationships with workers. The mother's request for practical help was seen as a way of making contact with her and establishing a relationship of confidence that would enable her to look at other problems. As a Norwegian participant put it, 'Practical assistance to the family, according to the mother's wishes, could be the key to co-operation with the family'. The Australian group thought that services needed to be non-threatening and responsive to the needs expressed as well as pursuing a professional agenda. 'Unless there's someone out there who the family trust, you won't get anywhere.'

Inter-Agency Co-operation

The effectiveness with which agencies were able to collaborate with each other formed an important component of many of the discussions of the groups. Identification of a key individual responsible for co-ordinating the delivery of service was important, but there was often debate as to who this should be.

In several countries, particularly Ireland, the UK and Italy, the GP (or equivalent) was seen as a potentially important co-ordinator. In both Ireland and Northern Ireland the GP was seen throughout as the key professional, knowing the family's history, linking resources and able to get access to services. In Italy the importance of collaboration was emphasised 'so as not to give conflicting messages—"scissors"—which is what normally happens'. In Italy, the *medico di base* would often be the case co-ordinator, although in complex cases it would be an employee nominated by the district health authority. There seemed to be flexibility in the system because it was suggested in the discussion that the case manager would be the person most trusted by the family. In Northern Ireland, too, 'the person who Mary trusts most' would assume the role of key worker.

In England and Australia it was strongly suggested that this family's needs could easily get lost without someone designated to act in some sort of case management role to ensure that they received the help they needed. The danger was that with a multiplicity of service providers 'what gets lost in it is maybe who is actually taking responsibility ... who is following up... who is taking responsibility for assessment and risk'. Or, in the words of an English worker, 'who is linking all this together, who is doing what?'. This became more pronounced at Stage 2 with the involvement of the school. The English child mental health group thought it unlikely that community mental health services would be made aware of such a situation. 'Complex cases could fall between the two services (children's services and adult mental health)', and the child's needs might be overlooked. Workers in Australia and England expressed the most anxiety over the difficulties of communication and co-ordination between different services, particularly between children's services and adult mental health. In England the mental health groups thought that at Stage 2 they would have no way of knowing that there were problems in this family. Such gaps in communication were highlighted particularly by the Australian child welfare group which noted that 'there is a great reluctance amongst professionals to seek a mental health assessment of a parent. There is also a lack of knowledge about the impact of parental mental illness on children ...'. The hope was expressed in England that co-ordination was likely to be improved with the development of the primary health care teams with a responsibility towards both parents and children. In Germany, as in Italy, the anxiety seemed to be more about confusion between agencies than about families falling through the gaps. 'It can sometimes be a right old "spaghetti" when someone is working with a mother and children and the children are "at risk" on account of the mother' (German group).

At Stage 3, many countries assumed that there would be inter-agency meetings. In Norway the Child Protection Agency would form a group of involved professionals, including health services, the school, mental health and child protection services to co-ordinate actions related to the family and for long-term planning. In Denmark the social services department would arrange this. The UK groups talked about holding a child protection conference at this point, but the English groups thought that the situation was too urgent and that there would not be time. An emergency planning meeting would be more likely. It was also acknowledged that the range of individuals and institutions involved could be confusing to families.

In France a service was being set up which would offer out-patient treatment and support on a flexible and part-time basis, called a *Centre d'Accueil Thérapeutique à Temps Partiel* (CATTP). This service, which could be linked to other services, such as short-term foster placements, would aim 'to forge links between the maternity unit, i.e. the medical services of the hospital, with the adult psychiatric services, the PMI [community maternal and child health service] and the social services'. Countries such as France which have a multidisciplinary child welfare service which includes maternal and child health and generic social work, showed less anxiety about communication although there were still problems over co-operation.

There was a particular concern voiced by English groups, but not elsewhere, in relation to specialisation. It was not only that specialisation, particularly in social work, made it difficult to communicate; there was also a regret for the time when social workers had had a generic training, and worked generically. Records had been held in one system, and information about social work contacts with any family members would be in the same file. At Stage 2, Mary's previous contact with the mental health services would thus have been very unlikely to go unnoticed.

Services for Ethnic Minorities or Refugees

At the end of the discussion of the vignette, the groups were asked a question that related to all stages of the story. What difference, if any, would it have made if the family had come from a minority ethnic group? The experience of the group members varied considerably. Some had worked with many different ethnic groups, some had not. In some areas the main experience was with refugees, in some it was with second- or third-generation immigrants. However, similar points were made repeatedly. There were difficulties over translation, which in some places were poorly resourced so that intervention had to be considerably delayed. The availability of translators and the funding for translation services were both potential problems, and standards of translation were unreliable as translators sometimes distorted what was being said. There was an awareness that the professionals might have different expectations of families from the service users. There was a tendency to expect that in ethnic minority families there would be more supportive and extended family networks. One of the English workers cautioned against making assumptions about this. She pointed out that a family who had been in the country for some time might not have maintained these networks, or might have fallen out with their relatives. The wider family was seen as sometimes helpful, but also as capable of preventing a family member from seeking help outside their network. There were several suggestions that families from ethnic minorities found mental illness more stigmatising, and would want to hide it.

There were specific problems about recognising mental illness in someone from another culture, partly because of language difficulties, but also because of differences in the way that an illness might be presented. There was a fear of both over-diagnosis and under-diagnosis. There were parallel problems about expectations of parenting, with fears that workers' ideas about 'normal' parenting might lead to fallacious assessments. The participants emphasised that they aimed to provide the same level of service for all users, and also that the law of the country was the same for all. The extent to which there were special service delivery systems varied. Some countries were providing information leaflets in a range of languages.

The responses of the groups depended to some extent on their experience of the ethnic minority groups that they had previously worked with. Within England, one of the boroughs had a number of different ethnic minority groups, mainly refugees. One borough had a large well-established group, and the third had both well-established groups and more recent refugee arrivals. Problems around translation and adaptation were obviously more difficult if a number of different ethnic groups were involved, and if they were new arrivals. There were great differences between the project countries in the numbers, composition and origin of ethnic minority groups, and in the laws relating to nationality and citizenship. For example, in Luxembourg, the largest immigrant group was from within the European Union, and they did not have problems in finding employment, but they did have social problems. In France there were immigrant groups from Africa and North Africa, some of whom were second or third generation, and some of whom were recent.

The Swedish groups, which worked in an area with a high level of immigrants from several countries, were very aware that their normal way of working was based on an assumption that the service users shared the same view of the relationship between the individual, the family and the state that they had. As described earlier in this chapter, when they were working with Swedish families, both sides made the assumption that social workers, as agents of the state, had resources to offer to support families, and that children were the concern of the state, and not only the concern of their families. Immigrant families, particularly refugees who had had different experiences of state power, were not likely to share these assumptions, and this had to be understood. It made it difficult for both the families and the social workers when interventions were offered which were meant to be supportive, but were experienced as threatening. Interestingly, this suggests that countries with a low level of state intervention might be experienced by immigrants as less threatening than countries with high levels of family support and an emphasis on preventive work. However, as immigrant and refugee families may be experiencing high levels of poverty and deprivation, they are also greatly in need of support.

Although there was a general consensus in the replies to this question, the groups who worked in areas with a large number of immigrants, and with wider experience of difference, gave more detailed answers that showed a greater depth of understanding of the complexities of the issues raised.

CONCLUSION

The major areas of variation between countries appear to be around the weight given to a number of different factors and concerns. These dominant issues were over the use and legitimacy of compulsory psychiatric intervention, the use made of the extended family and social networks to support the family, the role of family support services in helping maintain the family, the provision of services for the children as individuals, and the perception and diagnosis of risk. These issues formed the basis of the work of the Luxembourg workshop. Preparatory work for the workshop began in the second meetings of the professional groups, when they heard about the responses of another country. The next chapter is concerned with these reflections and the ideas developed in Luxembourg.

Chapter 7

Inter-Country Reflections

In the previous two chapters we have set out the responses of the groups in different countries to the situation described in the vignette. At a second meeting the groups were presented with the responses of another country and asked for their reflections.

It was usually the case that groups began by thinking that practice in the other country was not all that different from their own. This reflected the fact that the main structures of services available are similar throughout Europe; there are health services, social services and schools, there is child protection legislation and there is provision for the admission of people with a mental illness to hospital against their will. It also reflected a high level of shared professional ideology and a shared knowledge base. As the groups thought more about the other country's processes, they began to be more aware of difference. The reflections that we describe here are those where one of the pair was an English-speaking country.

Ireland was paired with Sweden, and as well as the scheduled meeting, they took part in a joint discussion group at the Luxembourg workshop. A group from Sweden later visited Ireland.

The first impressions of the Irish groups were that the two systems were 'not too different', but they went on to describe significant differences;

- mandatory reporting existed in Sweden;
- health and social services appeared to be better resourced in Sweden;
- Sweden appeared to have better/clearer co-ordination;
- the Swedish response was generally faster and more proactive;
- people were not waiting for something to happen before they intervened.

Participants from Sweden thought that:

- the existence of mandatory reporting in Sweden was the key difference;
- in Ireland the GP's role appeared to be very central, which was not the case in Sweden, although it was like that many years ago;
- the combination of health and social services as a single agency was very different from Sweden, where the services were divided and not based in one place;

• in Sweden there is no criminal responsibility for children under the age of 15, compared to age 7 in Ireland.

The Swedish group found the organisational structure of the Irish services confusing. The team did not appear to 'work together' and the Swedish group wanted to know why it seemed so loose. It was explained that the different professionals, although normally part of the same team, were often based in different buildings and that communication was very poor. Originally, they had worked in the same building, but as services had expanded, this had not proved possible. Sweden's impression of the Irish workers was that they were 'lonely'. The Irish delegates confirmed that distances and physical geography as well as professional culture created a gulf between the professions, even if they were nominally part of the same team. There also appeared to be a difference in legal responsibilities. In Sweden, the legal responsibility for a child's welfare rested with the child welfare team. In Ireland, it was the responsibility of the health and social services board.

Swedish workers were very surprised that workers or parents in Ireland could not contact child psychiatry directly. In Ireland, referral to child mental health services has to be made through a GP, and this appeared to them to be a 'road block'. In Sweden direct referral by social workers or others was possible. The co-ordinating role of the GP was seen as useful, but workers from Ireland qualified this, saying that although the formal position was that the GP would have the key co-ordinating role, this was sometimes a ritual. Certainly, if a case were very complex, there would be doubts whether it could be properly managed by a GP.

Some workers in Ireland felt that if mental health services intervened in child welfare issues, as they did in Sweden, they would be seen as 'going beyond their brief'. However, they thought that the Swedish approach was faster, better co-ordinated, and more effective. Ireland was impressed with the attention of the Swedish groups to the father's needs. The Swedish groups showed more awareness of his importance in relation to the children. The Irish noted and envied the Swedish residential facilities where parents could stay with their children.

The Irish workers were particularly struck by the statement from Sweden at Stage 3 that 'this could never happen here'. In Ireland they thought that the situation probably happened on a regular basis. There was great admiration for the Swedish approach; workers seemed to know what should be done, and did it. This was compared with Ireland where professionals were likely in the first place to go their own way, although they would eventually co-operate.

However, the Irish group had some doubts about the readiness of the Swedish services to intervene. One Irish worker suggested that the joint visit between the health visitor and child psychiatrist, suggested as a possibility in Sweden, was an attempt to 'ambush' the family. They thought that the family was seen in a different light in Ireland and treated as a privileged institution. When asked if the difference was to do with views about the family or views about the stigma of intervention by the health services, representatives from both Sweden and Ireland said that people did not want social work intervention. The difference was that Swedish people were more willing to accept the involvement of society via the state. The Swedes said that this was much more difficult with immigrants who might not subscribe to these values and with whom it was then more difficult to achieve real co-operation. In Ireland, the role of the state in child health services is based on legislation introduced around 1950 and certain groups in Ireland opposed the level of state intervention put in place by this legislation. The principle of subsidiarity, which is important in Ireland, means that problems and issues should be dealt with at the lowest level able to cope with them. The family would often be expected to resolve issues and there would be suspicion of the state having a larger role.

England was paired with Germany, but the German responses to the vignette were also shown to the groups in Australia and Northern Ireland owing to the difficulties in correlating the timing of the groups in different countries. Most of the following reflections relate to the English/German exchanges, because the Germans only heard briefly about the Australian and Northern Irish responses.

The German professionals thought they had the same problems over co-operation and communication as in England, but they saw important differences, such as the greater readiness in Germany to intervene in family life. The German group reflected,

> 'Whereas with us it seemed that such professional help would be organised for the family (at least in the daytime while the father was at work), the English teams operated on the basis that the family would have to rely on its own resources. This is a significant difference, which surfaced on several occasions. We think it might be that economic resources for such household services are even worse in England than they are for us.'

Clearly there were significant resource issues, but differences in intervention between Germany and England were more complex than that. Germany also had certain resource constraints: 'We have no community nurses. We have no mother and baby units. Both are a severe lack'. They also deplored the difficulty of providing home help which could only be provided where an illness had been ascertained by the health services.

The English thought the German services must be better funded. 'Here we'd really have to argue for funding based on risk, and there's a tendency to see risk more because it gives you more funding. … And if you have more money you can start thinking about issues of trust.' The English groups returned to resource issues in a variety of contexts. Discussing the German responses at Stage 3,

> 'There was a lot of emphasis on the fact that this was a long-term issue and would require long-term input which I don't think is the same here. Although perhaps in our hearts we know that's what is going to happen, it doesn't seem generally spoken about. It's definitely more short-term style here. We rather hope that nothing else will come up. …'

The English were concerned about the level of choice given to patients in Germany by the health insurance system, and thought that the lack of a GP system was worrying. They wanted to know who was accountable in the German system. If John went to the family doctor, would the family doctor be accountable? 'If things aren't going right, who decides about the threshold criteria?' The role of the judge in agreeing to compulsory hospitalisation puzzled the English groups. They thought it strange that, with such an emphasis on intervention at the lowest level, hospital admission should involve the courts. But one participant reflected, 'they're more worried about freedom, I think, than we are here. We're more worried about safety, perhaps'. The English thought that the Germans were slow to suggest hospitalisation for Mary.

The English groups noted different expectations of the family. The expectation that John would look after the children was seen as much lower in Germany at both Stage 1 and Stage 2. It seemed to them that it was assumed by their German colleagues that 'he [John] would be around until the support services could arrange some sort of support for Mary and they would step in and relieve John of his parental responsibility—that's how it sounded. … Our code is that a man stays home if needed. Is this just a social services department view?'.

The English groups envied the Germans the SPFH service, but they were ambivalent about it. They questioned the role of the SPFH service and wondered if it was considered stigmatising. They had a similar reaction to the Irish (who had questioned the Swedish level of intervention), and felt that the level of input of the SPFH would be intrusive. There was an apparent inconsistency between the English concern, on the one hand, that the SPFH service intervened too readily and, on the other, that the mental health services did not intervene readily enough. It was interesting that their definition of a low level of intervention by the mental health services related to the unwillingness of the Germans to promote hospital treatment for Mary, while, by contrast, at Stage 2 the Germans were astonished that in England no psychotherapy was sought for the mother. Taking mental health and child welfare services together, the overall level of intervention in Germany was high, with the SPFH service providing an alternative to hospitalisation. The English groups seemed to see the interventions of the services as separate from, rather than complementary to, each other. The fact that each country seemed to think that the other intervened too little on the mental health side, suggests that they may have had different conceptualisations of what constituted intervention.

Discussing inter-agency working, the Germans were dubious about formal child protection conferences and network meetings, saying that 'we work in a much less formal way—professionals get together as need arises in an individual case in various "help conferences"'. They found it interesting that the health team should delegate responsibility for the family to the children and families team, whereas in Germany both teams would feel responsible. The English felt that the German system was insecure and lacked a structure: 'it helps to have a framework when you are anxious'. At Stage 3, the German groups liked the setting up of a core group comprising both services and also the suggestion, from Northern Ireland, that the 'key worker' should be the person whom the mother most trusts. This contrasted with Germany where 'with us it would probably be the *Jugendamt* social worker who automatically assumed this role, and the mother's wishes would play no part in the matter'.

The Germans noted with some surprise the English teams' focus on the risk that Anna was being sexually abused and said, 'We didn't see sexual abuse or violence in the family as an urgent problem—the children have enough reasons for their unsettled behaviour, without the need for any further conjectures'. This comment can be paired with an English comment at Stage 2:

> 'It strikes me that they're much more confident about their ability to contain things than perhaps we would be. I think we would be more anxious and more concerned about the risks to the children and the mother. But they seem much more open to the ideas of the family and non-statutory support.'

The English teams noted that the German team spent much more time at every stage talking about the children's needs.

The Australian groups heard about both the English and the German responses. They commented on the fact that there appeared to have been major cutbacks in English services. They noted the difference between the English and the German responses to intervention. 'In the English discussion there is this expectation that the family will manage.' This echoed the comment of the English child mental health group at Stage 2 that they might never hear about Anna because 'the anxiety about this family is not high enough to ensure that anything gets done'. The Australians thought that the Germans were quick to bring in services and experts and they too were surprised and uncertain about such early intervention.

The Scottish and the Norwegian groups were paired. The Scottish first impression of Norway was that child welfare provision appeared to be more integrated than it is in Scotland, though it was thought that Scotland might be moving in the direction of more integrated services for children with the establishment of new community schools. The Scots were also impressed by the availability of residential services in Norway which would admit the family together. These would not be common in Scotland. There was some surprise in the Scottish groups about how much thought the Norwegian adult mental health team gave to the children and how they were managing while at home. The groups were unsure whether there would be this concern in Scotland, and they thought that the adult mental team, in concentrating on the needs of the mother, might forget about the children.

In terms of services to the mother it was considered that Norway and Scotland were very similar. Compulsory mental health admission processes seemed similar in both countries. At Stage 2, Scottish workers suggested that in Scotland the school and education services would be more involved than appeared to be the case in Norway, while in Norway it appeared that child mental health services would be more likely to be available.

Scottish workers felt that both countries had the same aims and generally went about getting there in a similar way. In both, inter-agency working was a problem:

'In both countries there appeared to be a frustration at this stage; all professionals could identify what needed to be done for this family but could not identify
who would have the responsibility for providing services, co-ordinating the
activities of the professionals, or ensuring that information was exchanged
among professionals.'

The Norwegian groups agreed that the aims of the groups in both countries
were the same, and that the types of resources referred to were similar.
However, they noted significant differences in the ways tasks were carried
out. This was summarised by the comment that the Scottish helping system
was more practical and instrumental rather than focusing on prevention.
They thought that in Norway they got involved earlier in the problems of the
family. In Scotland it seemed that the situation for the child had to be more
serious before child protection services were involved. Indeed one participant had the impression that in Scotland the child had to experience harm
before action could be taken against the will of the parents.

The Norwegian participants said that the Scottish participants seemed to
focus more on individuals than on the family as a whole, but also noted that
they did not give much consideration to John's lack of employment, and that
no attention was paid to the demanding behaviour of Thomas. There was
thus agreement between the observations of the participants in the two countries. Both thought that the Norwegians focused more on the family, under-
took more preventive interventions, paid more attention to the children's
emotional state and to the long-term needs of the family than did the Scots.
This was attributed partly to differences in legislation; the Norwegian child
protection legislation requires that support should be offered at an early
stage, and seemed to the Scots to give the parents less room to refuse help.
There were also differences in resources; the Norwegian child mental health
service is well resourced and has a low threshold for treatment.

THE REFLECTIONS OF THE ENGLISH-SPEAKING COUNTRIES

Threaded through the responses of all the English-speaking countries was a
shared anxiety about state intervention. They were all paired with well-
resourced countries, and even though they envied the ability of these countries to intervene early, they all had reservations about early intervention.
They thought it too intrusive, and expected that it would be regarded as stigmatising and resented by the family; the preventive aspect of early intervention was acknowledged, but carried less weight. This anxiety about help
being unwanted seemed to lie behind other reflections. For example, some of
the English child welfare social workers were worried about the German
reliance on voluntary agreement. 'The danger is it's still all voluntary on her
part. If it's that bad (i.e. bad enough to need such extensive services), then it
needs to have statutory support.' The implication was that they did not
expect to be able to work with a family in severe difficulties on a basis of trust,

because they did not expect to start work with the family until the risks were so great that it was too late to establish trust.

Subsidiarity was an important principle in both Ireland and Germany. One might therefore expect that the importance of the family as the first support-ive system would be the same in both. Yet both the Irish and the English thought that the readiness of the professionals in Sweden and Germany to offer formal supportive measures demonstrated a failure to take into account support from the wider family. This is interesting because with the emphasis that subsidiarity places on family support, it might be expected that the Germans would place more emphasis on the wider family as a source of help. However, the Swedish, Norwegian and German professionals all had the same expectation that state support was probably needed by the family in the vignette right from the start, whether or not there were wider family resources. The Irish and the English assumed that formal support for the family could only be given as a substitute where informal support was lacking, rather than as a supplement or complement to it. Whether this was a response to financial realities or a point of principle was well articulated by one of the Australians: 'It's probably a combination of both, under-resourcing and putting the onus on people to cope'. When talking about their own lack of resources, one English participant said that there was often no point in thinking about what might be needed because they knew that there were no resources; she then reflected that this meant that resources (or the lack of them) actually began to modify not only <u>what</u> you thought about cases but <u>how</u> you thought about cases. Some things became unthinkable; a rationale or a conceptualisation then had to be found that made sense in terms of what was financially possible. Another participant demonstrated the pressures behind this, saying 'everything is driven here by financial principles and reality, every minute of the day'.

The Australians shared the English view that the health-insurance-based German system would make it easier for a family to fall through the net, or for a person to avoid psychiatric treatment. The Irish and the Scots saw the statist Swedish and Norwegian systems as well organised, and offering more preventive work through early intervention. These perceptions may reflect the different qualities of subsidiaristic systems and statist systems.

The English groups did not all respond the same way to the account of the German discussions. While some thought that too much attention was focused on Mary and John (one said, '<u>our</u> client is Anna'), others thought that greater attention was paid in the German discussions to the needs of the chil-dren and to the family as a whole and approved of this. Thus some of the English participants showed a narrowly child protection focus on their work with the family, while others were reaching towards a more supportive way of working with the whole family. As described above, the Scottish groups were very definite about the greater attention paid to the children and the family perspective by their Norwegian colleagues, and rated it highly.

It was noticeable that all the English-speaking groups spent a great deal more time talking about procedures than any of the others. They spent less time talking about the functioning of the family, about ways of understanding what was going on, or about how to work with the family. Both the Germans and the Norwegians commented on the fact that not only were resources restricted in England and Scotland, but that their mandate of intervention seemed to be different, so that a child had to be in danger before action could be taken. An Australian participant described their situation as similar to the English, saying that sometimes 'the only way to access more intensive family support is through reporting (i.e. using child protection procedures)'. Whatever the explanation, the English-speaking countries appear as poorly resourced and comparatively unwilling to intervene, with high expectations of the family being able to cope; both these factors discourage early intervention. The English-speaking professionals had to focus on risk and danger because this was the only way to get resources. Formal procedures then gave some reassurance.

The English-speaking countries did not, however, all speak with one voice, and there were considerable differences between them. The Scottish groups did not talk as much as the other English-speaking groups about procedures, and placed much more emphasis on the importance of the school medical service and on working with the school. The school played a very small part in the English discussions, and the role of the school nurse, which was important in Scotland, was not mentioned in England. Northern Ireland and Ireland seemed to be more flexible in their approach and less inhibited by inter-agency boundaries, with stronger informal communication between professionals. The remark of the Northern Irish participant, that Mary should work with the person she gets on with best, was not replicated in England. England and Australia seemed most alike, with the most restricted resources, with the heaviest emphasis on procedure and with the most difficulty in working across boundaries. All the English-speaking countries referred to the importance of the GP and health visiting system, but in Ireland, and even more in Northern Ireland, there was reliance on the primary care professionals being able to take on a major role in supporting, monitoring and co-ordinating. There were other interesting similarities between Ireland and Northern Ireland. The most distinctive difference between the systems of Ireland and Northern Ireland and the other English-speaking countries is the structure of combined health and social welfare boards or trusts. The greater flexibility of Ireland and Northern Ireland in inter-agency co-operation suggests that the joint management structure may have some advantages in providing a more coherent and less fragmented system than the English and Scottish division between health trusts and local authority social services. To summarise, the Irish and Northern Irish groups shared the attitudes of the other English-speaking countries to the early intervention in child welfare of Germany and the Scandinavian countries, and showed the same preoccupations with procedures, but had more flexible agency boundaries and better informal communication.

THE LUXEMBOURG WORKSHOP

The research process ended with the workshop in Luxembourg, which was attended by the research partners, and a participant from each of the discussion groups. It was thus an international and multidisciplinary meeting and the issue of inter-professional and inter-agency working was the main focus of discussions. Certain aspects of the different systems were identified as important in facilitating co-operation.

In Denmark, Norway and Sweden it was thought that mandatory reporting of child neglect and abuse was a facilitator of co-ordination. As described in Chapter 2, mandatory reporting in these countries includes, for professionals, the reporting of anxiety or suspicion about possible child abuse, which leads to early intervention on a voluntary basis. The Scandinavian participants explained that the reason for mandatory reporting was that there was a very strong culture of confidentiality in health and social services, so that mandatory reporting was needed as a countervailing principle. However, there was a need for more informal communication as well as formalised teamwork between services and the rapid turnover of staff in the social services undermined co-operation.

France also has mandatory reporting but with different rules, which do not include anxiety or suspicion of abuse. In France the multidisciplinary teams in the social services include the maternal and child health nurses and the generically trained *assistantes sociales*. This aided communication and discussion; the exchange of information was not inhibited or limited by issues about inter-agency confidentiality. However, the staff of local social services had difficulty in communicating effectively with medical staff and often used different languages, so the generalist professionals, particularly social workers with a generic training, were important. In both France and Luxembourg, the *assistante sociale* expected, whatever her work place, to provide a generic social work response to all user groups. By contrast, English children and families teams were both specialist and monodisciplinary, which seemed to have led to the development, noted by the English professionals, of different 'languages' in child protection and mental health. It was agreed that multidisciplinary teams and regular multidisciplinary meetings that included workers from the health professions and social work facilitated communication and co-operation. For example, in Italy, a meeting of workers in health and social services had recently been instigated (as described in Chapter 3). This was providing a good focus for inter-agency co-operation. It was important that meetings were held regularly so that people got used to working together. The opportunity and time to develop informal contacts were also felt to be necessary in facilitating co-operative working.

The role of the primary care system and the universal services such as midwifery, health visiting, nursery schools and schools was of the first importance, if adequately resourced, and the lack of a universal health-visiting service was lamented by the German participants. However, this did not of itself ensure co-operation; in Ireland the primary role of the public health nurse and the GP was seen as very positive, but there was poor co-ordination between nurses and social workers. On the other hand, workers from different parts of the health and social services boards often worked in geographically close locations which was a great aid to good communication at an informal level. In Scotland the school system was an important part of the system for these families. The school health service provided a means of offering help to Anna that would be acceptable to her mother and the chain from school nurse to the school doctor to GP to psychiatrist provided connecting links between the services. A structure of liaison social workers between the social services, primary schools and some secondary schools was being developed. The Scottish emphasis on co-operation with education services was unique in this study.

The structure of joint Health and Social Services Boards and joint Health and Social Services Trusts in Ireland and Northern Ireland contributed to co-operation at local levels. By contrast, in England there were problems in co-operation that stemmed from budgetary arrangements boundaried according to the separate financing of the national health services and the local authority services.

Flexibility between agencies was valued; German delegates, who thought that their system was difficult to co-ordinate, were very impressed by the response from more than one country that the person in whom the family has most confidence should be the case manager. To the English, however, the German child welfare system seemed very flexible. Resources were also important in encouraging co-operation, and in Greece the shortage of workers was a major impediment. Germany and Luxembourg demonstrated that high levels of resources could compensate for the complexities of services that result from an insurance-based health service and subsidiaristic welfare services.

The remit of the Luxembourg workshop was to develop a European model for inter-agency co-operation in work with families where there is a mentally ill parent. The conclusion of the workshop was that, in spite of important differences in culture and structures between European countries, there were some underlying principles which would facilitate the development of better services (for further detail see Hetherington *et al.* 2000 and Sheehan *et al.* 2000). These were:

- The development of a 'whole family' approach by all agencies, supported by consultative use of child and adolescent mental health services.
- The development of a better knowledge base for child welfare professionals about mental health and for mental health professionals about child development.
- The development of greater professional awareness of the needs of families with a mentally ill parent and the children in these families.
- The development of links between universal services (primary health care and schools) and specialist services.
- The development both of formal links and regular meetings between health and social work agencies and of informal inter-agency contacts.

The use of these principles would develop co-operation and trust between agencies and between workers, on the basis of shared professional knowledge, shared aims and shared experience of working with their colleagues. Resources would be important in supporting the work, but the most important resource would be time to communicate and build trust.

The work of the Icarus project was based on inter-country collaboration and aimed to be as un-Anglo-centric as possible. It is obviously impossible for any project to shake itself free from a national perspective, but as far as possible the work was undertaken and the report written from a multi-national point of view. This has been reflected in the first part of this book. In Part II, the perspective shifts, and the focus is on England.

Part II

INTRODUCTION: WORKING WITH DIFFERENCE

THE INTERDEPENDENCE OF CULTURE, STRUCTURES, IDEOLOGY AND FUNCTIONING

In Chapter 1 we referred to the concept that in any country there is a constant and continuing interaction between the wider culture of the society, the structure of laws and systems that define, regulate and express that culture, and the way that these structures function. In looking at systems of health and welfare, we included professional ideology in the interactive circle, as being more than a specialised aspect of culture, and as forming a further force to be taken into account in considering the way in which health and welfare systems function.

In Part I, when describing the different reactions that we collected to the vignette, we did not look at what might lie behind these differences. At one level, the differences could be seen simply as the logical local response to the given laws, services, resources and administrative arrangements. But this did not seem to account for the nature of the discussions and the differences in focus of the responses to the vignette. In Part II we are looking at some of the factors that may lie behind the difference. One of the problems is that the work that has been done in the field of cross-country comparison of welfare regimes and other governmental systems has usually taken place at the macro level of policy development, or at a broadly theoretical level (see Baistow 2000). In attempting to use 'ground level' information to develop these analyses, we have difficulties owing to the variety of discourses involved and their different ways of referring to things that are possibly the same, certainly similar. An example is the term 'liberal' (as in Chapter 9, 'liberal welfare regime'), which is used to describe a political approach at the macro level. This is related to the approach discussed at the micro level in the following chapter which is there named as the 'case management approach' to welfare practice. Our thesis is that the wider political basis on which services are delivered is reflected in the approach to work at ground level. However, as will be demonstrated, the way that services are delivered cannot only be explained by the political philosophy of the state at macro level. Service delivery is also affected by laws (which do not necessarily express current policy), by the level of acceptance of official policy within the community, by the professional opinions and ideology of the workers in the services, and by the cultural climate within which the workers, the service users and the rest of the community operate.

To give examples from other comparative research (Cooper *et al.* 1995), the French provision for *adoption simple* (which is a limited form of adoption) could be used in situations of long-term fostering, but is not. The possibility is there in law, but it is not culturally syntonic to use it. To give another example, theories may be shared, but can be differently interpreted. Social workers in different countries show a high level of agreement about the importance of bonding between mother and infant—and, to support this, refer to Bowlby. The resources available to look after infants who are separated from their mother are, however, quite different. In France, infants in the state care are likely to be placed in *pouponières* (residential nurseries). In England these children would be first in line for foster care. This demonstrates how theory may be differently interpreted according to the culture within which the interpretation is taking place. The example given could demonstrate that fostering has a different place in English culture than in French culture (which is not to say that fostering is not extensively and imaginatively used in France, as the current project demonstrates). It could alternatively or additionally reflect different cultural attitudes to institutions. Whatever the explanation, it demonstrates how professional ideology responds to the culture within which it is sited, and the assumptions of that culture.

THE UNSTATED OR UNRECOGNISED ASSUMPTIONS

It is possible to identify differences in such things as laws, resources and organisation, but this does not explain why those laws have been passed, or why the choice has been made to fund those resources or structure organisations in such and such a way. Reasons may be given for those choices, but it is often hard to identify the different assumptions—often unstated, sometimes also unrecognised—that lie behind the choices. We see comparison as throwing some light on the nature of these assumptions. We regard it as important to try to uncover and identify these assumptions, because if we wish to introduce changes or new developments, they may have a decisive effect on the nature of the changes that are possible. This is not a pessimistic view that sees change as impossible because of pre-existing contexts, but a realistic view that sees a need, in attempting to make changes, to understand and take account of the existing context.

The comparative study of state intervention in child welfare is bound to raise wider issues. Children are dependent people in all European cultures;

they exist within a family (or family substitute) structure. They are also people who exist as citizens within a community and a state. Parents exist as people and citizens within the community and the state, but they also have a role as caretakers of other citizens—children. The roles of children and parents in relation to the state are thus ambiguous; they both have two possible roles, and at any time the state may respond to them in one or other of these roles. There is therefore room for wide variation in the interpretation of their roles and their relationship to the state, and this will be influenced by the general nature of the relationship of the state to its citizens. There is a shared rhetoric within Europe that the family is important and 'a good thing'. Reality suggests that the relationship between the family and the state is differently conceptualised and lived in different European countries, and that 'the family' is not everywhere the same construct.

The relationships between families and the state may, of course, vary within cultures as well as between cultures. We are looking here at the variation between countries because we can use the differences in laws, resources, organisation and the realities of practice to throw light on these differences in relationships.

Families will expect certain responses from the state. The state will expect and reward certain responses from families. The community has expectations both of appropriate family behaviour and appropriate state response. Professionals in the services for child welfare and parental health represent the state and are, or have been, in families; they both represent the state and are part of the community. They are at the meeting point of expectations which are reciprocal but not always reciprocated.

In the responses of our participants to the vignette, these expectations underlie their understanding of the situation, their views on the best course of action, on what is probable and what is possible.

We therefore identify certain areas of potential difference in the underlying assumptions that determine the structure and functioning of child welfare services:

- expectations of families
- expectations of the state
- expectations of the community.

Expectations of Families

Expectations of families derive from two interlocking sets of belief. Firstly, about the nature of the family; secondly, about the nature of citizenship. In the research into child protection which started our cross-country studies (Cooper et al. 1995), we developed a view of the differences in conceptualisation of the family in France and England, which we took further in work with other countries and with parents. Our initial understanding was that the family in France was a more robust and persistent entity than in England. English social workers worked with the hypothesis that a family was very important but was very easily destroyed. It was therefore important for

English social workers not to remove a child from the family, and very dangerous to do so, because it was likely that the family would fragment. If a child's family fragmented, it was necessary to find him or her a new family. French social workers worked with the hypothesis that the family was resilient, but also irreplaceable. You could risk taking a child out of a family, because you expected to be able to return the child. The corollary of this was that your family was your family for life; it could not be replaced through adoption, and everyone had to make the best of it. It was therefore necessary to put a lot of effort into supporting families. When we extended the research to include other European countries (Hetherington *et al.* 1997), we did not change this understanding of English and French differences in conceptualisation of the family. Moreover, it seemed to us that other European countries shared a concept of the family very much closer to the French than to the English. The current project supported our previous conclusions, and the comparisons in the following chapters will demonstrate the importance of these different ideas about the family.

Expectations of the State

There were two further factors that impinged on our understanding of the family: differing conceptualisations of being a citizen and of being a member of the community. Expectations of the state are one facet of citizenship. In referring to citizenship we do not intend to enter the vast field of studies on nationality and citizenship, and all the legal and historical background that this includes. But at the level of our research, it is clearly the case that what people accept as legitimate state activity in relation to themselves and their family, varies greatly from country to country. This appears to reflect assumptions about the 'correct' relationship between the state and its citizens. Silverman (1996) distinguishes between two underlying and contradictory principles of citizenship, the 'civil' (individualistic and market orientated) and the 'civic' (interventionist and solidaristic). The different conceptualisations of citizenship of the participating countries seem to demonstrate different 'weights' given to these principles. What people feel their state should do and may do is a complex issue beyond the scope of this book; but it is an issue that cannot be ignored when there are plainly important differences between countries which affect the responses of our participants. Levels of state intervention in families that are seen as socially acceptable in one country may be seen as inadequate in another. Chapter 9 looks in more detail at the connections between citizenship, the theorisation of welfare regimes and the responses to the vignette.

Expectations of the Community

Citizenship and the sense of being a member of the community, though related, are far from being the same. The Scandinavian countries had a very positive sense of citizenship, which seemed to include their sense of being part of the community. This was different from the approach to the community of other European countries. It is stereotypical to see a much stronger role for the community itself in southern European countries, but there was support for this stereotype. The community appeared as a much more important resource in the responses of our participants in Italy and Greece. This was not just that in those countries there was a much stronger expectation that there <u>must</u> be extended family members. There was also an expectation that neighbours would be prepared to get involved and that the community was a resource that could and should be mobilised by the professionals. Part of the role of the professionals was to do this. Savio's research into the role of community mental health nurses in Italy and England supports this observation (Savio 1996). This view of the professional role was also a factor in the responses of the French participants. Different expectations of the community and of the relationship between professionals, individuals and the community visibly affect the possible experiences of the vignette family.

The brief outline given above, of the areas in which underlying assumptions may differ, indicates the complexity of the task of trying to understand why professional responses to the same case are both similar and very different. In Part II we focus on comparisons between England and other countries in exploring some aspects of these differences. We start in Chapter 8 with a comparison between England, Germany and Italy—three countries which illustrate how differently the family might fare in different parts of Europe. Chapter 9 looks at state philosophies of welfare and their relationship to citizenship and the delivery of family welfare services. Chapter 10 takes this further and looks at a particular example, risk, which illustrates action at the meeting point between the concerns of the state and of the family, where state intervention may be necessary. Chapter 11 is concerned with the ways in which the co-ordination of services is affected by the structures of agencies and the professional ideologies and knowledge base of their workers.

Chapter 8

Comparisons: England, Germany and Italy

The information about the systems of the countries in the project, and the responses of the professional groups to the vignette, have been set out in the earlier chapters and this gives a basis for comparison of the responses of the different countries. There is a certain amount that is the same between different countries in the way that they respond. There are then some things that look similar, but on closer inspection are different in some important respects; and there are some things that are clearly different. In looking at what is the same and what is different, we always need to question: 'Why is it different?'. Is it because of differences in structures such as laws, in resources (or the accessibility of resources), in expectations or in something else not yet identified? Understanding the origins of these differences gives us new ideas about the reasons why our own system functions as it does.

In order to simplify the process of comparison we have selected two countries, Germany and Italy, to compare with England. Germany and Italy were chosen because they both had higher expectations of being able to keep the mother out of hospital than other countries, but they had different approaches in other respects. Both, although different from each other, are very different from England. The comparisons concentrate on the likely developments if Mary's illness was severe and if there was no help available from the grandparents or the wider family.

THE COMPOSITION OF THE PARTICIPATING GROUPS

As explained in Chapter 1, the groups comprised different professionals in different countries, reflecting the organisation, structure and staffing of services in each country. In England the adult mental health groups were drawn from community mental health teams and the child welfare groups from children and families teams in each of three boroughs (inner London, outer London and south-east England). In one borough there was also a group of child mental health professionals. The summary combines the responses of all these groups. The professionals taking part were, in the mental health groups, psychiatrists, mental health nurses, social workers and occupational therapists; in the child welfare groups, local authority social workers, children and families team managers and family workers (unqualified); and in the child and adolescent mental health group, psychiatrists, psychologists, nurses, social workers and specialist teachers. Germany and Italy had two groups each: one of mental health professionals and one of child welfare professionals. The German mental health group consisted of four social workers, two psychologists and one psychiatrist. Their child welfare group consisted of a consultant child psychiatrist, a freelance child psychiatrist, two adult daughters of mentally ill parents, two social workers, two social pedagogues and one residential social worker. In the Italian mental health group there were two social workers, three psychiatric social workers, three psychiatrists, one psychologist, one nurse and, in their child welfare group, five social workers and two psychologists (one from the child mental health service).

Stage 1

Interventions in the community

At Stage 1 there were similarities in the likely initial actions. All groups thought that the first source of help would probably be a generalist doctor (GP, 'family doctor', *medico di base*). He or she might visit, and might prescribe medication, but if the mother's illness were acute, she would be referred to the mental health system. All the participants were anxious, on the one hand, about the physical risk to the baby and, on the other, about the dangers of separating mother and baby. All countries considered the possibility that the mother might need to be hospitalised, and they were specifically asked to consider the likelihood of the use of compulsion and whether that would be possible.

Although England, Germany and Italy all thought that a generalist doctor was the likely first point of contact, there were differences within this. In Italy and England, the generalist doctor is the usual point of entry to the medical system. Germany has a health insurance model, and while many people, and especially families, have a 'family doctor', it is possible and quite usual to go directly to a specialist of your choice. The family doctor does not necessarily have the same position as a generalist practitioner in holding a summary of all medical information on his patient. It would have been possible (though it was considered unlikely because of the stigma attached to mental illness) for John to have gone straight to a psychiatrist when he was worried about his wife's state of mind. An alternative in all three countries was to have contacted the midwife, but it was thought likely that she would have contacted the generalist doctor, although referral by the midwife to the psychiatric system was possible. In either case, it was likely that a community mental health service would be involved. In Germany this would be a local authority service, the *SozialPsychiatrische Dienst* (SPD), in Italy it would be the *Centro di Salute Mentale* (CSM), the mental health centre which is the key service of their psychiatric system. The English equivalent is the community mental health team (CMH team).

In both Germany and Italy child welfare services would then become involved. In Germany this would be the SPFH (intensive family support service). This team would be able to work with the family to support the parents, and would be able to provide this service quite quickly and for several hours a day throughout the week. It was thought possible that there could be overnight support. These services are usually provided by NGOs, but the finance for such an intervention has to be negotiated with the *Jugendamt*, so the local authority social services for children would know about the family. In Germany, child welfare services are available to all, but health services provided by the local authority are means tested. The support for the family would therefore be likely to be centred on child welfare services. In Italy, the *Consultorio Familiare* (CF) would be involved with the family because they provide the maternal and child health service and are linked to the midwifery service. However, the leading workers would be likely to be from the CSM. They would work with the *medico di base* to try and put together support from within the community. The Italian groups commented on the lack of family support services, but felt that they would be able to find neighbourhood support. The English groups in all three boroughs, both those from the mental health services and from the child and families services, thought that it was very unlikely that the local authority children and families team (C&F team) would have been contacted. It was known to both primary care services and mental health services that the C&F teams would only respond if there were clear child protection issues. Table 8.1 summarises the community services and support available at Stage 1.

Using hospital care

The question whether hospital care was likely to be needed depended on two separate factors. The first was the availability of alternatives, and the nature of the hospital care offered. All countries started from the position that it was better for the mother to be treated at home, and that it was wrong for mother and baby to be separated. Resources clearly affected their ability to keep the mother at home. In Germany, where there were good family support services, keeping the mother at home was a much more realistic possibility, and could be managed with less risk than in England where no family support services were thought to be available. In England, the possibility of hospitalisation in a mother and baby unit also made hospitalisation a less detrimental alternative. In Italy, a proactive approach to community and neighbourhood support compensated for the lack of family support services. The workers from the CSM co-operated with the *medico di base* in finding a local solution.

Table 8.1 Community services and community support at Stage 1

Community-based agencies likely to be involved in (a) mental health and (b) child welfare		
England	Germany	Italy
(a) CMH team; joint health and social services community mental health team.	(a) SPD (*SozialPsychiatrische Dienst*); local authority community mental health service.	(a) CSM (*Centro di Salute Mentale*); mental health centre run by the local regional office of the national health service.
	(b) *Jugendamt*; the local authority service for children and young people.	(b) CF (*Consultorio Familiare*); multi-disciplinary service for maternal and child health with a wide remit, employing nurses, doctors, midwives, psychologists and social workers.
	SPFH (*Sozial Pedagogische Familien Hilfe*); intensive family support team staffed by trained social workers, usually NGO.	

Resources available other than hospitalisation		
Support from the CMH team.	Support from the SPD.	Support from the CSM.
Community midwife.	Intensive support from the SPFH, funded by the *Jugendamt*.	Support in the community from volunteers organised and supported by the CSM and the *medico di base*.
Health visitor.		Support from CF.
		Support from the social services (SSB).

The second factor was the attitude of the mental health workers to psychiatric illness and hospitalisation. Differences in conceptualisation of mental illness between the health professionals in the different countries were an underlying motif in the responses of the mental health groups. The clearest difference was between the English-speaking countries where there was in general a response based on physical medicine and the continental countries where an underlying psycho-dynamic framework was apparent (see Chapter 4). This observation is supported by Van Os *et al.* (1994), who researched the responses of psychiatrists to the diagnosis of schizophrenia in France and the UK. They found considerable differences in diagnosis and diagnostic categories between the two countries, and clear differences in explanations of aetiology: 'the French psychiatrists favoured psychoanalytically-orientated aetiological statements ... while their British counterparts scored high on items postulating neurodevelopmental and genetic causation' (Van Os *et al.* 1994: 183). The existence of 'psychosomatic medicine' in the German psychiatric system (Herzog *et al.* 1994) points to similar differences between the UK and Germany. The word 'psychosomatic' is used in a much wider sense in Germany than in the UK, to describe an approach with a holistic and psychotherapeutic conceptual framework which places more emphasis on psychotherapy and holds a specific place in the organisation of medical training and the provision of treatment. These differences in approach seemed to be reflected in a stronger drive to treat patients in the community. In Italy, the approach to mental illness was also affected by the philosophy of *Psichiatria Democratica*, the movement led by Francesco Basaglia in the 1970s which led to the closure of the Italian psychiatric hospitals and the development of the system of mental health centres (see Donnelly 1992). This philosophy, which centred on the re-establishment and retention of the civic rights of psychiatric patients, is embodied in the laws and regulations in relation to compulsory hospitalisation.

Compulsory hospitalisation

Information about the grounds and the procedures for compulsory hospitalisation was sought in the questionnaires and was outlined in Chapter 4. The possibility of the use of compulsion was an issue raised by the researchers in the groups (and prompted the comment by one continental group 'typical of the English, always wanting to know about the law'). The arrangements in England, Germany and Italy are very different. The process of compulsory hospital was not a problem for the English. Although they would have preferred home treatment, they thought that if Mary was very ill she would be best treated in hospital. If she refused to come into hospital on a voluntary basis, compulsion would be possible and necessary. There was the possibility of placement in a mother and baby unit, which made hospitalisation much more acceptable.

For the Germans it was not as straightforward. They seemed to feel more strongly about the importance of voluntarism. One member of the mental health group described a situation where she had tried to prevent the admission to hospital of a very ill mother. They had put in support workers, but this had not been enough and it became necessary for the woman to be admitted. However, it was worth while; because of the contact with the support worker, she now trusted them enough to agree that she needed hospital treatment, and came in as a voluntary patient. If the Germans did need to use compulsion, the admission had to be agreed by the judge of the guardianship court. In the situation in the vignette they were by no means sure that the judge would agree to compulsion. The relevant criterion would be that the mother was a danger to the baby; the judge might say that the situation could be made safe by fostering the baby, and that she could then be treated at home. If the baby was removed, the group thought that she might then become suicidal, in which case there would be grounds for compulsion, but by then the baby would have been taken away. At the time there were very few facilities for mothers and babies to be admitted together (although, since the research took place, these facilities have increased). The existence of the intensive family support service made it more possible to set up home treatment and avoid the use of compulsion, and the problems surrounding compulsion were an incentive to make home treatment work.

In Italy, although they had nothing like the German level of service for family support, they rated very highly the importance of keeping Mary out of hospital. They hoped not to medicalise her condition. 'Pharmacological care … increases the woman's confusion around her own experience. Ours must be the job of closing the gap which has been created.' At the same time the workers had to accept an element of risk. 'We have to see if she [Mary] can find a way of managing her children at home, above all if there can be a network of support. Therefore we workers must contain our anxiety and accept the margin of risk.' If hospitalisation seemed to be indicated, they did not think that there would be grounds for compulsion. The Italian law on compulsory hospital admission requires: (a) that a person has a severe mental illness such that urgent treatment is required, (b) that this treatment is not accepted by the patient and (c) that the condition cannot be treated suitably outside of hospital. The law does not include the question of the patient being a danger to him/herself or others, so that risk to the baby would not be a reason for compulsory hospitalisation. The maximum compulsory admission period of seven days creates a very strong incentive to develop alternative means of providing treatment, and to make the mental health services acceptable to the community. It is relevant that the Italians thought that it was possible that John would approach mental health services himself, and that the approach would be to the CSM.

Anxieties and preoccupations

In seeking to achieve their goal of treating Mary at home and keeping the family together there were some shared concerns, but there were differences in emphasis between countries and within countries between mental health and child welfare groups. There was concern about separating mother and baby and reference to the principles of bonding and attachment. This was the most widely shared theoretical position, held by workers in all the countries studied and by professionals in both mental health and child welfare. This might not have quite the same implications in all countries but, in this instance, it was one of the main reasons for trying to keep Mary out of hospital. In the mental health groups and particularly in Italy, there was less emphasis on this point because there was also a strong commitment to treating Mary at home in any case. Thus while all groups thought that bonding was important, it was more important, and more of a preoccupation for the child welfare groups, who were most concerned about damage to the mother–infant relationship. In England and Germany, there were different solutions to keeping mother and baby together. In England they could use (or hoped to be able to use) hospital-based mother and baby units, while in Germany they relied on the SPFH service. This contributed to a greater readiness to consider hospital treatment in England.

The main focus of many of the child welfare groups was risk to the children, particularly the baby. The mental health groups were also concerned about risk to the children, and in England they seemed more aware of risk to the baby than the child welfare groups. The English child welfare groups, which were mainly drawn from social services children and families teams, had a lower estimate of the seriousness of Mary's mental state than the mental health teams, and therefore rated the risk to the baby lower. However, the question of risk to the children was important for the English child welfare groups because, unless there was a risk, they were unlikely to be involved. If Mary's illness required hospitalisation, they expected John to cope with the children. If it did not require hospitalisation, then there was no risk, and the level of the family's need would not be great enough for them to intervene. The English mental health teams were well aware that this would be the reaction from child welfare. In Germany, risk to the baby was a concern and was the reason why the SPFH could be brought in. There was an expectation that John would need help; he would have to go to work, so he would have to have some support even if Mary was in hospital and there was no risk to the children. In Italy there was less preoccupation with risk to the baby, and more concern with the needs of the family as a whole. The situation as a whole was regarded by the Italian groups as risky, but the child protection issues were not stressed; the rationale for intervention was the distress of the mother and of the family, suffering rather than dangerousness.

Beyond the common core of concerns (which was largely shared between countries and within countries), there was greater divergence. The English groups focused on the need for an assessment of the family. This was potentially a problem for the mental health groups, who were in a double bind. They did not feel that it would be productive to refer the family to the children and families team because there were no clear child protection issues; but they needed to have some assessment of the family. They showed little confidence in their skills in assessing the family, and seemed to feel that they would be seen as trying to do work for which they were not qualified. This was not a problem for the German groups because of the immediate involvement of the SPFH. Nor did it seem to be an issue for the Italian groups, possibly because the CF service would be involved, and that includes social workers. The problem that preoccupied the English groups was how to achieve an assessment of the family, rather than what the assessment would tell them about the family. This preoccupation with getting a procedurally valid assessment seems to be related to the high level of specialisation in pre- and post-qualifying training of the English social workers. This specialisation has led to the very clear separation of tasks between workers with different groups of service users. These anxieties are in line with the report by Diggins describing a project in Lewisham (Diggins 1999), where they found that workers lacked confidence in their ability to transfer their skills to work with another service user group. Budgetary conflicts were another aspect of the problem, and the mental health groups could see no straightforward way of getting child-orientated service resources. Again this problem is echoed by Diggins who found a preoccupation with the issue of 'who has overall responsibility for a case, or budgetary responsibility' (Diggins 1999: 141). In common with the other English-speaking countries, the English groups generally spent a great deal of time discussing procedures. However, having little to offer in the way of family services, the

English teams had a realistic anxiety as to who should monitor the family if Mary was not in hospital.

Other countries spent much less time on procedures. In Germany, the concern was about the need to build trust with the different family members. There was an emphasis on working on a voluntary basis with the family, and for this it was necessary to establish trust. If Mary could be encouraged to trust them, she would accept the SPFH workers and it would be more possible to avoid hospitalisation. If she did need to be treated in hospital, she might trust them enough to accept it. They thought that all the family members needed help, and needed someone they could trust. Of all the groups, the Germans were most concerned about Anna, particularly the child welfare group. They thought that she needed someone she could talk to, and that there was an urgent need for someone from outside to be involved in the family because there might be no family member who could help her as they would have their own preoccupations. 'Someone who focuses on the needs of the child, who she trusts and with whom she could be open about her own feelings.' Trust, in relation to one family member or another, was a theme which the German groups revisited throughout their discussions. The Italian mental health group was concerned to establish trust with Mary, and they stressed her need to understand what was happening to her, as well as to have treatment. There was an extensive discussion of the need for thoughtful preparation for action and the need to take time to understand the situation, but this was in tension with the possibility that there would be a need for urgent action. The child welfare group showed a greater concern for Anna and a similar interest in the need to understand Mary's past experience. Table 8.2 summarises the anxieties and preoccupations of the professionals at Stage 1.

Table 8.2   Anxieties and preoccupations at Stage 1

England	Germany	Italy
Separating mother and baby.	Separating mother and baby.	Separating mother and baby/home treatment for mother.
Risk to the children.	Risk to the children.	
Assessment of the family.	Building trust with the mother and Anna.	Building trust with the mother.
Procedures.		
The need for someone to monitor the family	Anna's distress and anxieties.	Mother's need to understand what is happening to her.
	Father's need for support.	

Structures that promote integration, co-operation and liaison

As the focus of the research was on co-operation, we were interested to see what structures there might be for facilitating and supporting the working together of different agencies and services. At this stage of the vignette, no connecting links were mentioned by the English groups. The GP had a transitory role as the referring agent, and the health visitor was mentioned, but Anna was 6 and the baby was still too young to have been referred. There did not seem to be any expectation that the primary care team would form part of the treatment system. In Germany, there was no reliance on the family doctor as a link person, and there is no universal maternal and child health service. Mental health services had to rely on the family support services to provide the links. This could happen through the 'help conference', which is a meeting that takes place at an early stage in supportive interventions for children and families. It has to take place in order to get the agreement of the *Jugendamt* to finance the work of the agency (usually a voluntary NGO), and includes all those involved in the situation, family and professionals. A 'help plan' is agreed, which is then regularly reviewed. In both England and Germany, mental health teams are multidisciplinary. Child welfare teams in Germany are likely to be largely staffed by social workers and social pedagogues, and although they also employ psychologists they do not include other health professionals.

In Italy, the *medico di base* had a very important place as a colleague and formed a connecting link between the mental health service and the community. The maternal and child health service is located in the CF, which is a multidisciplinary team including health professionals, psychologists and social workers. There are thus links between primary and universal health care services and the mental health services. There is also, in one area of the locality of our study, a regular meeting between workers in the CF, the child mental health service (*NeuroPsichiatria Infantile*—NPI), the local hospital and the local social services (*Servizio Sociale di Base*—SSB). This was welcomed by the child welfare group members as providing a forum where they could meet regularly, discuss problematic cases and get to know each other. There was also the possibility that one of the CSM workers would take responsibility as key worker. Table 8.3 summarises the structures promoting co-operation at Stage 1.

Table 8.3   Structures that promote integration, co-operation and liaison at Stage 1

England	Germany	Italy
	Help conference (a care planning meeting which includes the family and relevant professionals).	*Medico di base.* CF multidisciplinary team. Health teams meeting. CSM worker as case manager.

Stage 2

At this point, the action moves into the child welfare sphere, and there was less knowledge in the mental health groups about what might happen. There were again important similarities in responses, but it was generally expected that the local authority children and families service or its equivalent would be involved. It was agreed that Anna needed help and that the problem would be to persuade her mother that this should happen. Offering the mother practical help was seen as a way of persuading her to accept help on a wider basis.

Services and resources

At the beginning of Stage 2, the school has an important part to play, but in all three countries this was largely ignored except as a source of referral. In England it was thought likely that the school would refer the family to the social services, possibly through the education welfare service. The school medical service was scarcely mentioned. It was not thought likely that the CMH team would still be in contact with Mary by this time, and there would be no way that the children and families team would know of any previous contact. Child and adolescent mental health (CAMH) services would not be likely (in the view of any of the English groups, including the CAMH group) to receive a referral. In one area the school psychological service provided behavioural management treatment for which the school might refer Anna. The possibility of contact between the school and the health-visiting service was not mentioned, although a health visitor would have known the family because Thomas was only 3 years old.

In Germany the school might refer Mary to the *Jugendamt*, and the school could also refer Anna to the school psychological service, which might be acceptable to Mary. The school psychological service offers counselling and treatment for emotional and social problems as well as for academic problems and testing. Although there was no explicit reference to this, the German social workers in the child welfare group would have been aware that if they thought it necessary, they could have interviewed the children without informing their parents (see Chapter 3). There would also be the possibility, if Mary could be persuaded, of referral for Anna to a private child psychiatric clinic paid for by John's health insurance policy. It would be possible that the PSD would still be in touch with Mary.

In Italy, the school would refer Anna to the NPI, and Mary to the local social services department for practical help. The CF would already be in touch with Mary because of her pregnancy. It was thought likely that the nursery school (and it was assumed that Thomas would be attending nursery school) would have contacted some agency with anxieties about Thomas. There would be a 'problem family' meeting which would include the CSM if Mary's previous contact with them were known about (and this would be possible because the CF would know).

The resources available to the English child welfare teams depended on the type of assessment undertaken as well as on the results of the assessment. All the groups thought that an 'in need' assessment would be made. This would be an assessment to establish whether, under s. 17 of the Children Act 1989, Anna and Thomas were children in need of services which could or should be provided by the local authority. If the children were assessed as being 'in need', as was thought likely, there were several services, but availability was limited. A nursery school or playgroup place could be found for Thomas, but there would not be much social work time to offer. A family worker (an unqualified worker offering family support) might be able to see them a few times, or the case might be given to a social work student (who would be able to offer more support, but probably only for a few months). They thought that the child mental health service would have a six-month waiting list, though in some areas an emergency assessment might be possible. The best resource was a family centre, which could provide support for Mary, and also work with Anna and Thomas. The English child welfare teams were among those who raised the possibility that Anna was being sexually abused. If further information suggested that this was so, the social services would have to make a child protection investigation. This would be a 'risk assessment', where the concern would be about the risk of abuse taking place and would have wider implications. There would probably be a child protection conference to see whether the children's names should be placed on the child protection register, and, if they were registered, a protection plan would have to be made. This would mean that more resources would become available, including the time of a named social worker. Raising the question of sexual abuse therefore had very specific practical and procedural implications.

The German groups expected that mental health treatment would be available for Anna, probably from the school psychological service. The only difficulty would be to persuade her mother that this should happen. Waiting lists were not mentioned as a problem. They again looked to the SPFH to work with Mary and to support the family as a whole. A kindergarten place could be arranged for Thomas, and they would put John in touch with a local self-help group for people with mentally ill relatives. Both groups wanted to make contingency plans because they felt that it was very likely that Mary would have a further breakdown after the birth of the new baby. They wanted to plan for increased support after the baby was born.

The Italian groups wanted to work with the whole family. They thought that Anna needed help, but they did not want to label her as the problem, and also felt that in order to reach Anna they had to work with her mother. The most important resource was the NPI, which works with a systemic family therapy approach. They hoped to be able to provide some home help (but this would only be practical help) and they would liaise with a local co-operative to help John to find employment. The Italian professionals, like the English, commented on the lack of family support services and social work time, but seemed less pessimistic than the English. Table 8.4 summarises the services and resources at Stage 2.

Anxieties and preoccupations

It was common to all the countries to see Mary's need for practical help as a 'way in'. This would give the worker the basis for gaining Mary's co-operation and trust, so that she would accept that Anna needed help. The English workers had the most formal system for doing this, with a specific

Table 8.4   Services and resources at Stage 2

Services or agencies likely to be initially involved in (a) child welfare, (b) adult mental health and (c) child mental health		
(a) School.	(a) School.	(a) School and nursery school.
Children and families team.	*Jugendamt.*	SSB.
Education welfare service.	SPFH.	CF (because mother is pregnant).
	School medical service.	
	(b) SPD, or some part of the mental health system might still have maintained contact with the mother.	(b) CSM.
(c) Behavioural treatment team of the school psychological service.	(c) School psychological service.	(c) NPI.
	Hospital-based or private child mental health service available through the health insurance system.	
Resources available		
Family worker or social work student.	SPFH.	Thomas would already have a nursery school place.
Playgroup	Kindergarten.	
CAMH (child and adolescent mental health service), but they have a six month+ waiting list.	Support group for father.	Home help.
	School psychological service.	Co-operative, to support father in finding work.
An earlier appointment might be possible for assessment only.	Hospital-based or private child mental health service available through the health insurance system.	NPI.
School psychological service behavioural treatment programme (only suggested by the CAMH group).		

assessment format. Their main anxiety was that when they had undertaken an assessment of need, they might have very little to offer. They wanted to work with Mary in order to persuade her to accept help for Anna, but they had very little social work time in which to do so. They did not think that the family would be allocated a social worker. Child mental health services were not seen as a realistic resource, because even if they could make an assessment, there was no service that could be offered in the immediate future. The child welfare groups were less concerned about Mary's mental health than were the mental health groups. The mental health groups thought that there was no likelihood that they would still be in touch with Mary, and that they would not know that the family was now in difficulties. The German groups were again concerned with gaining trust. At this stage the focus of the need to gain trust was to enable Anna to be helped, and there were services available if trust could be established. They also wanted to gain Mary's trust so that she would accept help for herself and enable them to set up a support system that would be in place when she gave birth. The Italians also wanted to gain Mary's trust in order to be able to help Anna, but their anxiety was that Anna was being labelled by the school, and might be labelled by the family as the 'sick' family member. They wanted to work with the whole family, and felt that work with Anna could not take place in isolation from work with her mother. They made a distinction between Anna's need to have her own space and feel supported, and treatment for the family as a whole. They saw problems over who should work with the family, and who should co-ordinate practical support. Of the three countries, they voiced the most concern about liaison between agencies at this stage: 'Every service sees the problem from its own point of view and tends to stop there ... we are not able to have in mind the dynamics of the whole family and inevitably we tend to create splits'. They particularly wanted a multidisciplinary link between the CF, the NPI and the mental health services. The Italian child welfare professionals were more concerned about inter-agency co-operation than the mental health professionals. Table 8.5 summarises the anxieties and preoccupations of the professionals at Stage 2.

Table 8.5   Anxieties and preoccupations at Stage 2

England	Germany	Italy
Persuading Mary to accept help.	Gaining Mary's trust so that she and Anna could be helped.	Persuading Mary to let them offer help to Anna.
Not having resources, especially time.	Anna's mental state.	The need to work with the whole family.
Lack of availability of CAMH service for Anna.	Mary's mental state and the recurrence of her illness.	Not allowing the school or the family to label Anna as the 'problem'.
	The need to set up a supportive system that would be in place after the birth of the third child.	Who should work with the family and the role of practical help.
		Problems of co-ordination between different services.

Stage 3

At the final stage of the vignette, the level of agreement between the countries and within the countries was highest. It was generally expected that Mary would need hospital treatment and that the children would need to be in care, at least temporarily.

Services and resources

The most important difference at this stage was that the German groups did not think that this situation was possible, on the basis of the support and services that would have been put in at Stage 2. They were not the only groups to have this reaction. The Norwegian and the Swedish groups felt the same, and for the same reasons. The Northern Irish and the Greek groups thought that it was highly unlikely because there would always be some neighbourhood support. The Italian groups also thought it unlikely, for the same reasons, but agreed that it was possible. The German groups (and the other dissenting groups) discussed the third stage on the basis that this family had newly moved into the area.

Apart from the addition of the child placement services that would now be needed for the children, no new services were mentioned. The child welfare services were seen as needing to take emergency action and as being the lead services. There was agreement that Mary would need hospital treatment, and even the Italian groups thought that compulsion might be possible. However, there was still a continuum between the English who thought that hospital was almost certain and the Italians who thought that it probably could not be avoided. The Germans were still uncertain about the reaction of the judge to an application for an order, and the Italians were not certain that it would be possible to make an order.

Anxieties and preoccupations

The anxieties of all the groups centred on the risk to the children and, once more, the dangers of separating mother and baby. They were all concerned about the difficulties of finding a placement where the children could be together. They all wanted to find John, as his involvement with the children was valued, and his agreement to their placement would be needed.

The differences were mainly of emphasis, within a shared framework of emergency action. The English groups spent time discussing the procedures that would be involved in emergency action. The concerns of the German groups centred on the emotional well-being of the children. They wanted not only to place them together, but also to find suitable therapeutic placements for them, and these two aims might be in conflict. Both the German and the Italian groups spent time discussing the support that would be needed to reintegrate the family. The Italian groups looked to the future and the child welfare group was anxious that the cycle of family dysfunction should not be repeated in the next generation. They were more open than any other group in contemplating the possibility that the family might not, and perhaps should not, be reunited. Table 8.6 summarises the anxieties and preoccupations of the professionals at Stage 3.

Table 8.6 Anxieties and preoccupations at Stage 3

England	Germany	Italy
Risk to the children.	Risk to the children.	Risk to the children.
Separating mother and baby.	Separating mother and baby.	Separating mother and baby.
Emergency procedures.	Anna's distress and anxieties.	Finding a suitable placement for the children.
Finding a placement for the children together.	Father's need for support.	Breaking the cycle of family dysfunction.
	Finding a placement for the children together.	The reintegration of the family.
	Finding a suitable placement for the children.	
	The reintegration of the family.	

Structures that promote integration, co-operation and liaison

At this point, for the English groups, the child protection system, the strategy or planning meeting and the child protection conference became important. All groups thought that the lead service would be the children and families service and that they would call meetings to ensure co-ordination between the agencies involved. They considered that there would be no time for a child protection conference at this point, but a planning meeting would be certain. In Italy and Germany there were no further liaison systems at this point than had been available earlier.

At all Stages

The consistency of responses between the mental health and child welfare teams

As expected, there was a noticeable difference of focus and emphasis between the two groups in each country. In all cases, the child welfare groups maintained a stronger focus on the children's needs and experiences, while the mental health groups looked in more detail at the mental health needs of the mother. However, within this range, there was greater or lesser agreement between the groups over certain topics.

In assessing the mother's mental health, the English child welfare groups consistently estimated the mother's mental health problems as less serious than the English mental health groups. In Germany the child welfare and the mental health groups had a similar estimate of the mother's mental health. In Italy both the mental health and child welfare groups thought that the mother need not be hospitalised at Stage 1. By Stage 3, the child welfare group thought that hospitalisation was certain, but the mental health group were less positive.

In relation to the needs of the children, all the English groups had very similar responses and prioritised the need to keep mother and baby together. In England, all the groups were united in a concern about child protection issues. The German groups both prioritised the need to keep mother and baby together, but the emphasis of the child welfare group on emotional support for Anna was far greater than that of the mental health group, although they too were concerned. In Italy both groups prioritised the need to keep mother and baby together and both emphasised the need for work with the whole family, but the Italian child welfare group discussion focused much more on the functioning of the family system.

SUMMARY OF THE COMPARISONS

The detail of these comparisons is complicated, and the differences are the product of many elements. Broad generalisations can be made, as long as the modifying importance of the detail is kept in mind. A typology can be constructed on the basis of these comparisons in which England demonstrates the characteristics of a system with delayed intervention by child welfare services, relatively scarce resources for family support, and an emphasis on child protection. Germany demonstrates a system that encourages early intervention by child welfare services and provides extensive resources for family support. Italy demonstrates a system where there is a high expectation of neighbourhood and community support and active intervention to mobilise this. To generalise this typology even further, these countries are, respectively, types of the child protection focused system (England), the child welfare focused system (Germany) and the family group focused system (Italy). All the English-speaking countries and none of the other European countries appear to have child protection focused systems. Child welfare is only one aspect of welfare systems and welfare regimes, but as we have indicated in the introduction to this part, it seems to us to have a particular importance. The categorisation of welfare systems has been theorised from a number of different perspectives, usually from the top down. In the next chapter some of these theories are discussed in relation to the material from our research.

Chapter 9

The State and the Family: Explaining Variations in Interventions

This chapter begins by looking at different conceptualisations of the welfare state in capitalist society. It draws upon studies of the development of welfare states in specific countries and comments on attempts that have been made to classify them. It then examines the extent to which the evidence obtained in this study supports these typologies and suggests how they may need amendment. Finally, there is an attempt to identify what appear to be the major explanatory factors that lie behind variations and similarities in interventions between different countries.

THEORETICAL APPROACHES

Capital

Traditionally, radical commentators have had some problem with the existence and function of welfare services in capitalist societies. Attempts to explain welfare service provision have tended to do so either in economic functional terms or as concessions wrung from capital by labour. These two explanations have not always sat comfortably together.

Some accounts (e.g. Warde 1987) have explained welfare services as a necessary component of the reproduction of labour power. This approach derives primarily from the writing of Marx on productive and unproductive labour. The argument is that as capitalism developed there was a need to have available a healthy, well-educated and productive workforce. The provision of services to ensure this was generally not profitable for any one faction of capital to provide, but such services were nevertheless necessary for the maintenance of the capitalist system as a whole. The state became the main vehicle for the collective financing, providing or organising of such services. Such a model explains welfare provision as a functional response to the needs of capital. Certainly there is a lot of evidence to suggest that desire for a healthy and disciplined workforce was a motivation behind many nineteenth-century reforms in health and education. However, there are some problems with such a functional interpretation.

The first is that, if such an approach were correct, then presumably differences in welfare provision would be due solely to differences in the relative development of capitalism. This would lead one to expect little or no difference in the levels of provision in modern capitalist countries, which in the light of the evidence presented earlier appears questionable. Second, it has been suggested that the level of provision is 'always at the minimum level' (Castells 1977). If this were true then it is surprising that so many commentators can talk about the 'rolling back of the welfare state' in the 1980s and 1990s since a capital-theoretical model could not explain how it ever rose above the minimum necessary level in the first place. A third problem with capital-theoretical approaches is that they do nothing to explain variations in the form that welfare provision takes in different countries, and have trouble acknowledging historical and cultural influences on how services are delivered and the way in which such services are legitimised.

A capital-theoretical approach is useful in that it highlights how, through the provision of collective services, the state meets the interests of the business community as well as the individual recipients of services. However, it seems better suited as an explanation of the state's role in areas such as transport, market regulation and education than for welfare services. Also, the extent to which the business sector gains directly from, for example, child protection legislation is likely to be minimal.

Class

An alternative formulation is to take the provision of welfare services as part of an ongoing class conflict between capital and labour. In periods where labour is in the ascendancy it is able to secure additional welfare services and achieve increases in the level of provision, and in periods where labour is weak, capital is able to claw back some concessions (e.g. Gough 1979). Such a formulation is better at explaining diversity both over time and between nations than capital-theoretical approaches. It has the advantage of siting the development of welfare services in a political process of conflict between classes over the role of state.

However, when such analyses focus on capital–labour relations to the exclusion of all other factors, this is a gross oversimplification of the political process. Even accepting that welfare provision is a locus of conflict between capital and labour, the conflict is not expressed in these terms and these forces do not operate directly. Instead there are political forces, ideological structures and justifications that have no necessary 'class belonging' that are a real part of the political process. They have their roots in civil society as it has developed in particular locations. These are not determined by the balance of

forces between capital and labour at any one specific given point in time but
are a cumulative residue of previous conflicts, compromises and social and
cultural innovations. Moreover, focusing exclusively on capital–labour relations can entail neglecting issues of gender and race.

A more sophisticated variation on this approach is given by Offe (1996)
who sees the relationship between citizens and states being made up of three
components:

- the rule of law 'the constitutional guarantee of freedom and liberty' (Offe
  1996: 147)
- representative democracy
- the provision of citizen security via the welfare state.

What is interesting about this analysis is that it describes a situation in which
the three components can be mutually supportive or mutually antagonistic,
depending upon the structural situation at the time. Thus the welfare state
can find support or antagonism from both the market economy and political
democracy. The two types of justification of the welfare state are as follows:

- *Economic justification*: Provision of skills, health, peaceful industrial relations and built in demand stabilisers generate necessary input for market
  economy and its further expansion.
- *Political justification*: Convergent pattern of party competition, reduction of
  intensity of political conflict, political integration of entire electorate, end
  of ideology, vanishing of political radicalism.

Offe sees a key factor in the development of social democracy in post-war
Europe as being the situation where representative democracy and the
welfare state were seen as mutually supportive. He suggests that this is no
longer an easy ideology to sustain because of a 'structural disintegration
process that leaves behind an interpretative pattern that is deeply distrustful
of social policies as "public goods" ' (Offe 1996: 172). Structural changes that
have derailed the political support for the welfare state are seen as: increasing
disparity in life chances between workers; the development of jobless
growth; the lack of pro-welfare political alliances; dissatisfaction with the
bureaucratic means of delivering public services; the growth of the salaried
middle class; and the disappearance of a mobilising political programme
within the European left.

However, the most useful aspect of this work is not the identification of
structural changes (which is hardly original) but the way in which Offe identifies the potential for positive ideological links between the welfare state,
representative democracy and the economy. The dominant ideology in the UK
over the last 20 years has stressed the destructive influence of the welfare state
on democracy and the economy, so it is helpful to be reminded that this was
not always the case. While Offe does not comment on this, it does appear to
point to an important factor that may be a feature of variation between welfare
states. In some countries the development of the welfare state may be legitimised more by reference to economic criteria, and in others more by reference
to political democracy. This could have effects both on the organisational form

and professional cultures operating in these countries, and is a point that will be returned to later.

Offe's work suggests that a more sensitive approach would be to look at the development of capital and welfare services in particular countries over a period of time. This would have the advantage of examining how different forms of welfare have been introduced and how, in their development, they have affected, and are themselves influenced by, established cultural and ideological norms about the relationship between the state and the family. Such a thoroughgoing historical analysis is outside the scope of this chapter, however some relevant themes are discussed below.

THE STATE AND THE FAMILY

A number of writers have emphasised the coercive nature of the state and its ability to promote specific family roles. For example, Fox Harding (1996) identifies different models of relationship between the family and the state and the different means that can be used to promote these roles. Although there can in theory be both authoritarian and *laissez-faire* models, Fox Harding suggests that in most countries the state influences family structure in one of four different intermediate models, these being:

- enforcement of responsibility in specific areas, e.g. via criminal and civil law;
- the manipulation of incentives (tax allowances and benefits);
- substitution for family roles, intervention with families (family support measures); and
- responding to individual needs and demands (i.e. services for individuals).

There are undoubtedly different ways in which the state can encourage particular models of the family, and a particular model may be pursued more or less comprehensively. However, such an approach seems very descriptive and does not suggest why, or in whose interest, such measures are pursued. There is a need to provide a fuller explanation of the imperatives behind any particular approach and the conditions whereby one may be more likely to be pursued than another. Nevertheless, Fox Harding gives a useful description of policy measures and reminds us that there are networks of legal fiscal and welfare measures that can, often with inconsistency, contradiction and anomaly, encourage specific family forms.

WELFARE REGIMES IN EUROPE

Esping-Andersen (1990) suggested a typology of three welfare regimes which have different origins, e.g. liberal, conservative and social-democratic. While not convincing in all respects, this typology provides a useful way of identifying clusters of different types of welfare state in capitalist societies and the different forces and ideological imperatives at work. It is therefore worth describing in some detail. A liberal regime reflects the classical liberal concerns to minimise the role of the state and to prefer market solutions. The organising ideology is said to be English nineteenth-century political economy. In such a regime welfare is seen as a residual 'safety net' targeted at individuals in need, rather than offering universal entitlements, often derived from a 'poor law' approach. It also tends to be selective in the areas that it covers and to encourage market solutions. Examples cited of liberal regimes include the USA, Canada, the UK, Ireland, Australia and New Zealand.

Social-democratic welfare regimes, although initially liberal, have gone beyond their liberal origins, and have increasingly (since the mid-1960s) adopted a comprehensive entitlement model. A social-democratic welfare regime is said to be characterised by universal services or benefits, comprehensive risk coverage, generous benefit levels and egalitarianism. Such a regime is also characterised by a deliberate effort to minimise market dependence. 'What, then, is uniquely social-democratic is, firstly, the fusion of universalism with generosity and, secondly, its comprehensive socialisation of risks' (Esping-Andersen 1999: 79). The only examples of such regimes he identifies are the Nordic countries of Denmark, Norway, Sweden and Finland.

The 'conservative' welfare regime is described as such because of the way in which states have attempted to conserve pre-capitalist social forms. The origins of welfare states in such countries often lie in either monarchical étatism, corporatism, or Catholic teaching, and their post-war development under the auspices of, primarily, christian-democratic or conservative coalitions. Characteristic features of these regimes are said to be corporatism (in the form of status divisions, and subsidiarity), and familialism. The status divisions take the form of different packages for different groups of people, often by employment groups. Subsidiarity has been mentioned in earlier chapters and involves services being organised and delivered at the lowest possible level by organisations outside of the state, such as church-related charitable organisations. Familialism was introduced as an additional factor and concerns the degree to which the welfare obligations are assigned to the household.

Familialism is discussed more extensively in Esping-Andersen's more recent work where defamilialisation (as opposed to familialism) is defined as 'the degree to which households' welfare and caring responsibilities are relaxed—either via welfare state provision or market provision' (Esping-Andersen 1999: 57). It is a process whereby the household takes on a reduced care burden and the individual's dependence on kinship reduces. After looking at expenditure levels on family services, day-care coverage and home help coverage, Esping-Andersen contrasts the highly familialised southern Europe (Italy, Portugal and Spain) with the uniquely defamilialised Nordic countries. Defamilialisation can take place via the welfare state or through the market. The USA is cited as one country in which the market is able to provide child care because of the availability of cheap labour. In other countries, such as Sweden and France, affordable child care is available because of state provision or subsidy.

It is suggested that conservative regimes, like liberal regimes, possess a degree of residualism, but that 'liberal residualism means picking up bad risks left by market failure; conservative residualism, in contrast, is primarily a response to family failure' (Esping-Andersen 1999: 83). The conservative label is applied by Esping-Andersen to the countries of continental (western) Europe—examples mentioned being Germany, Austria, France, Belgium, the Netherlands, Italy, Portugal, Spain—and possibly Japan. The characteristics of the three regimes are given in Table 9.1 (Esping-Andersen 1999).

Table 9.1 Characteristics of welfare regimes

	Liberal	Social-democratic	Conservative
Role of family	Marginal	Marginal	Central
Role of market	Central	Marginal	Marginal
Role of state	Marginal	Central	Subsidiary
Mode of solidarity	Individual	Universal	Kinship, corporatism, étatism
Locus of solidarity	Market	State	Family
Degree of decommodification*	Minimal	Maximum	High (for the breadwinner)
Modal example	USA	Sweden	Germany, Italy

* Provision of entitlements independent of market participation.

There is little doubt that this typology is very illuminating about some of the differences between the welfare regimes of different countries. In particular the attention paid to familialism and the role of the state and family may very well be of use in explaining the different interventions followed by welfare agencies in different countries. However, there are some areas in which the model appears to be strained.

The main problem is that the conservative label appears to cover quite a broad range of welfare arrangements. Indeed, Esping-Andersen himself states that 'France's (and Belgium's) membership is problematic in that familialism is less dominant' (Esping-Andersen 1999: 82). Elsewhere it is also noted that the countries of southern Europe (Italy, Portugal and Spain) are considerably more familialistic than the rest of continental Europe (Esping-Andersen 1999: 94, note 20), but this is seen as more of a position on a continuum than indicative of an additional regime.

The form of these divisions may, however, be enlightening. Esping-Andersen explains the high degree of familialism in terms of the historical response of nations to the emergence of capitalism.

> 'To conservatives of the absolutist, Hegelian, mould, it was mainly hierarchy and state authority that were under siege. In the Catholic (or East Asian Confucian) tradition, however, communitarian-familial solidarities were at stake. ... Hence to a Confucian or Catholic social reformer de-commodification is desirable if it bolsters family piety and interdependence. But it is suspect, indeed ruinous if it encourages individualism and independence.' (Esping-Andersen 1999: 44).

Thus it appears that within the 'conservative' regimes there may be some that attach a higher degree of importance to maintaining the family and discouraging independence. Certainly such an approach may reflect a different conceptualisation of citizenship.

CITIZENSHIP

The contrasting concepts of citizenship as they have evolved within different European states provide a useful prism through which to consider the different forms of welfare provision in Europe. Bouamama (1995) contrasts the emergence of nationality in Germany, France and Britain. He traces the formation of the German state in 1871 as conflating citizenship, nationality and statehood so that the three appear inseparable. In Britain, by contrast, there was little concept of nationality until the twentieth century. Instead, in Britain and the Commonwealth there was recognition of common allegiance of subjects to a monarch which 'resulted in a dissociation of the concepts of nationality and citizenship' (Bouamama 1995: 57). France, following the French Revolution, constructed a concept of citizenship based upon the association of individual citizens free and equal in rights. French attitudes to citizenship are explained as a result of a tension between this political definition of a citizen and the concept of nationality.

A simplistic 'reading off' of welfare regimes from these concepts would suggest that the German emphasis on intervention may be a product of a predisposition towards sustaining community and social cohesion while French nursery and health care are explained by a predisposition by the state towards universal equal services. However, by contrast, French, Italian and Greek services focused their interventions very much at the level of the family while Germany was much more ready to look at individuals in their own right. For the former the needs of the individual citizen were more closely bound up with their family unit—the opposite of what would perhaps be expected. While this is too simple an explanation of the interventions we have seen, the different conceptualisations of citizenship do appear to influence how services are provided.

Silverman (1996: 148) unpacks the term and finds that:

> 'Within the term "citizen" there is, then, a whole cluster of different discourses pulling in different directions yet whose problematic nature becomes obscured within an apparent coherence of purpose and design.'

In particular, he points out that between the twin pressures of localisation and globalisation the national state is increasingly superfluous. Silverman goes on to note that citizenship is becoming equated with consumerism. Certainly this seems correct with the term 'social exclusion' often being used to describe market exclusion without any examination of the richness of someone's social contacts outside the market place. Thus it is generally assumed that the vehicle for participation in society is the market.

We would suggest that while the nation state may be increasingly impotent, welfare regimes are predominantly national in their development and can constitute a major component of national identity. For example in the Scandinavian countries the social-democratic welfare regime appears to be bound up with a sense of national identity. For care professionals, and possibly the general public, the bargain between citizens and the state now appears to be among the key definitional elements of the state. This partly explains why the Swedish professionals said that they had trouble engaging with immigrant families who did not always share their model of the state's obligation to intervene in family life, and who may have had very negative experiences of the state in their country of origin. Similarly in England political parties vie for the status of defender of the NHS, the health service having huge practical and symbolic importance.

APPLICATIONS OF THE 'THREE WORLDS' MODEL

In an empirical comparison of European social attitudes, Taylor-Gooby found little to support the 'three worlds' thesis. A study of public attitudes towards the role of the welfare state found that 'British opinion does not appear to be strikingly less supportive of welfare in general than in corporatist countries' and that 'there was no evidence of convergence of public opinion in different European States' (Taylor-Gooby 1998: 71). Thus the differences may be present less in public beliefs than in legal and organisational forms.

In Esping-Andersen's depiction of the 'conservative' welfare regimes the mixture of corporatism and étatism appears to be a little strained. The delivery of services in France does not appear to be very subsidiaristic, but appears to be very centrally directed. Similarly one would also be sceptical of the restriction of corporatism to the conservative bloc. For example, one could argue that in Sweden there is a very high degree of corporatism in selected areas—for example, in the involvement of trade unions in the provision or financing of services such as housing (Duncan 1991).

In the field of mental health services the 'three worlds' model has been used to explain difference in mental health policy. For example, Goodwin (1997) describes mental health policy in these regimes as having the following emphases:

- *liberal regimes*: rehabilitation—independence within a market economy;
- *conservative regimes*: subsidiarity—maintaining the status quo;
- *social-democratic regimes*: rights of citizens to receive social benefits.

This suggests that the 'three worlds' model may work quite well at the policy level. However, it is not so certain that it is very suitable as a tool to help to explain variations in service organisation and intervention. Certainly the forms of organisation and methods of intervention that we have identified previously did not follow the patterns that one would predict using a pure form of the 'three worlds' model.

The liberal and social-democratic models appeared to be the most robust with a clear set of similarities in the intervention and approach used within these blocs. Even there, both parts of the island of Ireland, along with Scotland, appeared to be less residual than England and Australia. The countries of continental Europe showed considerable variation in the way they intervened. It may be that one of the main fault lines was, as Esping-Andersen suggests, at least related to the strength of familialism (see above), but even this did not supply a perfect match.

Certainly it is the case that familialisation does not automatically equate with a family-focused method of service delivery. This may partly be due to different conceptualisation of the family and the roles that needs to be supported; for example, although Italian professionals talked a lot about the family as a unit, interventions appeared to be focused on the mother, rather than the father and children in their own right. Family failure was seen as a likely consequence if the mother's role was not somehow fulfilled during her period of mental ill health. The working assumption appeared to be that if the mother's role was being fulfilled the family would be all right. In Germany and Scandinavia the family was seen more as a collection of individuals with their own needs as well as their needs as a family unit, while France appeared to occupy a position mid-way between.

AN EXPLORATORY MODEL

The data of the previous chapters suggest a typology of the interventions described along the following dimensions:

- statist vs subsidiaristic
- interventionist vs reluctant to intervene
- focused on the individual vs focused on the family.

The typology will be described and an effort made to determine the extent to which these relate to the characteristics of the three regimes described above.

Statism

By statist we are referring to the propensity for interventions suggested to be undertaken by state employees rather than the voluntary sector or other non-governmental organisations. The countries that would be described as statist would be those in the first column of Table 9.2.

Table 9.2   Statist vs subsidiaristic

Statist		Subsidiaristic
Denmark	Italy	Luxembourg
Norway	Greece	Germany
Sweden		
France		
Australia		
Ireland		
UK: All		

It is worth noting that Ireland, although it has a tradition of subsidiarity, appeared to almost exclusively suggest the use of public sector employees to meet the needs of families. Similarly, although Greece relies extensively on non-governmental welfare organisations, most of the action discussed related to governmental agencies. In almost all of the countries surveyed in this study the main mental health services were provided by the state. Where subsidiarity did exist it was more often in relation to services for children and families.

Interventionism

'Interventionist' refers to the propensity of official agencies to intervene rather than leaving the family to resolve the situation on their own. It may relate to thresholds above which intervention with children and families will take place. Alternatively, readiness to intervene can be a readiness to provide preventive and supportive services. This spread of readiness to intervene is shown in Table 9.3, where it can be seen that Greece, Italy and Ireland occupy the middle ground although they were ready to intervene at an early stage. In Ireland their intervention appeared to be coupled with a degree of ambivalence about how coercive this intervention should be. In Italy they were ready to intervene but very unwilling to use compulsion. All three appeared to be fairly ready to provide services in support of the family, with Greece constrained by lack of resources. England and Australia demonstrated relatively high thresholds to state intervention but, interestingly, the same was not true in Scotland or Northern Ireland, which appeared much more willing to contemplate intervention at a lower level.

Table 9.3   Interventionist vs reluctant to intervene

Interventionist . . . . Non-interventionist		
Denmark	Italy	Australia
Norway	Greece	England
Sweden	Ireland	
France	N. Ireland	
Luxembourg	Scotland	
Germany		

It is interesting to compare this typology with the typology constructed by Millar and Warman (1996). In their review of systems they identified three tiers of services:

- crisis intervention
- support for parents experiencing difficulties
- support for parenting and some recognition of autonomy of children.

Looking at the countries in our study, they placed Ireland, Greece, Italy and Germany together as characterised by crisis intervention. The UK was placed alongside France and Luxembourg as offering support for parents experiencing difficulties. The difference between the above typology and that of Millar and Warman may be explained by the fact that they were looking at systems, whereas this study looks at practice. Thus while social services departments in the UK have statutory duties to provide support and counselling to children in need, the UK groups (particularly in England) could not offer services on this basis; services became available when children were at risk, which we would define as crisis intervention. Indeed, in England and Australia the emphasis in the discussion groups was over whether or not the situation met the child protection criteria. In these two countries there was a clear reluctance to intervene unless specific thresholds had been reached. Another anomaly was Germany, which appeared to offer a range of inputs to families, at a very early stage, and was clearly interventionist—in contradiction of the Millar and Warman typology.

This suggests that policy studies can only be of limited usefulness in determining the character of welfare states. Policy may instead do more to satisfy political and ideological imperatives than to satisfy the needs of those people to whom the policy is ostensibly targeted. Policy interacts with a complex of organisational and professional cultures and practices, which appear to have just as much impact on the services that people receive.

Individualism

The balance of services to the individual and to the family is probably the most difficult of all to determine. Participants from some of the countries talked a great deal about 'the family'; however, it became clear that they did not always mean the same thing. Table 9.4 indicates the distribution of countries on this axis.

Table 9.4 Focused on the individual vs focused on the family

Individual		Family
Denmark	France	Italy
Norway	Luxembourg	Greece
Sweden	N. Ireland	Ireland
Germany		
Australia		
England		
Scotland		

German and Scandinavian workers talked about securing services for all family members—but usually on an individual basis. By contrast, in Italy, Greece, Ireland and Northern Ireland there was a lot of reference to the family, but the primary recipient of services appeared to be the mother. As mentioned above, it was apparent that, for the Italian participants especially, supporting the family meant supporting the mother's ability to act as the principal caregiver, and maintaining the family unit until such a time as this role could be resumed. It was not about supporting individual family members or changing roles within the family to cope with the new circumstances. The mother was seen as the key element in the family and she was to be helped to take responsibility for the family. In those countries where welfare and caring responsibilities had not been so fully shared with the state or the market, there was a correspondingly greater emphasis on family-based solutions that would maintain the ability of the family as a whole to provide care and welfare. In this sense the variations in the balance of response between individuals and the family may be seen as a result of the degree of defamilialisation in the country concerned. In Australia and England the emphasis on the ability of the family to cope without the need of state support could be seen as demonstrating defamilialisation in a liberal welfare regime.

UNDERSTANDING THESE GROUPINGS

It is apparent that we are seeing a fairly complex set of patterns. One might have hoped for a simple and consistent spread of countries, but this has not been the case and there is no easy combined typology. The 'three worlds' model, although of some help, has been found wanting, and Table 9.5 combines the three sets of patterns discussed above.

Table 9.5   Patterns of welfare

Country	Statist	Interventionist	Individualistic
Denmark	High	High	High
Norway	High	High	High
Sweden	High	High	High
Australia	High	Low	High
England	High	Low	High
Scotland	High	Medium	High
N. Ireland	High	Medium	Medium
Ireland	High	Medium	Low–Medium
Greece	Medium	Medium	Low
Italy	Medium	Medium	Low
France	High	High	Medium
Luxembourg	Low	High	Medium
Germany	Low	High	High

The Scandinavian countries came out as statist, interventionist and individualistic in their approach, as would perhaps be expected. Greece, Italy, Ireland and Northern Ireland clustered together as fairly interventionist, family-orientated services, with Greece constrained by resource availability;

however, they were very different in terms of their involvement with the family and their management of risk. The Irish approach to an escalation in problems was likely to lead to a shift from family support to specialist individual work. In Italy there was a far stronger commitment to keep the work community based and non-specialist and a willingness to accept an element of risk to achieve this.

The real anomalies appeared to be France and Luxembourg—with the addition of Germany, which did not appear to fit readily into any of these clusters—but neither could they be clustered together. Germany could be characterised as interventionist, subsidiaristic and individually focused. Its main difference from the interventions in Scandinavian countries was the lack of centrality of the state in providing the intervention and the large role of non-governmental organisations. Germany also appeared, if anything, to be slightly more focused on individuals within the family than the Scandinavian countries.

In a country where the 'male bread winner' model of the family receives considerable financial incentive and where child care opportunities for working mothers are so limited, it is interesting that the interventions we found were so individually based. One possible explanation may be that the nature of subsidiarity in Germany may be qualitatively different from that in other countries and may be less concerned with preserving the family than with maintaining social cohesion—leaving more scope for work dealing with individual pathology. Esping-Andersen suggested this when referring to the Hegelian desire to maintain the authority of the state. In Germany there is a model of the 'three pillars of society' in which the churches and other organisations act as a series of checks and balances against the state. Another source of this difference is the strongly established legal principles around the rights of the individual which have been a feature of German civil law and administrative practice over the past 50 years.

France also stood out as fairly statist, fairly individualistic and very (to fairly) interventionist. The inclusion of France in the most interventionist camp is not completely unqualified. Overall, France appears to be middle-of-the-road. One study has suggested that 'as far as services for children are concerned, Belgium and France could hardly be more different from Germany and the Netherlands', with Belgium and France having an 'extensive day care and pre-school system, which is the most comprehensive in the whole of Europe' (Anttonen and Sipilä 1996: 97). However, in this study France was not found to be as interventionist as Germany or Scandinavia. One reason why French workers did not appear to be so dramatically interventionist may be because the presence of a universal system of family support means that there is a whole layer of involvement that is already initiated, whereas in Germany they would have to begin to establish just such a level of support.

England was both very statist and very individualistic in its approach; the major difference was in its lack of interventionism. Indeed, in both England and Australia there was an air of pessimism about the efficacy of the intervention itself, whereas in other countries there was much more optimism about the intervention. It is interesting to note that both of these countries are among those that Esping-Andersen designates as 'liberal'. However, he points out that although Britain occupies this camp, this was not always the case. 'Had we made our comparison in the immediate post-war decades, we would almost certainly have put Britain and Scandinavia in the same cluster: both were built on universal flat-rate benefit programmes, national health care and a vocal commitment to full employment.' However, this is not the case today and 'Britain is an example of regime shifting or, perhaps, of stalled "social democratisation" ' (Esping-Andersen 1999: 87). Further support for this interpretation of events in Britain is provided by Anttonen and Sipilä (1996). A similar explanation is offered by Esping-Andersen for Australia and New Zealand (Esping-Andersen 1999: 90).

It may be the case that the culture of the social work and care professions in the UK and Australia is a product of a social-democratic or proto social-democratic welfare regime. But this is a professional culture that exists in what is now a liberal welfare regime and the pessimism of the professionals in these countries may be a consequence of this mismatch. This begs the question of whether similar tensions exist in 'conservative' welfare regimes—that is, is the culture of social work necessarily social-democratic and at odds with, or at least poorly suited to, any other welfare regime? The responses of our participants would not support this hypothesis. In this study practitioners from continental Europe appeared to be every bit as optimistic about the efficacy of their intervention as those from Scandinavia.

This is not to suggest that care professions are necessarily at odds with the liberal regime. The not-for-profit sector in the USA suggests that there do appear to be models where a well-motivated set of professions can exist within a liberal welfare regime. Rather the point is that the professions as constituted in England, but not the rest of the UK, do not appear to have a great deal of optimism in their ability to perform and effect change in the context of the UK welfare regime. This mismatch could in theory be overcome by either changing the welfare regime or changing the professional ideologies.

UK and Irish professionals did not describe themselves as particularly envious of the Scandinavian social-democratic welfare regime *per se*. However, there were positive comments, chiefly about the level of resources that these countries enjoyed, the universal school meals and after-school services, and the acceptance by the population of the legitimacy of the state's intervention. Certainly these demonstrate the principles of universalism and the citizen's arrangement with the state, which are central to the social-democratic welfare regime. The underlying principles and the resources implied by the social-democratic model appeared to be attractive to professionals in the British Isles.

An important caveat must be made here in relation to Scotland, where generally the approach was much more positive than in England. It is interesting to note the comments of the Scottish groups on the proposed interventions in Norway:

'Generally both groups were struck by the similarity between Norway and Scotland in the types of services that would be provided and in the ways that the family would be treated. It was felt that both countries were trying to get to the same end and generally went about getting there in a similar way.'

The Scots clearly did not feel that the approach in a social-democratic welfare regime was particularly different from their own. Once again this suggests that the welfare regime is less important than the expectations of professionals about how they should respond to specific situations.

This raises a number of problems for our suggestion that the UK professional culture is at odds with the liberal welfare regime in which it finds itself. Interpretations of the Scottish response could be:

- the regime type is relatively unimportant in determining interventions;
- Scotland has a different welfare regime to the rest of the UK;
- the professional culture in Scotland is different to the rest of the UK;
- these results are unrepresentative and should be 'swept under the carpet'.

While the fourth option is attractive, it would be overly convenient. However the first two are not as problematic as they first appear. Firstly, our groupings based upon the three loci—statism, interventionism and individualism—have already found a mismatch between the clusters observed and the 'three worlds' model. Secondly, although it clearly does not have a different welfare regime, Scotland does have important differences from the rest of the UK in its service provision. The Scottish social work departments were set up with a much wider remit than the English social services departments. They were established to respond to requests for help, not to assess need for help—much more like the continental model. These differences look set to increase following the establishment of the Scottish Assembly. Thirdly, in some respects, particularly in the structure of the legal system, Scotland has long had a more continental European culture than England, and this may be reflected in differences in professional culture. Thus the observation made by the Scots may not be fatal for the model outlined above.

CONCLUSIONS

This chapter has summarised some recent thinking about welfare regimes and determined the extent to which the responses from the different countries in this study appeared to concur with these theoretical approaches. Overall there was not a perfect match and the 'three worlds' model in particular may be flawed. However, these models do illuminate some key explanatory factors and have allowed us to identify the following dimensions that help our understanding of the nature of international difference. These are:

- statism vs subsidiarity
- readiness to intervene vs reluctance to intervene
- focus on the individual vs family focus.

It also provides a hypothesis that can explain some of these characteristics in England, and to a lesser extent in other parts of the British Isles, as a consequence of the tension between a professional culture that is essentially social-democratic within a welfare regime that is liberal. The potential importance of this hypothesis will be examined in the final chapter.

Chapter 10

Risk, Childhood and Mental Health

One of the most important issues facing practitioners working with difficult issues such as mental health and child protection is the management of risk. Discussions about risk were central in virtually all the groups, and the different approaches to managing and working with risk formed one of the central themes of this project. This chapter will explore the notion of risk and how it was approached by the different groups.

It is now considered axiomatic that we live in a 'risk society'. Risk dominates our existence, and permeates our culture. Perhaps the leading contemporary theorist of risk (and the person who invented the term 'risk society') is Ulrich Beck. Beck (1992) acknowledges that humans have always lived with risk, but, he asserts, the difference is that in the past the risk was *personal* and *local* whereas in our society the risk is to *humanity as a whole* (or even life itself). Of course, Beck is talking about such risks as nuclear destruction or global warming through pollution, but it is easy to see how his thinking can be extended into the area of child welfare and mental health.

Beck sets out five theses which summarise his position.

1. Risks induce systematic and often irreversible harm, generally remain invisible, and initially only exist in terms of the knowledge about them. They are peculiarly open to social definition and construction.
2. Some people are more affected than others by the distribution and growth of risks. Risks also contain a 'boomerang effect'—those creating risk for others can themselves become subject to risk.
3. There are losers and winners in risk definitions, but they are not the same as economic losers and winners.
4. One can possess wealth but one is *afflicted* by risk—thus knowledge (of the risk) becomes all important and creates a power of its own.
5. Risk politicises what was previously the apolitical domain of professionals and technicians.

Although risk is usually contrasted with 'safety' or 'certainty', there are other ways of conceptualising it. In particular, 'risk' can be contrasted with 'dangerousness'. Although these are often seen as synonymous, they are conceptually quite distinct. Firstly, dangerousness implies an act by a person, that someone has committed harm or that a person has expressed an intention to harm. Risk relates less to *individual people* and more to *factors* (so-called actuarial risk). Another crucial difference is that in some contexts risk implies choice. In one context a person or situation can pose a 'risk' and this is synonymous with being dangerous. This does not involve choice. However, 'taking a risk' does involve choice. If there is no choice or no escape from the danger, then it is not possible to take a risk. Thus Beck and others maintain that risk (or current perceptions of risk) is part of the modern 'Enlightenment' world view which has replaced fatalism with doubt and uncertainty.

One of the key problems for welfare professionals, which was reflected in the vignette, is how to manage and 'distribute' risk. In many countries child care and mental health work is now carried out in an environment where decisions about children and families are no longer accepted as being 'in good faith', but are held to be accountable in terms of their outcomes and costs. There is a sense in which welfare has become analogous to industrial production. In the modern era, industry produced goods to meet the needs of the population, and welfare similarly met the needs of those who could not otherwise look after themselves. However, in the post-modern era, industry itself has come to be seen as a risk—technology is not necessarily the saviour of humanity, but each technical advance produces unknown risks for the future. Similarly it is now acknowledged that welfare interventions, even when they help in the short term, can create long-term deleterious effects. Sometimes these effects are known, and can be weighed up at the time decisions are made, but others are more subtle, and cannot be calculated. These second kinds of risks are much more insidious and are the cause of much difficulty for professionals in child welfare and mental health. Alaszewski *et al.* (1998) point out that risk is not always negative—positive risk-taking can be beneficial for users. They also argue that providing welfare services always entails risk. However, it is the defensive attitude to risk which undermines the delivery of services.

The vignette in this study addressed a number of different risk situations. The more explicit risks were:

- the mother's mental illness causing her to hurt the children in the first and third stages
- the father's alcohol abuse
- the risk of physical harm coming to the children due to lack of sustenance
- the risk of the mother's illness becoming worse if not effectively treated
- the risk of the mother's illness deteriorating if the children are removed or she is hospitalised against her will.

There were, however, a number of implicit risks that were discussed by the participants. These were more problematic because they involved more complexity than the immediate risks, which were dealt with mainly by balancing known risks. The implicit or potential risks included:

- father sexually abusing Anna
- domestic violence

- mother's paranoia about father may be justified
- removing the children would be harmful to mother.

A third kind of implicit risk in these scenarios was the risk to the practitioner. There were, in fact, a number of risks for professionals. In some systems, notably in the English-speaking countries, implicit and sometimes explicit anxiety was expressed about 'getting it right'. The most immediate risk here was the risk of having their careers affected either by being seen not to protect the children or, conversely, being seen to act too precipitously by institutional-ising the children or the mother and thus breaching their rights. This is gener-ally known as the 'damned if we do/damned if we don't' syndrome. However, this well-known dilemma was not the only one for practitioners. There were, for example, the perceived risks of stepping over professional or organisational boundaries. For example, in Stage 1 the English child welfare group felt that this mother did not meet their threshold for action, and by acting in a case like this they would be seen to be breaching agency policy. By intervening in a low-level situation such as this they were, potentially, preventing more serious cases from being dealt with and were mis-using scarce resources. The irony of the situation—that by NOT intervening they were allowing more serious problems to develop which would cause them more difficulty later—was not lost on these practitioners. Nevertheless the agency imperative was much too powerful for them to do anything about this.

Within the helping professions, the archetype of the kind of risk which Beck discusses is that of child sexual abuse. Hacking (1999), in his discussion of the social construction of child abuse, makes the point that abuse has historically been seen as a kind of psychological or social pollution. In many ways, child sexual abuse is the 'nuclear waste' (the ultimate pollution) of the helping professions. Like nuclear material it is seen as being 'too hot to handle', possessing so much risk that even to talk about it becomes risky. This was confirmed in the research, when some of the participants from continen-tal Europe admitted that even though in the discussions of the vignettes there had been no mention of sexual abuse, they had in fact thought about it but the consequences of mentioning it would have been the break-up of the family. They considered the risk of naming the abuse to be more dangerous than the abuse itself. Unlike other forms of child abuse, sexual abuse is seen as poten-tially existing undetected and then 'exploding' into the public domain with incalculable results for the child, the family and the social worker.

However, attempts to 'scientise' abuse and the interventions aimed to address them have proved less than successful. Despite popular and profes-sional beliefs, we know little about the real extent of abuse, its causes, the consequences for the victims and their families. We know even less about effective prevention and treatment of sexual abuse. Despite the enormous effort put into preventive programmes (MacMillan *et al.* 1994; MacIntyre and Carr 2000) there is still no research that demonstrates their effectiveness in the long term. Also, most adults who have been sexually abused have said that their abuse could not have been prevented (Wattam and Woodward 1996). Virtually all our knowledge has been gained from clinical material relating to a small range of cases.

One reason sexual abuse is so risky to professionals is its politicisation and the consequent media attention which it attracts. In the UK since the Cleveland affair, and in continental Europe since the Dutroux affair, the media and politicians have never been far from expressing opinions about sexual abuse and the interventions aimed at preventing it and policing its perpetrators. Beck's fifth thesis—the politicisation of professional and technical information—has come to dominate the thinking about child sexual abuse (and to some extent mental health work as well).

Another reason is the intense emotion which sexual abuse often engenders in the workers themselves. Sexual abuse touches aspects of our personalities which we would rather leave alone. For the average welfare professional (as for the public as a whole) it is relatively easy to imagine drinking too much, having a 'nervous breakdown' when under pressure, lashing out at children when they are persistently demanding, etc. Deliberately targeting a child for sexual abuse is in a different category altogether, both morally and cognitively, and admitting to oneself that one could possibly be in a situation where one could perpetrate child sexual abuse is too difficult for most professionals to deal with. Parton (1998), although drawing on Foucault rather than Beck, agrees with Alaszewski *et al.* (1998) that perceptions of and responses to risk are part of the fabric of the delivery of welfare services, and that the management of risk goes beyond the normal discussions about child abuse.

In recent years in the UK there has been an upsurge of public anxiety about violent mentally ill people randomly murdering members of the public. This 'moral panic' has, in some ways, followed a similar path to that of child abuse in the 1970s. A small number of well publicised incidents have caused great media attention followed by high profile enquiries, new government regulations and a whole new risk assessment industry (e.g. NACRO 1998).

Taylor and Gunn (1999) note that 'the public and politicians believe, or are being encouraged to believe through the mass media, that unless people with a mental disorder are once more segregated, the streets will not be safe'. Both child protection and adult mental health have therefore become areas of practice in which risk management has come to dominate practice and where practitioners perceive themselves and their assessments to be in the public gaze.

In this research there emerged two contrasting approaches to managing the risks presented by this family. All the groups explicitly acknowledged the risks to the children and the mother, and there was also a fair degree of consistency about the differential risks presented by the three stages of the vignette.

The first stage presented a dilemma to all the groups. Did the mother represent a big enough risk to the baby to justify forced institutionalisation for herself and/or the baby? Would alleviation of the short-term risk of harm justify either the long-term risk of damaged relationships between mother and children which might result from her institutionalisation or the risk to the mother's mental health if the children were removed?

The second stage was more problematic for all the groups. The risks here were implicit rather than explicit, and the risk factors more difficult to assess.

Significantly this stage involved the perceptions of the child, which were not seen as being as straightforward as those of the mother in the first stage. The role of the father also became much more ambiguous, and many groups discussed whether he presented a risk, or whether he was a potential mitigating factor in relation to risk.

The third stage presented a more paradoxical response. On the one hand, the circumstances were more dangerous for the children, who appeared disturbed and neglected, and for the mother, who was obviously ill. On the other hand, there was less talk of risk, because for most groups heavy intervention (if not institutionalisation) became inevitable, and so there was a lot less of a dilemma for professionals. This is an example of the differences between dangerousness and risk alluded to above.

This (relative) convergence in relation to the issues of risk disappeared when the groups moved to discussing the management of risk. In these discussions clear divisions emerged. The most important division was between the approaches of the English-speaking countries and those of continental European countries.

The fundamental difference was that the English-speaking countries tended to take a *case management* approach to the work, which was characterised by risk *assessment/avoidance*, whereas continental countries tended to take a *therapeutic* approach, in which the main feature was concern with risk *management*. The case management approach tended to manage risk by *diagnosis* whereas the risk management groups approached risk management by building up relationships and therefore basing intervention on *trust*. We are not trying to make an absolute division between these two approaches. It is very likely that if one would ask English or Australian practitioners if their aim was to build trusting relationships with their clients, the answer would be 'yes'. Similarly, Italian and Swedish workers would almost certainly confirm that they are heavily dependent on assessment to inform their interventions. However, the material, which was based on what workers spontaneously responded to in the vignettes, did demonstrate clear differences of emphasis between countries.

Risk assessment was not necessarily a formal process or activity, but rather it was a frame of mind or an approach to the work. The English-speaking countries tended to focus the discussion around criteria for involvement, the boundaries between agencies, budgets, etc. When discussing the family they tended to focus on the short-term consequences of action or inaction, and whether action could be justified. The preoccupation was therefore with thresholds and interventions.

The Italian groups provided a contrast to this position. Their primary aim was to establish a good relationship between the workers and the mother, the rationale being that only by doing so would they be able to help the family in the long term. They were concerned to work with and understand the mother's subjectivity, rather than labelling her fears as simply symptoms of mental illness. They acknowledged the risks inherent in this approach, but these did not disable or hamstring their interventions. A related leitmotif in the Italian discussion was the imperative to keep the mother out of hospital.

The rationale was that the stigma of hospitalisation and diagnosis would be more damaging to the mother's self-esteem and parenting ability than the immediate protection of the children would justify. The Italians explicitly sought to avoid diagnosis for the mother so that she would not feel stigmatised and would trust them more. This required them to work with uncertainty and could be seen to increase the dangerousness, but from their point of view the risks of intervening in a statutory manner were even higher.

The relationship between *diagnosis* and *risk* in all of the countries was particularly significant here. The contrast was most apparent in the first stage, when many groups debated whether Mary was suffering from post-puerperal psychosis and the extent of her illness. Diagnosis is the ultimate aim of assessment, and provides (the illusion of) objectivity and certainty. Once a patient is diagnosed, prognosis and treatment immediately fall into place. Doctors take control and other professionals then become reactive to the primary task of treating the illness. This aspect relates to Beck's fourth thesis: in risk management, knowledge becomes power, and if the knowledge is medical then the power is that of the doctor. (The exception to this is the diagnosis of sexual abuse, where the power relationships are shifted from the doctor to the social worker or the police. However, the consequences of a diagnosis of sexual abuse are even more momentous than those of mental illness—see the discussion above.)

Diagnosis did not entirely end the discussion, and there continued to be debates about the appropriateness of different forms of intervention, but these debates were much more delimited and contained. Diagnosis also raised another aspect of the relationship between risk and danger. In the Australian mental health group, one member, while arguing for institutionalisation, made the comment 'We know how unpredictable and volatile these [post-puerperal depressive] women can be'.

This comment illustrates two things. Firstly, 'these women' have now become a category, and Mary has become one of a group whose characteristics are known. She loses some of her individuality. More importantly the statement illustrates an increase in danger but a decrease in risk. On the face of it this is a contradiction—surely if Mary is more dangerous she must present a greater risk. However, the danger is known and therefore manageable, whereas risks are much more insidious. Thus, even though the diagnosis raised the stakes in some ways, it lowered professional anxiety, helped focus the discussions and allowed decisions to be made about the best form of intervention. Indeed there was much discussion in some of the groups (England/Ireland/Australia) about the relationship between diagnosis and access to services. In some cases diagnosis was a prerequisite for services such as community psychiatric nurses or mother and baby units, and in these cases there was a clear incentive towards crossing the threshold of diagnosis. The corollary of this, however, was a focus on the treatment of the illness, and the tendency, noted in Chapter 12, for particularistic rather than holistic thinking about the family and a lack of focus on the subjectivity of the children.

Diagnosis does, nevertheless, have some clear benefits for the patient, even when there is no easily identifiable treatment. It gives her an identity and

GOVERNORS STATE UNIVERSITY
UNIVERSITY PARK
IL 60466

places her within a group of people. More importantly perhaps it gives her a language with which to talk about her difficulties.

Thus diagnosis has consequences for the patient, the family and the professionals. Some of these consequences are negative but there are also benefits for all those concerned. The main importance of diagnosis for this discussion is that it provides a comprehensive approach to managing risk. In the UK and the USA this way of thinking has become all pervasive. The USA has moved towards the 'actuarial model'—the quantification of risk, especially in child abuse cases. (For a fuller discussion of the 'forensic' approach to assessment see Katz 1997; Parton *et al.* 1997; or Cleaver *et al.* 1998.) The UK has moved away from this 'forensic' approach towards a more holistic needs-based assessment model. However, *Working Together to Safeguard Children* (Department of Health 2000b) and the *Framework of Assessment of Children in Need and their Families* (Department of Health 2000a) entrench the role of assessment and diagnosis into children's services, in such a way that assessment can become more or less the only intervention possible. There are well-documented dangers of intervening without assessment: reactiveness, drift and inappropriate intervention (see Department of Health 1995; Reder and Duncan 1999). Too much assessment, however, results in 'paralysis by analysis'. In this study none of the groups was advocating an actuarial approach, and all the discussions about risk assessment acknowledged, to some extent, the broader family and social context. Nevertheless, what they actually meant by holistic assessment differed considerably between countries and, to a lesser extent, according to the focus of the services. Children's services groups tended to acknowledge and discuss the family as a system more than adult mental health (see Chapter 8 in relation to England, Germany and Italy).

There are, therefore, clear problems with the assessment/diagnosis approach to risk which is bound up with the case management approach to practice. The therapeutic approach was based on very different premises. For these practitioners the major task was to gain the trust of the family (especially Mary) and the biggest risk was to lose that trust. The discussions, particularly in the Italian and Swedish groups, were remarkable. The following quotes are taken from the Swedish and Italian mental health groups, discussing the first phase of the vignette. A Swedish participant pointed out that 'You must build up a relationship first with such a frightened woman as this one—you can't just wade in'.

The Italian contribution raises several issues, some of which will be discussed below. The situation was summarised by one of the psychiatrists who outlined two possible ways forward. Either they would activate resources, including Mary's mother who could support her and give a positive connotation to her anxieties about the baby—it is right to feel anxious about small babies. This would reframe Mary's response and protect her from seeing her anxieties as illness. Alternatively, the medical services could provide pharmaceutical treatment, but this would label Mary's anxieties as illness. This would be undesirable. The *Centro di Salute Mentale* should work to help Mary to reconnect her feelings of fear with her husband's attitude, with her relationship with her mother. 'Pharmacological care … increases the woman's confusion around her own experience. Ours must be the job of closing the gap that has been created.' At the same time the workers 'must accept an element of risk'. Either there is compulsory hospitalisation, or there is support and observation. They have to see 'if she [Mary] can find a way of managing her children at home, above all if there is a network of support. Therefore we workers must contain our anxiety and accept the margin of risk'.

Practitioners in these groups were concerned to understand the subjectivity of Mary's experience, rather than simply to understand the factors which were likely to endanger her or the children. They were also prepared to negotiate with her on the possibilities, and to help her to understand the nature of the situation.

One interesting feature of these discussions was the attitudes of the different countries towards the risks and benefits posed by their own interventions. In Chapter 5 and Chapter 8 we have already noted that some countries had a lot more difficulty believing that the sequence of events portrayed in the vignette could have occurred. In Germany and Sweden in particular, and in several other countries, the participants felt that if they had done the things they said they would do at Stages 1 and 2, then the scenario presented at Stage 3 would not (or could not) have occurred. This optimism about the consequences of professional intervention was far more pronounced in those countries which adopted a therapeutic approach, and freed the workers to feel less concerned about the consequences of their interventions and more able to confront risk rather than avoid it. They were therefore shielded to a greater extent from the boomerang effect of risk mentioned by Beck.

In England at least, professional optimism has been progressively undermined over the past 20 years by a succession of political and media attacks and by questions by groups of its own practitioners and managers about the efficacy and equity of its traditional methods, especially the therapeutic approaches. These have been attacked from the right as lacking cost-effectiveness and an evidence base, and by the left as demonstrating bourgeois, patriarchal and ethnocentric attitudes towards service users.

Perhaps the most explicit attacks on professional optimism, at least in the social work profession, have been those of Dale *et al.* (1986) and Dingwall *et al.* (1995). Dingwall *et al.* devote a great deal of attention to 'the rule of optimism', which, they assert, governs child protection work in the UK (or rather governed it in the early 1980s when their research was conducted). The rule refers to the (unfounded) optimism of practitioners about parents' ability to change. In particular, the rule asserts that parents who do not display overt hostility towards their children and who are willing, even at a superficial level, to comply with the worker, do not present a risk to their children. Dingwall *et al.* found that in these circumstances practitioners consistently overestimated the ability of parents to care for children, and underestimated the damage of their inadequate parenting.

The two most important aspects of the rule of optimism are cultural relativism and natural love. Cultural relativism is the belief of social workers that they are unable to accurately assess the risks in families from minority ethnic families since they lack the benchmarks to do so. They invariably gave these parents the benefit of the doubt, assuming that behaviour which would be considered abusive by UK standards was culturally appropriate child care practice for the parents. Natural love is the belief that parents naturally love their children, and therefore that an act of child abuse is a contravention of the laws of nature, and the abusers are therefore sub-human. This creates a disincentive for workers to recognise abuse, especially when parents assert that they really love their children. This argument is close to the earlier discussion of the risks of identifying sexual abuse.

Although the rule of optimism does not refer to the optimism that the worker's intervention will be successful, it has been an important milestone in the history of British social work, and has contributed (with other historical events such as high profile deaths, etc., see Parton 1985) to a generalised pessimism about the effectiveness of intervention. In reaction to works such as this, British social work also became much more pessimistic about the abilities of parents, and, to some extent, now operates a 'rule of pessimism' which asserts that parents are unlikely to change, and that intervention is unlikely to succeed. Thus the case management approach combines a pessimism about intervention with a pessimism that families can change. The only way forward is to intervene in a crisis, when there is no choice for either party. In these circumstances there is very little risk because the intervention is that of rescuing. When a child or adult is rescued the risk of intervening becomes self-evidently smaller than the risk of not intervening, and the outcomes are also self-evidently better for the child or mentally ill person. Thus from the point of view of the professional, rescue is a very low-risk type of intervention.

The work of Dingwall *et al.* is interesting in another way for this analysis. Their theory asserts that the rule of optimism is not a psychological attribute or failing of individual social workers. Rather it represents an aspect of the relationship between the liberal state, the family and the child. Their analysis takes forward the work of Donzelot (1980) whose thesis was that, historically, the state had been involved in policing the public domain, while the family had been used by the state to police the private domain. This was done by giving the father unlimited power over his wife and children. Modern capitalist societies, however, demanded that the state had to extend its policing into the private domain, and so a range of 'psy' professions was developed to deal with issues internal to the family.

Dingwall *et al.* accept this analysis, but claim that the rule of optimism is a way of mitigating this state power over the internal workings of families. There is now an understanding between the state and parents which entails practitioners, as representatives of state power, giving parents the benefit of the doubt in return for the parents' co-operation in the intervention. It is interesting that, although Donzelot's analysis was of French society and Dingwall *et al.*'s research was conducted in England, neither acknowledges that there may be differences, at least of degree, between these systems. Both seem to imply that their analysis is true for any liberal democracy.

Our research shows, however, that there are indeed differences between different countries with respect to the way the rule of optimism works.

Although, as stated above, the optimism is not about the perceived effective-ness of the work, it is clear that this is an aspect of it. There is a willingness of workers using the therapeutic approach to intervene at an early stage and a belief that intervention is effective, justified and legitimate. In contrast those using the case management approach tend to back off, believing that the risk of meddling in people's lives is greater than leaving well alone.

However, there are limits to the optimism of the continental Europeans, and these bear on Dingwall *et al.*'s notion of 'cultural relativism'. Those countries who were most optimistic about intervention, also conceded that they had great difficulty engaging families from minority ethnic communities. As noted in Chapter 6, this was particularly the case in Sweden, which was arguably the most interventionist country of all. Although the participants agreed with the initial premises of Dingwall *et al.*'s argument—that practitioners find these families difficult to assess and engage—the consequences were the opposite of those described by Dingwall. Because the therapeutic approach depends fundamentally on trust and the ability to make relationships, it requires the family to fulfil their part of the 'social contract'—i.e. that they should trust the worker at least to the extent of being willing to be involved in the work. Minority ethnic and immigrant families do not share the host culture which nurtures this understanding. In addition they may well have experienced interventions from authorities with other than therapeutic intentions. This means that the tacit understandings involved in the therapeutic approach are much less likely to work with these families. Rather than giving them the benefit of the doubt, therefore, the workers in these systems felt compelled to intervene in a more heavy-handed way.

These observations are very important issues for the therapeutic approach to interventions in families. They imply that 'culturally sensitive practice' has certain limits (see Katz 1996, 1998 for a fuller discussion of the limits of cultural sensitivity in child protection). No matter how culturally relativistic or culturally sensitive is the content of therapeutic practice, it is bound to be ethnocentric in the sense that members of minority ethnic (and possibly other 'deviant') communities are excluded in some ways from the basic 'contract' on which this type of intervention is based. The consequence is that non-crisis intervention with these groups is likely to be less effective. The case manage-ment approach has attempted to overcome these problems by instituting 'partnership' practice and using such devices as written agreements, risk checklists and other frameworks of assessment, all of which are designed to make professional judgements more objective and less based on intuition or prejudice. However, the success of these measures is itself open to question. It may be that there is no perfect trade-off between fairness and transparency on the one hand and relationships on the other.

One crucial element left out of the discussion thus far is the thorny ques-tion of resources. We do not have accurate statistics about the relative spend-ing of each of our 13 systems on child welfare and adult mental health. Nevertheless, plenty of information is available about the overall state spending on health and welfare in different European countries. This shows that the Scandinavian countries, France and Germany have high levels of spending whereas southern European countries and English-speaking countries broadly have much lower levels of provision. Obviously high levels of resource are likely to reduce the risk of interventions in that practitioners in well-resourced systems have a lot more options available. Inter-agency tensions are likely to be lowered in situations where agencies are not competing for scarce resources.

It would be a mistake, however, to believe that there is a linear relationship between risk and resources. This is because, as Beck has said, risk is largely a matter of perception. We have already noted that in the UK and Australia practitioners have a much higher perception of risk than practitioners in Italy and Greece. This is despite the fact that the former countries have higher levels of resource, especially in primary prevention. One explanation for this is that practitioners in England are not comparing their resources with those of Italy or Greece, but rather with what they themselves had been used to in the past. In the UK there has been a steadily increasing number of children and families in poverty and requiring welfare services (Lobmayer and Wilkinson 2000). There has also been a decrease in spending on provision. Added to this have been the constant structural reorganisations designed to provide the same level of service for less money. These factors have combined to create inward looking and organisation-obsessed health and social services. It is this perception of increasing need and decreasing resource which is particularly damaging for professional self-confidence and which raises the perception of risk.

This research therefore confirmed a growing literature which contrasts the 'solidaristic' approaches of other European countries, based on family and community, greater state involvement with families and negotiation, with the English-speaking countries whose systems are based on litigation, individual rights and a 'catch-net' philosophy of welfare. However, generalisations are hard to make, and it is becoming apparent that, at least outside the confines of the helping professions, other European countries are in some cases even more concerned with risk than English-speaking countries. We should not forget that Foucault and Donzelot are French and Beck is German. The BSE affair is a good example of a situation in which the UK authorities' approach to risk was much more lax than those of the other European countries, who were portrayed in the British press as obsessed with safety to an unhealthy degree. Similarly, the different responses of the French and British aviation authorities to the recent Concorde disaster portray a higher concern for risk avoidance by the French. Thus it would be a mistake to portray risk-taking by practitioners as part of the culture in other European countries and that risk avoidance is somehow imbued in the culture of English-speaking countries. Much more important than any cultural or historic conceptualisations of risk *per se* is the cultural and historic relationship between the state (as represented by health and social services practitioners), the individual and the family, and the particular professional culture in each country which, as the previous chapter shows, are only partly related to their national cultures and are particularly in tension with each other in the liberal welfare regimes in the English-speaking world.

Another important issue to bear in mind is that the subject of the research—the relationship between the state, the family and the child—is not static in any country, and that there are indications of convergences in structure and functions across Europe which are likely to lead to less observable difference in practice over time. The Dutroux case in Belgium and the recent debates about paedophiles in Italy (Willey 2000) show that questions of the risks posed by child abusers are not only Anglo-Saxon preoccupations, and are likely to have repercussions for practice in continental Europe. Similar debates around mentally ill people, although less politicised, are also likely to occur.

Both 'child abuse' and 'mental illness' (Hacking 1999; Foucault 1967) are 'socially constructed' phenomena. The terms are imbued with meanings and connotations which go beyond mere neutral descriptions of human behaviour. Both have histories and their definitions have changed over time to reflect the concerns of society in different eras. In this sense they are both prime examples of the kinds of phenomena open to 'risk' interpretations described by Beck. Indeed, Alaszewski *et al.* (1998) have shown that the history of mental illness has gone through phases in which therapeutic optimism has been alternated with 'realistic' pessimism. We see in front of our eyes that these issues are changing day by day, and the public perception, understanding and response to the risks posed to children and the public by mentally ill people is being 'socially re-constructed' all the time. The issue is also becoming more politicised. This means that the risk-related dilemmas discussed in this chapter are likely to exacerbate rather than decrease over time.

Chapter 11

Co-operation and Communication

COMMON CONCERNS

Collaborative working can take place at a number of levels, from policy making to the delivery of services at ground level. Our interest in the central importance of inter-agency collaboration in supporting families where there is parental mental illness mirrors the emphasis placed on it in the UK in recent years (see, for example, Falkov 1996, 1998; Weir and Douglas 1999; Reder *et al.* 2000). New developments moving towards the integration of social and health services (for example, in Hertfordshire and Camden) demonstrate the concern of policy-makers to facilitate integrated working. All the participants in the Icarus Project agreed that inter-agency and inter-professional co-operation are vital in two important ways. Firstly, in helping families to deal with the difficulties associated with parental mental ill health and, secondly, in trying to resolve the problems posed by these families for the agencies and professionals working with them. Indeed these common concerns initially prompted our participants' involvement in the project and during the process of the research it became clear that while co-operation was seen as essential, the means to bringing it about were not straightforward. The central dilemma of how to balance the family members' needs for one another with their individual welfare, formed the focus of these concerns.

This is most obviously illustrated by the question of whether Mary should be hospitalised. Whether she is hospitalised or not, there are threats both to her civil liberties and to her need for care; there are challenges to her rights and responsibilities as a parent; there are risks to the baby's safety if she remains with him unsupervised and to the attachment process if she is separated from him; and there are threats to the long-term well-being of all the children. In addition, John's alcoholism and minimal involvement as a father raise questions about the degree to which the family is or can be integrated.

These kinds of issues were brought together in two key principles on which participants were in accord:

- The desire to maintain the integrity of the family if possible and a reluctance to split-up the family. In some countries (Norway, Italy, Luxembourg, Australia, Ireland) there was an espousal of an holistic approach to the welfare of the 'whole family' (especially early on in the case) but this came more from child welfare than from mental health teams.
- The importance of developing and maintaining an effective relationship of trust between the family and professionals, particularly with Mary; and its corollary, the voluntary involvement of Mary with a range of services.

Participants agreed that what was needed to operationalise these principles was a co-ordination of services which could ensure the provision of appropriate 'whole family' support by linking the activities of different professionals. Especially important was the effective communication of information between agencies, and between professionals and the family. What became clear, however, was that there was a range of factors which could militate against inter-agency and inter-professional co-operation, such as the structure of services, resource levels and professional motivation. The effects of these were often mutually reinforcing, and they influenced outcomes to different degrees in different countries.

INTER-COUNTRY DIFFERENCES

Given the multiple and sometimes apparently conflicting needs of families with mentally ill parents, our interest lay in finding out how agencies in different countries already collaborate and how different professionals within the same agency work together to meet these needs. Our analysis revealed a range of different ways that agencies and practitioners work together and though no one approach was singled out as a model of good practice, comparisons between them enabled us to identify factors which serve to hinder or facilitate effective co-operation.

Generally, inter-*professional* collaboration was more common than inter-*agency* collaboration. This was most likely to take the form of multidisciplinary teams, for example, the community adult mental health teams in England and other countries, the multidisciplinary child welfare teams in France such as the CISS (*Circonscription d'Interventions Sanitaires et Sociales*—an area team which includes social workers, health visitors and community paediatricians) and the child mental health services in all countries. Depending on their specialism, these teams were typically made up of practitioners representing psychiatry, nursing, social work, paediatrics and psychology. Child mental health teams frequently included specialist teachers and speech therapists. Multidisciplinary teams were valued as sources of shared knowledge and joint decision-making. Inter-*agency* co-operation, though also seen as very desirable in all countries, was generally viewed as more likely to be a source of difference, frustration and difficulty. This was most evident in the relationships between adult mental health and child welfare agencies. Teams differed in their perceptions of what constituted the 'problem' and thus the focus of their concern. They also differed in their assessments of the seriousness of Mary's illness and of risks to the children. Information-sharing could be difficult and raised concerns about professional confidentiality. Importantly, in most countries there were mutual uncertainties between teams as to who should co-ordinate services for the family.

There were exceptions to these expectations that inter-agency co-operation would be difficult; in Sweden, Germany and Northern Ireland, for different reasons and with different service structures, inter-agency and inter-professional collaboration were not seen as a problem. In the case of Germany, in spite of what practitioners described as a 'labyrinth' of agencies, their responses to the vignette demonstrated a high level of consensus between adult mental health and child welfare teams and a flexible attitude towards ways of working, which meant that professionals expected to be able to get together, as need arose in an individual case, in various 'help conferences'. In Northern Ireland too there was an expectation that co-ordination would be achieved in a straightforward way. This is partly attributable to structures providing conditions that are conducive to collaboration—in this case the existence of Health and Social Services Trusts, where the two services are represented, and multidisciplinary teams. But also, according to participants, it could be attributed to open channels of communication, both horizontal and vertical, which meant that inter-professional and inter-agency contact was straightforward.

Some countries, including Australia, Greece and England, were much less sanguine about the possibilities of collaborative working. In spite of positive attitudes in principle, both the child welfare and adult mental health teams in England were pessimistic about the possibilities of inter-agency collaboration and at all three stages of the vignette they emphasised the problems of working co-operatively, especially since the development of specialist services. For them specialisation was associated with very distinct and potentially incompatible focuses of concern and a lack of shared knowledge. In their view these difficulties were compounded by the geographical separation of different services. For participants in Greece, a number of structural factors—a scattered population, an absence of multidisciplinary teams, especially in child welfare, the fragmentation of services and the lack of any means to co-ordinate them—meant that co-operation between agencies and professionals was problematic and unlikely. However, although the French responses were optimistic about co-ordination at some levels, they indicated that the existence of multidisciplinary teams does not necessarily ensure inter-agency collaboration. While the multidisciplinary PMI (*Protection Maternelle et Infantile*) is seen to play an important role in child and family welfare and the *assistante sociale du secteur* has responsibilities for the well-being of adults as well as children—two factors which bode well for collaboration—participants also suggested that the structural gap which exists between mental health services and social services could make co-ordination between them difficult and consensual definitions of roles problematic. In

Luxembourg, the *assistante sociale* was viewed as a key professional, holding information and liaising with other services, but co-ordination was still seen as a potential problem because of a lack of shared information between different agencies.

HINDERING AND FACILITATING FACTORS

Service Structures

One of the most powerful factors affecting inter-agency collaboration is the way in which services are structured. This not only demarcates the territory of service delivery through the allocation of roles, responsibilities and accountability, but also encompasses resources, budgets, communication channels and knowledge bases. Thus the way in which the delivery of health and social care is organised creates a range of connected conditions which make collaboration more, or less, possible. Our study indicates that the division of services into 'free-standing' units, with specialised remits (as in England) tends to reinforce a fragmented approach to the problem, described by Douglas (1999: 188) as 'formalised fragmentation'. Where there are more integrated service structures together with flexible working practices (as in Denmark), or where health and social care are organised under the same broad umbrella either nationally or locally (for example, the health and social services joint boards and trusts in Ireland and Northern Ireland), or where multidisciplinary teams exist within child welfare services (such as the French CISS), then the possibilities of inter-agency collaboration are greatly enhanced.

While the specialisation and separation of services promotes clearly defined boundaries which, in other contexts of care, may be an advantage, comparisons with alternative ways of organising services suggests that, for a number of reasons, in this area they may be counter-productive to a 'whole family' approach. Precisely specified territorial service divisions are reinforced by strong budgetary boundaries which have implications for financial, as well as professional, accountability. In the cost-aware culture of the purchaser–provider model found in England, questions regarding the resourcing of inter-agency work are inevitably focused on asking 'who is paying?' and there is an accompanying reluctance to spend without a tangible agency-related outcome. Access to resources in England is governed by an adherence to procedures and legislation which not only militates against flexible and creative targeting to meet the needs of the family within agencies, but also between them. Reconciling these requirements to split and divide with a unifying 'whole family' approach therefore becomes a contradiction in terms. Furthermore, the legislative requirements of different agencies are connected to different and sometimes conflicting procedural priorities. As we have noted in previous research, given the procedure-bound nature of the work in England compared to elsewhere in Europe (Cooper *et al.* 1995; Hetherington *et al.* 1997), these differences act as powerful constraints to inter-agency work. While there may be policy directives urging professionals to 'work together', the possibilities of doing so in a straightforward, routine way are hampered by structures which in reality make it very difficult.

Organisational separation may also be mirrored in geographical separation, with agencies being located not merely in different buildings but on different sites. Geographical separation makes it more difficult for agencies, and the professionals within them, to set up formal meetings for collaboration and the sharing of information. In the experience of our participants this often proved to be unsatisfactory for reasons of time and conflicting commitments. However, they suggested that even where there were formalised opportunities for joint working, informal contact could promote more effective communications between professionals and could set the scene for working together. Participants from Northern Ireland, for example, stressed the important part played, in their view, by the physical proximity of colleagues from different agencies. Working in the same building did not just mean having access to shared information and shared social space; informal contact opened up real possibilities for practitioners to get to know more about one another's work. When agencies were geographically separated (which participants in England typically reported) informal contact or chance meetings thus became even more vital but much less likely to happen. As a result, knowledge-sharing and the kind of human contact that facilitates co-operation, suffered.

Shared Knowledge

One of the most important factors in facilitating inter-agency and inter-professional work that emerged from this study was shared knowledge which, in this context, takes various different forms; a knowledge base regarding mental health and child welfare and development; knowledge about each other's agencies and other available services; and information about the family itself. A lack of such shared knowledge reinforces territorial divisions and aids in the process of fragmenting both the problem and solutions to it. Compartmentalised knowledge is associated with a lack of shared discourse about the family (Douglas1999). Tye and Precey (1999: 168), writing about a project to promote inter-agency co-operation, describe how helpful it was that 'the mental health social worker working with the community mental health team helped her colleague within the children and families team to understand psychiatric language'. The separate discourses of child welfare and adult mental health can serve not only to fragment the family's problems but also to introduce a greater potential, for professionals and family members alike, to experience the concern and interventions of different professionals in terms of conflicts of interest.

On the whole, and perhaps predictably, where there were specialised services with few generic roles, participating practitioners felt unfamiliar with knowledge relating to the other field. As a consequence they also felt uncertain about making assessments and professional judgements that might call upon this knowledge, though some did venture opinions. However, while they knew that their knowledge of either child development or mental health problems and the related services was limited, some did not necessarily think that this was a bad thing; it was the responsibility of the other professionals to have a detailed knowledge of their field. Nevertheless, it became clear that while it is unrealistic to expect specialist professionals to have detailed knowledge of another field, for families where there are parental mental health problems, the professionals in child welfare needed some understanding and knowledge of mental health. Similarly the professionals in the mental health field needed to know about child development and to have some confidence in their own ability to talk to children and understand them. Both needed to know more about the structure and functioning of other agencies and the services they could provide. This points to the necessity of ensuring that, at the very least, practitioners acquire a broad but solid common base of knowledge, preferably during pre-qualifying training, in order that it can be built on subsequently and also that its existence can be taken for granted, as a routine basis of good practice and thus part of the 'cultural' expectations of all professionals.

There are a number of ways that this can take place. Generic training, particularly for social workers and community nurses, can provide a broad, shared knowledge base but even specialised training can offer an initial basis of shared knowledge before specific pathways are followed. There have been national and local initiatives to provide shared post-qualifying training to overcome the problems caused by early specialisation, and as part of strategies for increasing inter-agency collaboration (see, for example, Falkov 1998; Mayes *et al.* 1998; Bernard and Douglas 1999; and Lindsay *et al.* 1999 in relation to Bath and north-east Somerset). In other European countries and in Australia, the pre-qualifying social work training is at least three years and in most European countries is a generic training. While the content of courses varies within and between countries, a three-year generic training course has the opportunity to lay down a common knowledge base shared by workers who have later developed a specialism. In an international context, specialisation in pre-qualifying social work training is highly unusual, and in this research its disadvantages are apparent. In all the countries studied, social work professionals operated at the interface between institutions and the community, or between agencies with different remits. It was therefore particularly important for social workers to have been equipped with an extensive generic knowledge base and wide-ranging information about resources.

However, the nature of professional training, whether specialised or broad, does not exist in isolation but needs to be understood in relation to changing social, political and economic contexts; it reflects, and feeds back into, policies of welfare delivery and associated professional remits. In France (and in Luxembourg), for example, the *assistante sociale du secteur*, the generic social worker of the local authority social service, has a patch-based responsibility for children and adults, whatever the nature of their problems, and a generic training which provides the wide knowledge base that is necessary for the work. In England, the absence of a professional role for generalist community practitioners negates the need for broad-based training. The demise of generic social work training, reflecting as it does the changes in the organisation of social care and welfare during the 1980s and 1990s, has meant that, apart from those trained before this period, a shared knowledge of mental health and child welfare issues is rare (and implicitly unnecessary) among practitioners whose duties are narrowly prescribed. In our study this was reflected in limited knowledge of mental health and illness in child welfare practitioners and little knowledge or professional interest in child welfare issues from adult mental health teams. These practitioners recognised that, on the whole, they had little knowledge of the ways in which the other services operated and were sometimes confused as to what they might be able to offer to family members. As has been described elsewhere (Diggins 1999), this lack of shared knowledge regarding both child and adult health and welfare and related issues of service provision was linked to uncertainties and fear of treading on others' professional territory, particularly with regard to assessments. The lack of a shared discourse about the family can have repercussions beyond professional roles and sensitivities. Given the reflexive relationship between discourse and practice, divided services and separate discourses not only create the conditions for mutual suspicion and possible conflicts of interest between professionals and between agencies, they can also influence the way that family members think about and experience the family's problems and their own relationships with one another and with practitioners. These views in turn can affect those of practitioners; but professional relationships do not have to replicate familial ones. Shared aims and objectives—which denote 'a common sense of purpose'—rather than oppositional ones, as Douglas (1999: 187) points out, can only come from considering the needs of the family as a whole, even when the needs of individuals within the family may appear to be in conflict. It was noticeable, for example, that there was a high degree of consensus between the adult mental health and child welfare teams in Germany and Italy, and also in Northern Ireland. In these countries both teams showed a balance of concern between Mary's mental health and the welfare of the children and, importantly, they saw both issues as interlinked.

Confidentiality

The relationships between family members, professionals and agencies is further affected by the matter of confidentiality which emerged in this study as an important factor in knowledge-sharing, communication and co-operation. Confidentiality can emerge as an issue in various ways, but there are two basic types of situation when it becomes important. The first is when a family member wishes the information shared with a professional to be withheld from another family member. This is particularly important when it is a child who wishes to maintain confidentiality from a parent who has responsibility for that child and, therefore, has some rights to the information. The second important situation is when a person shares information with a professional and, for some reason, that information becomes important to other professionals, either to those involved in providing a service to the client/patient or to other members of the family.

Confidentiality can be paradoxical in its effects: it can form the basis of trust but it can also work, through secrecy, against openness. For most professionals, confidentiality is a fundamental principle, and sharing information with colleagues from another profession is viewed with hostility. For the most part, professionals only share information on a 'need to know' basis, and with the explicit informed consent of the client or patient. This in turn affects the content and quality of communications between professionals and between them and family members. Critically, muddles about confidentiality, as Douglas (1999: 188) points out, can result in important information not being passed on. Confidentiality is seen as important both for ethical reasons and for practical reasons. The ethics are based on the belief that information shared in professional relationships should not be used for any other purpose than to help the client or patient, and that the client should control what happens in the relationship. The practical importance is the belief that users will not engage with professionals if they believe that sensitive and private information will be shared with others.

It seems, however, that a distinction is made between sharing information between different professions working in the same team. For some practitioners, for example in England and Australia where there are specialist child welfare teams, issues of confidentiality posed more uncertainties than for those in other countries such as France where information-sharing was not seen to be limited by the need for confidentiality to the same extent. One factor which interacted, in some countries, with attitudes and practices concerning confidentiality was mandatory reporting: the legal obligation on professionals to declare knowledge of child maltreatment. In the Scandinavian countries, where professionals have to report not only abuse but suspicion of abuse, the participants had clear views about the value of information-sharing and the means to put it into practice. There were two aspects to reporting. On the one hand, it enabled them to offer help at an earlier stage, and was therefore linked to preventive early intervention; on the other, it was suggested by participants from these countries that in fact mandatory reporting existed to counteract a strong service culture of confidentiality; it was needed as an important, explicit principle in stimulating teamwork between sectors. The responses of Danish participants exemplified this point of view and the associated dilemmas. They thought that in spite of mandatory reporting—which meant that the GP and psychiatric services would have a duty to report the situation to the social services—workers might nevertheless fail to contact other services for fear of losing Mary's trust or of jeopardising their alliance with the family. Australia, France and Italy all have mandatory reporting (but not of suspicion of child abuse), but confidentiality was a more difficult area for the Australian participants than for the French and Italians, who have multidisciplinary child welfare teams. It seemed that the structures and professional culture could be more important than the legal provisions of mandatory reporting.

Confidentiality also poses different issues for different professions. The structure of the research in this project did not allow us easily to extrapolate the issues for different professions, but it did seem that adult mental health professions had more issues than the child care professionals. Adult psychiatry, as a profession, has a particularly strong tradition of working with individual patients and not viewing the patient as part of a holistic system.

Communication and Co-operation

At each stage of the case, the participants from all countries agreed on the vital role played by the quality of communications between professionals and the family and between different groups of professionals; regular communication made co-operation possible. It also helped to build up trust. While formal channels of communication were an important pathway, for example through regular meetings, it also became clear that informal contacts, even opportunistic ones, were more useful in developing a shared understanding of the family's needs and a shared sense of responsibility in meeting them. Thus in Sweden and in Italy, for example, where structures were seen as conducive to co-operative working, practitioners still saw an important role for individual contacts, even though this might in reality give rise to wide variations in levels of collaboration. Participants across different countries agreed that informal contact was more likely to happen if practitioners already had a history of working together or, as we saw earlier, if their offices were located in the same building. However, in the experience of the participants in England there were few opportunities for informal contact; the structural division and geographical separation of different agencies meant that there was little or no chance of meeting outside formal, pre-arranged settings. Moreover, formal meetings, such as the child protection conference, did not provide the best opportunity for building up collaborative practice because they were essentially reactive, crisis-driven and case-specific. The over-riding factor which made it very difficult to set up extra inter-agency meetings or to act opportunistically to do so, was lack of time. There was little or no flexibility in anyone's daily or weekly schedule to fit in another meeting.

Professional Time

As a resource, professional time was a critical factor in co-operative working, in establishing and maintaining good communications between colleagues and building relationships of trust and confidence with family members. Time gives practitioners the chance to be creative in their work. As well as enabling non-urgent and unscheduled meetings to take place, time is needed to 'network', to make and develop contacts and to carry out preventive groundwork. It is also necessary in building and consolidating relationships with clients and with colleagues. Previous comparative research with service users in England, France and Germany suggested that being able to form relationships with professionals who they felt they could trust, was highly valued by clients in both countries and an important ingredient in the perceived 'success' of the intervention (Baistow and Hetherington 1998; Baistow and Wilford 2000). A key feature of the 'trustworthy' professionals was their accessibility; they made time to listen and gave time to their clients who felt that they were being taken seriously. In the current study there was a consensus among participants that it was important to gain and work with Mary's voluntary involvement and that this could be best achieved by gaining her trust and persuading her that she and her family would benefit from help. This was important, an Australian group suggested, not only to fulfil professional agendas but also because services should be genuinely non-threatening and responsive to the needs expressed by the family. This might entail offering family support, especially practical help, early on, as in Norway, where participants thought that offering supervised home-help assistance to Mary according to her wishes would be the key to co-operation with the family. Similarly, in many countries, the mother's request for practical help was seen as a way of making contact with her and establishing a relationship of confidence that would enable her to look at other problems. In Northern Ireland where, as we have seen, inter-professional collaboration was not seen as a problem, it was thought that the best person to co-ordinate work with the family was the worker whom Mary trusted most irrespective of his or her professional designation or agency. The same response was given by the English child and family mental health team, but the adult mental health and child welfare teams did not respond so flexibly and seemed to be bound by the formal responsibilities of agency roles. Italian and Greek participants also thought that Mary's confidence and trust needed to be gained but, in their view and perhaps reflecting the greater cultural value placed on the family in those countries, the best way of doing this initially would be to introduce services to Mary through a family member or friend whom she trusted, and who could persuade her that she needed help.

Participants agreed that these relationships of trust need time to develop. However, one of the clearest resource differences between participating countries was in terms of the amount of time that practitioners could 'afford' to devote to their clients. Professional flexibility, responsiveness and availability to talk and to listen take time that, for practitioners in some countries such as Greece and England, was a scarce resource to be carefully rationed. The shortage of professional time that participants from England reported, not only reduced their availability to meet with colleagues, it also affected their accessibility and involvement with families in a number of ways. Our research strongly indicates that family support services are vital in ensuring the welfare of children with mentally ill parents but it was clear that in England there was much less professional time than elsewhere to spend with family members and the time that was available had to be saved until it was most needed. This had repercussions for assessment and for the timing and nature of interventions, which were likely to be left until there was no alternative. While there were objective assessment criteria in operation, assessments were also based on comparisons of need and a hierarchy of severity which offered a basis for dealing with cases in order of priority. In England (and in Ireland) participants thought that at Stage 1 the family's difficulties were not severe enough to warrant intensive support, which had to be saved for more extreme cases. By the later stages, when the problems had become more serious, support might be offered, but once again the time of qualified professionals was rationed. Support to the family would be generally undertaken by the least qualified (and lowest paid) member of the children and families team, i.e. the family support worker, whose time was cheapest. It was also likely that she would use behavioural approaches in a time-limited way, for example for a three-month period, to help Mary to deal with basic aspects of child care. In contrast to this situation, participants from those countries with more expert and more thorough family support—for example Germany, Norway and Sweden—found Stage 3 of the case vignette to be a very unlikely scenario; sufficient support services, involving extensive use of professional time, working on a number of aspects of personal and family life, would already have been put in place in response to Stage 1. This could mean intensive support at home by qualified social workers on a daily basis, including in Germany and Sweden, support for the family if Mary was hospitalised. In the view of practitioners from these countries, this kind of early expenditure of professional time would have prevented the later, more serious developments and would have provided a longer term basis for trust to be established.

There is also increasing clinical and research evidence, from both sides of the Atlantic, that the most effective time to take preventive action to promote child mental health is during babyhood (Child Psychotherapy Trust 1999). Identifying vulnerable babies (and their mothers) and implementing effective infant mental health interventions which are preventive rather than reactive, rely on anticipatory approaches which

- are sensitive to a range of risk factors;
- offer specialist support in the community;
- intervene early to work with the mother to focus on her relationship with the baby; and, importantly
- represent the baby's point of view and best interests to professionals and agencies.

The mother and baby unit in Denmark (Lier *et al.* 1995; Lier 1997) offered all these.

A NETWORK OF UNIVERSAL AND TARGETED SERVICES

As we suggested at the beginning of this chapter, practitioners from all participating countries saw collaborative work between professionals and between agencies as a key to supporting families where there is parental mental ill health. However, the ways in which this collaboration might be organised, and by whom, were various and there was no single answer. Family support services, based in the community and consisting of different professionals, were seen to be a very important resource with the potential to be the key site of inter-professional collaboration and a 'whole-family' approach. While they existed in most participating countries, they varied tremendously in terms of their remits, personnel, resources and availability. The countries notably differed in their relation to Mary's hospitalisation: in some countries family support was used to try to keep the family together; in others, it was seen as a way of enabling the other family members to cope in her absence. In some countries, for example, Australia and Ireland, family support services existed largely for crisis intervention and for families with more extreme problems, and participants doubted whether this case would be considered a priority. In others, such as Germany, a large number of services was available, for example the SPFH. The key to family support measures was Mary's willingness to accept them. However, the children were the main focus of concern and the primary aim of using these services would be to support the family and ensure that the children's needs were being met rather than to keep Mary out of hospital. A wide range of possible services existed in France too, which could be combined together in various ways depending on the family's needs and the changing nature of their problems. In other countries, like Scotland, limited support was available, in the form of home help, if Mary was hospitalised. However, the Scottish teams like their Scandinavian counterparts thought that by Stage 3 a raft of support services would already have been made available, so that the situation might not have reached this crisis point. In Scotland, as in Germany, there was a focus on the short- and long-term physical and emotional developmental needs of the children, but in Scotland a particular emphasis was placed on the school as a key provider of stability. In Luxembourg support services were more likely to be available on Mary's return from hospital. In contrast in Norway and Sweden, as we saw earlier, the family support team was seen as a preventive resource, to be brought in as a first rather than a last resort. Norwegian participants, like the Germans, saw intensive family support as a way of keeping the family together, by helping to prevent Mary from being compulsorily hospitalised and the children from being accommodated.

Our analysis suggests that while specialist family support services clearly have a vital role to play at various 'stages' of the case, depending on the family's changing situation, there is nevertheless space for a more proactive approach which anticipates rather than reacts to these needs. In our view, the services that are well placed to support these families are those universal ones to which all citizens are entitled as a part of the normal welfare provisions of the state, such as family or generalist medical practitioners, maternal and child health services, schools, nursery schools and school medical services. They are often the first to know that a child has a mentally ill parent, and workers in these services can play a key part in providing support or informing specialist services. Being essentially community-based they can more easily be in contact with and draw on the 'natural resources' of the family— relatives and friends—who can be vital (and valued) sources of family support, as participants from Greece and Italy described. Furthermore, because they are universal, contact with them bears less stigma and is generally more acceptable to families who may be experiencing difficulties but are afraid of the possible consequences if, as a last resort, they ask for help, or fail to do so. Our participants in Northern Ireland, where collaboration and co-ordination were not viewed as a problem, saw the primary health care team as playing a pivotal role, as the least intrusive service, in initial assessments and in co-ordinating the role of other services. In England, the GP, health visitor and primary health care team were also viewed as important but currently under-used resources, with real potential for information-sharing and co-ordination. More widely, participants agreed that GPs are well placed, in principle, to provide the basis for a 'whole family' approach, though in practice, shortage of time and large case loads prevent them from developing this role.

One universal service, which in most countries was an under-used source of support to Anna, was the school. The exception was Scotland, where responses to the vignette emphasised the importance that participants there accorded to school in providing emotional and social stability in Anna's life, in the face of uncertain and unstable circumstances. They also pointed to the key part that it could play in monitoring and fostering her health and welfare, as well as her academic education. Thus the school, the school health service and the educational psychology service would be involved as integral to the provision of support to Anna.

In addition to generalist services, and complementing them, our study also highlighted the important role played by specialist services which could be targeted towards different aspects of the problem. Some of these are costly, but not all of them, and some can operate at the local, small-scale level. Importantly, they have the potential to be both preventive and supportive. As well as the key resource of intensive family support teams described above, specialist services included residential mother and baby units in mental health settings (Denmark, Germany, Australia, Ireland and England), support groups for children (Sweden and Germany) and specialist fostering services for children with a mentally ill parent or whose parents may have repeated hospitalisations (Sweden and France).

At an intermediate level, and bridging the gap between universal and specialist services, examples from other countries showed the positive part that can be played by multidisciplinary child welfare teams, such as the French *Circonscriptions d'Interventions Sanitaires et Sociales* described above. These teams are routinely involved with other community orientated services such as primary health care, and in partnership with voluntary organisations, often promote local initiatives for the development of targeted services.

THE ROLE AND POTENTIAL OF CHILD MENTAL HEALTH SERVICES

Another important service which everywhere has the potential to play a more active role is child and family mental health. Offering as it does a combined knowledge-base of child development and mental health, together with a multidisciplinary team approach, it is well placed to integrate the two discourses and meet the evident need of other professionals for consultancy and advice in work with these families. However, in all countries these services tend to be under-used as consultancy resources, even if, as in England and elsewhere, they are over-stretched in other respects.

As well as undertaking their own assessment, treatment, training and research, child and adolescent mental health services have a particular contribution to make. In many ways they are Jacks of all trades and masters of none, but this can be a source of strength when considering children and families. Different members of the service have links and expertise with different aspects of the child. This capacity to understand the complexity of the world of the child enables the service both to hold the child in mind (or at least to recognise more quickly when the child is invisible), and to speak to or link with a range of experts and practitioners. So discussions with teachers in school, social welfare agencies, children and family, adult mental health and medical specialists, paediatricians, neurologists, and those with learning difficulties can all be done with familiarity and hence confidence.

The richness of the training and the diversity of the professionals and their skills make them an invaluable resource for consultation to anyone in the related or linked professional groups. Where that happens, it works well. In the UK, however, the service is small—for example, there are 400 child and adolescent psychiatrists in the UK and about 300 child psychotherapists. Services feel under siege, referrals have risen dramatically and providers have had to prioritise. In addition, some services have decided that complex child protection cases or cases where there are adult mental health problems should be dealt with by other agencies to enable them to focus on neuro-behavioural childhood psychiatric disorders such as autism, Aspergers syndrome or ADHD (Attention Deficit Hyperactivity Disorder).

DEVELOPING PREVENTION AND CONSULTATION

Child mental health services in the Scandinavian countries with their emphasis on early intervention and the large infant mental health service have prioritised early detection and prevention. Italy and Germany have extensive therapeutic provision and Germany provides impressive family support. A model of service provision could be envisaged rather like the four-tier model proposed by the Department of Health in England and Wales but, more specifically, for children and families in need and children in need of protection:

- *Tier 1*   Self help and the use of local community networks.
- *Tier 2*   Universal services (GPs, teachers, health visitors), social workers, family support.
- *Tier 3*   Individual child mental health professionals providing services and consultation, assessment and therapeutic input.
- *Tier 4*   Specialist services, out-patient, day and in-patient, which also provide consultation, training and research.

But, instead of mainly service provision, the focus could be the provision of consultation. By the dissemination of understanding and by providing time for discussion and training, this would enable the front line professionals to increase their awareness and skills when working face to face with children and families. At the same time, sufficient service provision should be maintained to provide assessment and treatment as required by the complex worrying cases.

In France it seemed that this was more or less what was happening; there was a tiered model although not specified as such. In the UK, where the social services intervene at a later stage, the work does not start until tier 3 or 4, and the child and family mental health services then feel overwhelmed by the extent of the problems and the work needed. Scandinavia, Italy, Germany and Greece focus most of their resources on family support and therapeutic work (tier 1, tier 2 and tier 3).

PROFESSIONAL ATTITUDES AND THE WILL TO CO-OPERATE

As well as highlighting the important role played by a range of structural factors in hindering or facilitating professional co-operation, it also became apparent from participants' responses to the vignette that a vital ingredient of collaboration was a will to co-operate on the part of professionals. We are not suggesting that this is purely a matter of individual motivation, although without this, true collaboration is likely to be very difficult to sustain. The will to work together is nonetheless connected to the contexts of organisational structure and policy, to professional training and to professional confidence; so that, as we mentioned earlier, cultural expectations develop which provide a basis to inform and stimulate collaborative practice, even in the face of obstacles. In Germany, for example, conditions exist, which on the face of it do not seem conducive to inter-professional collaboration; there is a multiplicity of agencies, many of them not organisationally connected because of the high level of NGOs. The German participants described this as a complex, labyrinthine network. However, their responses made it clear that they did not view collaboration as a problem. Moreover, there was a shared sense of responsibility, an expectation of working together and a desire to do so which meant that they worked flexibly to circumvent potential obstacles.

In England, by contrast, participants' responses indicated that while there is an interest in working collaboratively to develop 'whole family' approaches, there is also a pessimism about the possibilities of doing so. This seems likely to be connected to the issues of pessimism and optimism discussed in previous chapters. Current conditions are perceived as making it difficult to translate principles into action. However, we also detect a narrowing of professional imagination and a lack of inspiration concerning how things might be done differently. In recent years these have been dulled by procedural and budgetary preoccupations which have begun to shape our thinking about the 'problem' as well as our responses to it. As described in

Chapter 7, one English participant reflected, after hearing about the resources available in Germany, 'so resources—or lack of resources—begin to limit the whole way you think about something, the ideas that you can have'. Realistically, these conditions are unlikely to go away. It may well be that other European countries will also increasingly face reductions in welfare spending. However, although these factors may act as powerful constraints to developing new ways of working together, by increasing the imperative to think creatively they can, paradoxically, also serve to broaden our imagination, stimulating new ideas and professional resourcefulness.

PART III

INTRODUCTION: DEVELOPING NEW INFORMATION

Writing about information, Geoffrey Bateson made the following statement, which locates 'information' as something that can only be produced through comparison:

> 'It takes at least two somethings to create a difference. To produce news of difference, i.e. information, there must be two entities (real or imagined) such that the difference between them can be immanent in their mutual relationship.' (Bateson 1979: 78).

The implication of this statement for comparative studies is important. The concept has been developed elsewhere in relation to the use of cross-national comparison as a learning tool (Hetherington 1996) and by Cooper (2000) in relation to the child protection research referred to in Chapter 1. Bateson points out that to arrive at information, you must have two different things to compare. Thus all information is based on comparison. If we wish to have new ideas about how we encourage inter-agency co-operation, we need to think about how our system works at present. In order to have new ideas about our system we therefore have to describe it as it currently is. This 'information' (because a description is information) will be based on an implicit comparison between the 'real' system (the system that we think we are describing) and an 'imagined' system which forms the basis of our description. We are not usually aware of the imagined system, but it must be there to enable us to describe the real system. Comparison with other 'real' systems provides the opportunity to describe our system, not in terms of an imagined system (probably derived from our own past experience) but in terms of an existing but different system. In Bateson's thesis, there must be enough closeness between the 'things' compared for difference to produce information; as he says, the difference has to be 'immanent' in the relationship of the two systems; that is, the relationship has to contain 'sameness' as well as 'difference'. In comparing the responses of professional groups in different countries to the same situation occurring within similar (but not identical) social, economic and political frameworks, we have been looking for differences within systems that contain sameness but are not the same. We use difference to develop new information and thus a new description of English structures and practice. We 'discover' new information about how our system works, hoping that this new information may generate new ideas for change and development. The value of the comparison is not to do with learning from the other system because it is better (or worse), it is about learning from difference how to see our own system differently.

The above discussion focuses on comparison between two things. Comparison of more than two things opens up different possibilities. If when faced with the same situation, professionals in a number of countries with different systems all experience different problems, it is likely that the problems they experience are related to the differences between their systems and the functioning of their systems. Thus, while the Germans thought they might have problems with the judge if they wanted a compulsory hospitalisation order, the Swedes had no such anxieties. If the professionals in all the countries have the same problem in spite of their different systems, it is more likely that the problem is intrinsic to the situation. For example, all countries found that services needed by these families were provided by a range of different agencies and that there was a risk that these agencies would not be able to co-ordinate their input. With a large number of countries to compare, it becomes possible to make tentative suggestions about the ways of functioning that facilitate the task of the professionals, and to identify the difficulties that are intrinsic to the human situation they are faced with. This has practical significance. If existing structures and ideologies are generating less efficient functioning, they can be modified to respond more effectively, and inherent problems, if recognised, can be tackled with awareness and given the concentrated attention that they require. However, culture, as well as structures and ideology, affects the functioning of systems (see Figure 1.1 in Chapter 1). Cooper describes culture as 'the sleeping variable'. Working within one country we may be able to discount its effects, but, he comments, 'Cross-national comparative research can make no such assumptions. Rather … it works to disturb and awaken the sleeping variable of culture, and reveal it as a powerful shaping force potentially acting upon every level of data' (Cooper 2000: 95).

As described in Chapter 1, in undertaking this research we set out with four objectives. The first was descriptive and exploratory, to discover about the functioning of services and inter-agency co-operation in some other European countries. This map-making provided the material for Part I. The second objective was to identify the nature of problems over inter-agency co-operation. Our way of doing this was through comparisons between the ways that systems functioned in different countries. By comparison of the ways in which co-operation was achieved, or problems were experienced, we sought to distinguish the problems that were experienced everywhere—the intrinsic problems—from those that seemed to occur in conjunction with a particular system—the extrinsic, system-dependent, problems. Part II therefore concentrated on comparisons, with a focus on comparing other countries with England.

Our third and fourth objectives were linked: to identify things that were particularly problematic in this country, and the difficulties that might be encountered in trying to make changes. We have used comparison, as Bateman implied, to develop new information and understandings for our own purposes. Through seeing our own system differently we may be able to begin to understand why we do things the way we do, and why we have particular difficulties. In Part III we continue to look specifically at the English scene. In Chapter 12 we consider the situation in this country for children with a mentally ill parent, the needs of the children and difficulties that the research partners experienced in responding to the children's situation in the vignette case material. Chapter 13 looks at the resources and services described by our research partners from the point of view of parents, and reviews the resources available in different countries. In conclusion, Chapter 14 reviews the factors in the English system that seem to promote a good outcome for these families and the factors that make a good outcome difficult.

Chapter 12

Invisible Children

> In Brueghel's Icarus, for instance: how everything turns away
> Quite leisurely from the disaster; the ploughman may
> Have heard the splash, the forsaken cry,
> But for him it was not an important failure; the sun shone
> As it had to on the white legs disappearing into the green
> Water; and the expensive delicate ship that must have seen
> Something amazing, a boy falling out of the sky,
> Had somewhere to get to and sailed calmly on.
>
> (W.H. Auden: 'Musée Des Beaux Arts')

The poem quoted above, with which we opened this book, describes a painting of the death of Icarus. All that is to be seen of Icarus is his body disappearing into the water as he plunges into the sea. In the front of the picture, a man ploughing a field barely looks up from his work. A ship sailing near the falling Icarus shows no sign of having seen him. Icarus seems to be invisible. He falls from the sky, and the world barely remarks on the happening, and goes its way, asking no questions.

Our study reflects this process. All the groups except one had difficulty in responding to the children's world. The exception was a group where two participants had had a mentally ill parent. Other groups did not ignore the children, but attention to the experience and feelings of the children was hard to sustain. The participants in the groups knew the focus of the research in which they were taking part. They could be expected to show an above-average ability to centre on the children. But the groups had been asked to say what they thought was likely to happen to the family in the vignette, not what they wished would happen, or thought ought to happen. Their responses were in terms of current realities. Even if they as individuals might have been able to respond to the children, they did not see that as the likely process and described very few services that targeted the children. The picture presented was of a world where the services, in struggling to respond to the needs of the family, focused on the mentally ill person. Although there were differences between countries in the amount of attention paid to the children's needs, within each country there was little difference in this respect between adult mental health and child welfare groups. The adult mental health groups spent more time discussing the needs of the mother, the child welfare groups spent more time discussing the risk to the children and problems of working with the mother; both spent less time on considering the experience or the needs of the children.

It is only quite recently that surveys and handbooks on child abuse and child protection have begun to include mentally ill parents as a category. In earlier research (for example, Packman *et al.* 1986), they do not appear. A careful consideration of the impact of parental mental illness is more likely to be given by authors writing about neglect or emotional abuse. Thus O'Hagan (1993: 88) writes:

> 'The experiences of many mentally ill people are such that the emotional and psychological abuse of their children will be inevitable. The definitions [of emotional and psychological abuse] we have been using are a virtual echo of the lives of many of these children.'

On the mental health side, there seems to be less awareness. In a selection of standard community mental health texts, the needs of patients as parents, and the needs of their children, are rarely mentioned. Howe (1998), writing on living with mental illness, describes the situation of a mother with two small children, but does not mention the children's needs. Adamec (1996) in 'How to Live with a Mentally Ill Person' only makes one brief reference to children. In a chapter on users and their relatives, Perkins and Repper (1998) point out that the siblings of people with mental illness are often very much affected, but that 'there is a dearth of literature concerning their role and the problems that they face'. The children of mentally ill parents, of whom the same could be said, receive no mention. Perkins and Repper (1998: 113) close their chapter with the words:

> 'It is critical that all facets of a person's social world are considered: all may be important to the individual, all may be lost if not actively included and supported, all may be of value in helping and supporting the person, all may be central to the individual's quality of life.'

For mentally ill parents, the welfare of their children is indeed a central facet of their world. But, as Sayce (1996) pointed out, the Care Programme Approach lacks reference to child care, and child care facilities are rarely available in mental health day centres (see also Connor 1999).

PREVALENCE

Perhaps the lack of any statistics about the prevalence of the problem can be seen not just as part of a general failure to collect statistics, but as a failure which reflects the problem. Only our Scandinavian colleagues in other countries were able to provide figures for the numbers of families where there is a mentally ill parent, for the number of children coming to the attention of child welfare services who have a mentally ill parent or for the proportion of children having a mentally ill parent who experience problems. We described in earlier chapters the way in which these families can be lost between the mental health and children's services. The problems of establishing prevalence echo the problems over services. In the UK, there are some figures about mentally ill adults who are parents. There are some figures about children in need of protection who have mentally ill parents. But these figures do not join up. As was recently pointed out by Cleaver *et al.* (1999: 21): 'The information concerning the prevalence of mental illness ... in families with dependent children is incomplete'.

The information that we have on the potential numbers of children and families who might need support is very patchy, so that we do not know how many mentally ill adult patients have dependent children, and we do not know how many of the children on the child protection register or looked after by the local authority have a mentally ill parent. Are the children known to the social services a large proportion of the children who have a mentally ill parent or a very small minority? What information we have lacks consistent criteria and is dispersed through a range of different reports and surveys.

There are three different questions to answer (each of which has sub-categories). Firstly, how many parents with dependent children have a diagnosed mental illness? Secondly, how many children involved in child welfare interventions have a mentally ill parent? Thirdly, how many of the children who have a mentally ill parent are in need of support from outside the family?

Prevalence of Parental Mental Illness

Cleaver *et al.* (1999) summarise the information from the OPCS (1996) statistics on mental illness among parents. Combining the figures for neurotic disorders and functional psychoses, there is a rate of 15.9% for couples with children and 29.1% for lone parents with children. Weir and Douglas (1999), taking figures from separate local studies, give varying estimates of about 30–35% of patients with a mental illness who have children. None of these figures gives any estimate of the numbers of children each patient might have. However, a conservative estimate would be for an average of 1.5 children for each mentally ill parent. On that basis, for every 100 admissions, about 40 children would need to be considered.

Summarising the UK figures, Mayes *et al.* (1998) suggest that about 30% of mentally ill parents have dependent children. Research carried out in Stockholm (Skerfving 1999) found that a fifth of the in-patients in the Beckomberger psychiatric hospital had children under the age of 18; the children were mainly living with the other parent or were in foster care. A survey of out-patients found that a quarter of the patients had children under 18, and that most were living with their children.

Some of these children will not need any outside help, some will need a great deal. Most would benefit from information and from the knowledge that their place and their importance in their parent's life was recognised by the professionals who were now so crucial to the life of the whole family.

Families With a Mentally Ill Parent Known to the Social Services

At the other end of the problem, there are the children known to the child protection services who have a mentally ill parent. Surveying recent research, Cleaver *et al.* (1999) summarise some of the figures from research relating to the 'heavy end' of child welfare. These suggest that in England at the first referral stage (pre-inquiry) 13% of children referred have a mentally ill parent, 20% at first child protection enquiry, 25% at initial child protection conference and 42% at care proceedings. These figures are taken from several different studies with all the uncertainties about comparability that this entails. They may also refer to a changing group of children, because, as Cleaver *et al.* point out, more parents seem to become identified as mentally ill as enquiries progress. These figures cannot be directly related to figures for the mental illness of couples and single parents from the OPCS, but they suggest that parental mental illness may initially, at the referral stage, be under-recorded and/or that the discovery of a diagnosis of parental mental illness is a significant factor in the decision to initiate care proceedings. It appears that the process of child protection investigations may lead to the identification of more families with a mentally ill parent as being 'in difficulties'; thus confirming the fears of these parents that involvement with the services is dangerous. Thoburn *et al.* (1995), studying families involved in child protection procedures, identify 32 families (14% of their total) 'where the main carer was described as having some degree of mental illness' and comment 'our data almost certainly underestimates the extent of mental illness' (Thoburn *et al.* 1995: 91).

Stroud (1997, 2000) and Reder and Duncan (1999) review published studies of mentally ill perpetrators of filicide. Stroud (1997) analyses the Anglophone literature (up to 1996) in detail, and Stroud (2000) reviews studies from Denmark, Norway and Sweden in relation to current and forthcoming UK research. Reder and Duncan consider selected studies in relation to their own work on 'Part 8' reports. However, there are problems in using the figures as quoted in any of the studies that they survey for assessing the extent of parental mental illness in fatal child abuse. The base numbers are often small and the basis for selection varies. The studies analyse different populations and include different sub-categories within mental illness. For example, the total numbers of cases in different studies may or may not include substance abuse, personality disorders and subnormality. In these reviews, the studies most closely aligned in population are those by Falkov (1996), and by Reder and Duncan, both of which are based on 'Part 8' reports (and which, Reder and Duncan report, have a small overlap in cases). These give a figure of 18% for the occurrence of parental mental illness in 'Part 8' reports on filicide.

In the mental health field, Reith (1998) lists and reviews 28 mental health inquiry reports, published between 1988 and 1997. Out of these 28 cases, only one involved filicide (two children). The report on this case makes recommendations about co-operation between services, better education for social workers in mental health and guidance for psychiatric services on what is expected of them when a severely mentally ill patient has children. Two reports (Woodley Report 1995 and Armstrong Report 1998) make specific recommendations regarding the need for greater care and attention to be given to the children of mentally ill parents; these are both reports about mentally ill adults whose illness is linked by the report writers to their experience of disrupted and destructive parenting from a mentally ill parent. The Woodley Report recommendations are quite specific: 'That the Department of Health should give greater emphasis to *preventive support work* to children with parents with severe mental problems, and commission and publish research' and

'That local social services and health authorities address *the support needs of parents with severe mental health problems*, and the needs of their children, in community care plans and in children's services plans, and allocate resources. In so doing that they review *the distribution, co-ordination and access to specialist mental health services for children and families*.' (Reith 1998: 66; our emphasis)

Except for the OPCS data on mental illness among couples, all the studies referred to have problems of small base numbers and differences of definition. However, there is some consistency between them. Broadly, we are looking at a picture where about one-third of mentally ill patients have dependent children, and where over one-quarter of children who are placed on the child protection register have a mentally ill parent or carer. These are substantial numbers, but parental mental illness appears in the child protection literature as one sub-category of parental problem among many. There are more studies concerned with parental mental illness and child homicide than with parental mental illness and child abuse in general. It takes murder for these children to become visible.

Children and Families who Cope

There are also the children in families which do not get caught in the child protection net, but who are in need of help. They may be in contact with family centres, support groups or health visitors. They may eventually be given an 'in need' assessment (as the vignette family did at Stage 2), but they do not appear in child protection statistics. Frost *et al.* (1996) studied the families who were involved with Homestart. Some of these families had been involved in the child protection system, but in the main they were families where the concerns were not at this level. The children were in need rather than at risk. In these families, 'twenty four out of the 46 women were recognised by a health professional as having a current mental health problem' (Frost *et al.* 1996: 123). Of these, 12 were receiving medical treatment for mental health needs. The families with whom Homestart is concerned have many social and economic problems which compound any mental health problems they may have.

> 'Research has shown that adults with mental health problems are two times more likely than those without such illnesses to be unemployed, live in rented accommodation and be separated or divorced (Meltzer 1995), the very characteristics of the people in our sample.' (Frost *et al.* 1996: 57)

In the 'Homestart' research, over half the families had a parent with mental health problems recognised by a health professional.

There are also families who do not quite make it into any studies, who do not get counted at all. Some of them show up in research about carers. Children of mentally ill parents who are carers are identified by Dearden and Becker (1998, 2000). It is not only the older children who are involved as carers; the youngest carers of a parent with mental illness found in one study were three and a half years old (Frank 1994). Even the carers are not the whole picture. These children are probably also present in the groups of children who benefit from schemes like the Pyramid Project (Makins 1997) which runs groups for primary school children who are not a problem but are a concern to their teachers, underachieving but not disruptive. The numbers of these children who cope, and the extent of their problems, can only be inferred from other information or deduced from a logical consideration of other known factors, such as the numbers of parents with mental illness referred to above. But their problem should not be ignored because a statistically exact statement of its extent cannot be made.

This lack of statistically 'pure' information should not excuse us from making what use we can of the figures we have. Commenting from the perspective of community adult psychiatrist, Poole (1996) had no statistics on how many of his patients were parents, but he estimated that one-third of them had children under 18 years; and he conceded that to consider the possible existence of children considerably complicated his practice. A quarter of all children who are considered to need an initial child protection conference have a mentally ill parent (Farmer and Owen 1995). Not all of these children will be registered, but to get as far as a child protection conference, there need to be serious concerns. This leaves out entirely all the children where the family has a 'needs' assessment, but where the children are not thought to be 'at risk'. The estimate for these families suggested by Frost *et al.* (see above) is that in about half of them there may be parental mental health problems. We are talking about a large number of children; and yet there are, as our study demonstrates, considerable difficulties in providing services to support them and for their parents in negotiating very difficult, confusing and sometimes dangerous experiences. These children are not 'seen' by the adult psychiatric services and only an unknown proportion of them are visible to child welfare services.

In spite of an increase in academic and clinical studies, and the development of a more detailed knowledge base about the effect of parental mental illness on children (both their ability to survive it and the nature of the problems it leads to) our response to these families does not seem to change much over time. The opening address of Professor Tizard to the twenty-second Child Guidance Inter-Clinic Conference (Tizard 1966) could equally well describe the current situation:

> 'The problem of mental illness in the family, and its effects on children is one that we are becoming increasingly aware of. The reasons for this are clear. Mental illness is, after all a common phenomenon. It is also a fact that most adults who suffer from it are married persons with children. Now it is obvious that a disorder which affects personality and behaviour is likely to have an impact on other members of society, and that it is particularly likely to affect members of the sick person's family.'

Tizard goes on to look at some of the available figures, and then the relationship between parental mental illness and the child's well-being.

> 'We also know something of the factors that are associated with the illnesses of children who have mentally ill parents. The severity of parental disorder is not of itself of great significance. But where the illness bears directly on the child— for example, where a mentally ill parent has a personality disorder, long standing disorder or hypochondriasis, or delusions which involve the child—the disorder is likely to affect the child's behaviour. … It is not sufficient to consider only the condition of the patient. We must also consider society, and in particular the family.' (NAMH 1966: 9)

What is striking about these words is not just the succinct statement of the problems, covering in a few paragraphs prevalence, effects and social responses, but the fact that it was made nearly 40 years ago. The figures on prevalence referred to earlier in this chapter add very little to Tizard's statement that 'Mental illness is, after all a common phenomenon. It is also a fact that most adults who suffer from it are married persons with children'. Recently, Duncan and Reder, writing in 2000, echo Tizard's analysis of the impact on children when they propose that 'the most useful way to consider how children experience their parents' mental health problem is to focus on the impact of parental *behaviour* rather than their *diagnosis*' (Duncan and Reder 2000: 88; their emphasis). It is the application of this thinking to practice that is elusive.

Implications for the UK

We have been referring to the figures for the UK, more specifically, England. The lack of statistical information that we find here is largely shared with other European countries, although there is more information for Denmark, Norway and Sweden (Stroud 2000). What is different about the situation in other European countries is the extent to which services are made available to families on the basis of need rather than risk. If families can, at their own definition of need, access services more easily, there is less requirement for figures to prove that the families need help. In England (more than in Scotland, and possibly more than in Northern Ireland) the provision of social work services for children and families is dominated by the heavy end of child protection in a way that is not in evidence in other European countries. Gilbert (1997) points out that the important difference between the child welfare systems that he surveyed was not whether they had mandatory reporting laws but whether they focused on family services or child protections. Of the countries included in his work, only the English-speaking countries had a child protection orientation. Hetherington *et al.* (1997) and Pringle (1998) reached similar conclusions. In fact, in response to our case vignette, only one other country was less able to provide *supportive* services than England, and that was Greece, where the economic and resource problems were of a different order. There seems to be a much greater need in England than elsewhere in Europe to provide *proof* that certain children, a specific population, are suffering before provision can be made for them as a category.

However, it emerged very clearly from the research that in all the countries involved, professionals had difficulty in consistently 'seeing' the children and identifying with their perspective on the events that were taking place.

THE IMPACT OF PARENTAL MENTAL ILLNESS ON CHILDREN

In 1984, Rutter and Quinton found that, over a four-year period, one-third of the children of consecutive new psychiatric patients showed a persistent disorder, one-third had transient difficulties and one-third did not show any emotional or behavioural problems. The most frequent problems presented by the children were behavioural problems. They found that psychiatric patients were twice as likely to be single parents with more separations and divorces, there was more marital discord and where there was a second parent they too had problems, frequently a personality disorder. They suggest that it was the psycho-social factors that increased the risk of damage to the children. The impact of parental mental illness has been known for many years and documented in increasing detail (Göpfert *et al.* 1996; Reder *et al.* 2000).

Barnes and Stein (2000) consider the effects of parental psychiatric illness on the development of the child. They suggest that the disorders in the children may resemble those of their parents but they are of the view that the children have a much broader range of problems; that is, there may be a genetic link but the environment plays a considerable part. The parental mental illness may directly impact on the child, as delusions, hallucinations, obsessions but much more frequently it is the parent's preoccupation and unavailability that are more damaging. Alongside the mental illness there are likely to be other difficulties, marital/relationship problems, housing and financial problems, or substance and alcohol abuse. Where a parent is depressed the impact on the development of the child may be even greater. Children of depressed parents have not only a three-fold greater risk of major depression but also a similar increased incidence of phobias, panic attacks, alcohol dependence and social problems. They also have an increase in behaviour problems and substance abuse.

A depressed parent is unavailable and preoccupied, and so the attachment needs and the emotional and psychological needs of the child are not met. The parent's warmth, sensitivity, capacity to be responsive and to establish reciprocity are lacking. Where a parent has an eating disorder, is very anxious or has a personality disorder, the impact on the child is particularly damaging, because of the parent's preoccupations, their distorted views of their own needs and the needs of the children, and their considerable relationship and social problems. This is both because of the parent's mental health problems and also because the difficulties may be less obvious to others. The children are more likely to be allowed and expected to remain without support.

SEEING THE CHILDREN AND RECOGNISING THEIR NEEDS

Given that there is a wealth of knowledge and awareness of the impact of parental mental health problems on children, there is a need to try to understand why it is, in reality, so difficult to 'see' the children.

The UN Convention on the rights of the child has been signed by all countries except the USA and Sudan. This spells out very clearly the physical and emotional needs of the child, what children should have as a reasonable expectation in terms of education—their social, cultural and religious environment. It also is very clear about the need for children to be seen and recognised as individuals with their own rights, yet children remain marginal in most thinking and planning unless they cause problems. A disruptive child in school, children stealing and vandalising the environment, teenage pregnancy, suicide and substance abuse all produce fear, rage and a need to blame by adults.

At an early age, children need an environment, in the family and the community, that meets their needs and values them as individuals with a right to have their own thoughts, their own feelings, their own dignity and self-respect. Separations of mother and child, disruptions such as frequent house moves, marital discord and violence with various partners, and financial difficulties, leave children vulnerable. Children have massive developmental tasks to undertake; they need containment—that is, a sense of an adult who understands, cares, is consistent and reliable and can tolerate the child's pain, rage, envy and destructiveness as well as the child's longing for love, warmth, affection and physical contact. The child needs an adult who can respond, putting the child's needs first ahead of his or her own and whose view of the world is based on reality with appropriate concern—an adult capable of fun, enjoyment, content with themselves most of the time. This may be unattainable but many parents can provide most of these most of the time, that is, they are good enough parents. And yet, in these families this is what is so often not available psychologically alongside the risk factors mentioned earlier. Children in these families are not seen, services are not joined up and health, in whatever country, has adult mental health and child and family mental health set up as separate services.

Social Services similarly divide the service provision between adults and children—called children and families, and adult mental health. This refusal to see children in their families in the community must be a means of avoiding engaging with vulnerability and pain. To make the needs and the problems manageable they need to be divided up—the links, the connections, the emotional repercussions and damage have to be unseen, perhaps because young children protest very little; and if, when older, they do indirectly protest, parents and teachers can be blamed.

Children need a secure, stable environment with their attachment needs met and their emotional and psychological development facilitated. Then they can develop the capacity to think, to learn, to make links to conceptualise. However, before this can happen the adults around need to be in a healthy mental state. Perhaps it is not only the mentally ill parent but society in general that has problems with this.

THE ICARUS PROJECT

As explained in Chapter 1, the research team wanted to see what could be learnt from systems across Europe using a standard vignette. It explores events in a family where a mother has a child by one father (Anna) and, over time, two further children (Thomas and then Jane) by her husband.

As indicated, 'seeing' children is a problem. They are physically smaller; they are more difficult to communicate with; and adults are much more at ease talking to adults. A child's way of showing distress can be seen as developmental delay or being difficult, such as wetting, soiling, failing to concentrate and work at school and withdrawing from social activity. Their time scale is also different; three months in the life of a young child is a very long experience, three months in the life of an adult is brief.

How did the professionals in the different countries see the children in this vignette? At the first stage the impact on Anna of the arrival of the new baby, the first child of this marriage, was mostly not considered. Anna's possible feelings of exclusion from this new family, and her mother and stepfather's preoccupation with their new baby, was not mentioned. No attention was given to the stepfather's relationship with Anna and what might be available within the family in terms of support for Anna, as is usual in families where mother is preoccupied with a second baby. There was concern for the baby and the need to maintain the mother–baby relationship and proximity. The impact on the baby of mother's bizarre beliefs went unremarked as did the impact on Anna of her mother's bizarre ideas and mother's hostility to Anna's stepfather.

Recognising a postnatal psychiatric episode should be in the minds of all those involved in postnatal care; the midwife perhaps should have realised that something was wrong (and in some countries this was the expectation). Where there was home visiting, the home care nurse, community doctor or other home-visiting professional who has expertise with babies, children and nursing mothers would also have been concerned. There was, however, potentially a gap between the end of postnatal obstetric care and the start of community maternal and child health care. In some countries there was no universal health-visiting service, which could leave the family quite isolated. The father seemed to be left unsupported and it was little remarked that his previous experience of pregnancy, birth and postnatal states might have been nil, as Thomas was his first child.

Child welfare services in the UK countries and Greece did not expect to be involved, the children were not seen. In contrast, in Germany and Sweden intensive family support would be offered. Anna was ignored except by the German group (where they were influenced by two participants who had personal experience of a mentally ill mother). In Norway and Sweden professionals were expected to evaluate the children's needs and perhaps in Denmark use their parent–infant psychotherapy service, but only the German group, from the start, offered Anna the opportunity to obtain help for herself in her own right.

At the second stage more concerns for Anna were raised. Since most of the concerns were raised by the school, intervention by the school psychological service was suggested (Denmark, Norway, Germany, England and Scotland). In many countries the school doctor or nurse might be involved. It was interesting that, in Scotland, there was a high expectation of the school medical service, while in England it was scarcely mentioned. However, the preoccupation of all countries was how to encourage mother to seek help for her daughter Anna. Except in the Scandinavian countries, it was felt that if mother did not recognise Anna's need, little could be done.

In Denmark, Norway and Sweden there is mandatory reporting of concerns for a child's welfare where abuse might be a possibility, thus the mother's refusal to seek help for Anna would prompt referral to another agency. Other countries depended on the school health service to provide links through the school doctor to the general practitioner, which worked well in France and Scotland.

Sweden and Germany again had intensive family support. UK countries had as a resource the possibility of a day nursery place for Thomas or family centre attendance. Anna's needs were now considered but in England the possibility of help was felt to be slight. In many countries (and particularly in England) child mental health services were felt to be swamped and unlikely to be able to offer help. The English professionals (and others) did consider the possibility of child sexual abuse of Anna by her stepfather. In England, this would have opened doors to services because it would have provided grounds for a child protection investigation, with the possibility of registration. Without registration, the family did not meet the criteria to be offered services beyond those mentioned above.

The indications were that Anna was becoming quite a troubled and disturbed child. We know from studies (Barnes and Stein 2000; Cleaver *et al.* 1999; Reder *et al.* 2000), that children of mental ill parents, of parents with personality disorder and in families with marital and financial problems are at high risk of developing disorders themselves. The problems may be genetically linked to those of their parents but are generally due to environmental factors. The mother at this stage of the vignette sounds depressed and pre-occupied, and it is questionable whether she is getting support from her husband. Her avoidance of help for Anna is evidence of her lack of awareness and her own anxiety and possible guilt. The place of her husband as the step-father of Anna and father of Thomas needs exploration. It is clear that Anna's needs are again largely ignored except in Germany, unless the alarm bell of possible sexual abuse is pressed. In Italy, her needs are acknowledged, but a direct response to them is deflected into a need to avoid labelling her as the 'ill' person, and an imperative to work with the whole family.

By Stage 3, Anna and Thomas are displaying behaviours that are cause for serious concern, and their mother is again expressing bizarre ideas. Father has been drinking, is irritable, and there are financial pressures; then he leaves home. It still seemed to be hard to see the children. In some countries (Sweden, Germany and Greece) there was a refusal to believe that the situation could have happened, although there was some acceptance that a family who moved house or a family from another culture could fall through the net. One of the Swedish professionals, who had worked in other countries, felt that it was very unlikely in Sweden, but quite possible in the other places where he had worked. In Greece, it was the strength of the wider family and community that was seen as preventing the escalation of the family's problems from going unnoticed.

Of course, it would be ideal if this were so, if generous state services or a strong community could prevent such a situation; but one must question this and wonder if denial is playing a part. To be so sure that there is no poor family, no refugee or displaced family, no rural or inner city family like this is hard to believe. Perhaps to realise the plight of some children was too painful and a belief in the state system or the strength of the community had to emerge.

Other countries hoped that this situation would not arise, but thought it might (Northern Ireland and Ireland). The remainder thought that Stage 3 was entirely possible. All the professionals in all the countries saw this as an emergency. Keeping the children and, if possible, the family together was seen as very important and now the father's importance was stressed, but there was still little thought about the individual children and their needs. Anna clearly is physically neglected and this was often attended to, but there is also her emotional and psychological neglect. Thomas is also physically neglected; he is displaying disruptive overactive behaviour and is violent— one wonders what he has witnessed or experienced. Emotionally, the children are neglected both by their parents and by the professionals.

A full mental health assessment was needed for the family, for Anna, Thomas and father as well as for the mother. It may be that Anna needs a specialist placement, day or residential, to help her. She needs good physical care, educational help and psychological help, and she may well be a trauma-tised child given her mother's state and the family situation. Thomas also was likely to need help in his own right. Family work and possibly family therapy would be needed. Family therapy had been suggested by the Italian professionals at Stage 2, although availability was a problem, but was not mentioned at Stage 3. The German professionals again took the children's needs more seriously than professionals in other countries.

Whether there was denial that the situation could ever arise, or blindness to the situation until it became a crisis, the end result for these children was that their distress was not properly acknowledged until the damage had become quite serious.

REFLECTIONS

We know that children of mentally ill parents, or parents with personality disorder, alcoholism and substance abuse are at risk. There is a wish to break the cycle of disturbance and yet so frequently it does not happen. One of the Italian participants was very clear about this:

> 'My main anxiety is to try to understand—and that's difficult—if these children are potentially likely to be carriers of the same sort of problems towards their own children. Therefore we must give them serious help now and not just patch it up and hope for the best in the future. … We must not give half-commitment as is often given if, for example, a professional follows a case for a year and then abandons the case.'

Some countries see the children as the future of the state and have very considerable services available, the Scandinavian countries in particular. The Scandinavian countries were able to back up their use of mandatory reporting with the offer of both practical and emotional support. Germany has a vast range of services available which are non-stigmatising and do not have mandatory reporting. They talked about the necessity of building trust so that the family could use services on a voluntary basis. At Stage 2, the social workers 'would have to go into the whole family and see what each of them needed. And they would have to try to motivate each and every one of them'. Greece sees the extended family as providing what is needed. Italy, and to a lesser extent France and Luxembourg, have services for children and families, and are aware of the individual children. The UK countries can do little, until florid child protection issues or adult mental health issues prevail.

The major facts of life, according to Money-Kyrle (1968), are that there is life and death, male and female, child and adult and we could add to this, sanity and madness. It is possible to envisage that society, and the individuals as represented by the professionals acting on behalf of the state, find these 'facts of life unbearable'.

In this case life and death are being played with; the mother could have committed suicide, or could have committed infanticide to 'protect' her babies. Father too was being self-destructive. Gender issues were an important factor in several discussions. What is expected by professionals, as agents of the state, of a vulnerable mother, or of a father and stepfather? Was it expected that Anna as the eldest child and as a female child, would become a young carer? Many 6- and 7-year-olds live in this way.

That there are adults who must take responsibility—either parents, or when they cannot, professionals—seems to be the major 'fact' struggled with here. Allowing children their childhood when perhaps the parents' and professionals' own childhoods were difficult and distressing makes it hard if not impossible to see the child's needs, pain and vulnerability. The adults, if present, are blinded by their own unmet or unresolved issues. Perhaps the view persists that 'After all, children are resilient and robust; we had to be'. When we add to this the fear of madness, the confusion of the mother's fluctuating mental state and the impact on the professionals, then the reluctance to see and intervene in this situation is more easily understood. Where services were fragmented, it was all too easy to see the problem as belonging elsewhere.

In those countries with considerable early input available, it was perhaps unbearable to see that this help was not enough or had not been targeted sufficiently. In those countries with little to offer at an early stage, services that have constantly to pick up the pieces have low expectations and feel undervalued. They see their task (perhaps correctly) as keeping demand down and offering the minimum possible, unless there is a situation that will cause a scandal. Understanding and communicating with children is painful, and recognising their need has huge implications. Early interventions for most families must be the better way, if it can be done without idealisation of what is possible. There also needs to be the possibility of good assessments for the various cases that do not respond to family support and early intervention. Good appropriate interventions need to follow these assessments when there are concerns, and resources need to be targeted. Interventions that only take place following emergency situations must inevitably only be hoping to reduce damage rather than prevent it. The long-term implications for children—the next generation of parents—can too easily be overlooked or ignored. What the project demonstrated was that each country could 'see' some pieces of the jigsaw, but not the whole. An integrated service model using the strengths of each system would provide a much better, perhaps good-enough, service for these children and families.

Chapter 13

Meeting Needs

If we try to consider now, in the light of all the information that has been gathered, what innovations and developments we have seen, we can then consider how some of these responses might be integrated into a European model of support for families with a mentally ill parent. The aim and hope would be that such a model could prevent or limit the likelihood of damage or abuse to any children with a mentally ill parent. This is not to imply that having a mentally ill parent will not trouble, distress or disadvantage a child; of course, it will, but services and attitudes could reduce the difficulties to a minimum.

Services that support families, support children. When there is a mentally ill parent, all or any of the other family members may need particular services, relevant to them in their role within the family. In this work, in order to concentrate attention on the children, we have looked at the services for the family as a whole, as well as the services specifically related to children. We have not looked at the mental health services except in relation to their response to Mary as a mother, and we have scarcely touched on the services and support that might be needed by John. It was very noticeable that there was little consideration given to John in any group. The exception to this was one of the Swedish groups, where the need to give John help in his own right was maintained throughout. It was foreseen in this group, that if John did not get support at Stage 1, there would be problems later. This prediction (they did not know how the scenario would develop) was borne out. The lack of consideration for John illustrated the difficulty for all the professionals in moving between support for the individual and support for the family. Support for any individual may be vital to the well-being of the family. This was clearly accepted in relation to the needs of the mother, but much less well acknowledged in relation to the father and the children. With a few exceptions, help for the father tended to be seen pragmatically as a means of keeping the show on the road at any given moment, rather than as a long-term strategy. Help for Anna was seen in terms of her own well-being, but helping Anna was potentially of benefit to her mother's mental health, and therefore to the family as a whole. It was never discussed in those terms. The situation is a little different with regard to the babies (Thomas at Stage 1, and Jane at Stage 3), where the needs of mother and infant were seen as one. But

Thomas's needs at Stage 2 were rarely recognised—it was his mother's need for help that was the stated rationale for intervention.

The services and structures that help the family affect the individual family members. Anything that helps the family as a whole may help individual members; but it may also confirm family patterns that help the family as a whole at the expense of individual members. Or, it is possible that help for individual members may confirm an unhelpful family pattern. This was feared by the Italian child welfare team, who argued against directing therapeutic intervention primarily towards Anna at Stage 2, as they feared that this would label her as the problem and enable Mary and John to avoid acknowledging their difficulties. These complex interactions between the individual, their family role and the family as a whole need to be kept in mind; they affect all the services described below.

THE NEEDS OF THE FAMILY

The people with the most intimate knowledge of what is needed are the parents and children. It was not possible in this project to work with service users, although we were able to review our findings with one mental health service users' association in the UK. However, a research and development project in Melbourne, Victoria, initiated by the Early Psychosis Research Centre of the University of Melbourne, worked with parents who had experienced psychotic disorders and collated their views on what services and forms of help were most necessary (Cowling 1999a). The research design included both a postal survey and a number of focus groups, and collated the parents' views on what was most needed by their children and what they themselves most needed as parents (Cowling 1999a: 40).

Children's needs identified by their parents
- Continuity of care and least disruption to home and school when parents are hospitalised.
- Explanations of events surrounding their parent's illness.
- Someone available for the child to learn to trust and talk to about fears, guilt, confusion.
- Programmes where children can meet with other children.

Parents' needs identified by parents
- Continuity of relationship with supportive worker.
- Reassurance about the quality of their parenting.
- Quality care for their children.
- Suitable place for children to visit parents in hospital.
- Parent support groups.
- Understanding of mental illness in the community, including their own families.

This information relates to only one of the countries in our project, but we argue that it can be generalised to the others. Recently published research by

Göpfert and Mahoney (2000), carried out with parents who were mental health service users in the Liverpool area, reached similar conclusions. Previous research into parents' experience of child welfare in three European countries indicated that there was a common core of experience for families seeking support; parents in all three countries valued the same aspects of helping services (Baistow and Hetherington 1998; Baistow and Wilford 2000). It is interesting that the needs identified by the parents in the Australian research are very similar to the objectives described by many of our professional teams, although the professionals tended to use different terminology and sometimes a different rationale.

The Children's Needs

Continuity of care and least disruption to home and school when parents are hospitalised

The children's needs, as described here by the parents, can be identified in the discussions of our participants. The need for continuity and security was a recurrent theme, and the provision of continuity and security was very dependent on resources. It was met, or attempts were made to meet this need, in a variety of ways, essentially by trying to maintain the family as a unit, or reconstitute it as a unit after Stage 3, when it was assumed by everyone that it had broken down. The most effective means of supporting the family (if the wider family could not be looked to) was either the use of a family support team such as the German SPFH or active intervention to mobilise the community network (Italy and Greece). If either of these interventions were possible, the child's need for continuity and lack of disruption could be met. An adjunct to this security would be the work done within the school to mobilise support, as was suggested in Scotland, and/or by a 'social teacher' in the school in Norway. If at Stage 3 it was not possible to maintain the family unit, the continuity that could be offered in foster care or in residential care in a small group home became important. Participants talked about the possibility of having a foster family that could remain available to the family as a respite care resource and take the children again if their mother had further illness. This was often thought not to be possible because of the shortage of fostering resources. In France, however, there was a specialist fostering agency which might have been able to offer this kind of flexible and consistent support. Another support that was available in France, which could help both to prevent family breakdown and to facilitate reintegration, was the *Centre d'accueil thérapeutique à temps partiel* (CATTP—centre for part-time therapeutic care), which offered part-time and flexible day care and treatment, with facilities for children to be looked after while their parent attended. This could be used in conjunction with foster care, or to help the father to look after the family. In Denmark, as the mother was in hospital, it would have been possible for the father to use the mother's entitlement to paid maternity leave, which might have enabled him, with support, to look after the children.

Explanations of events surrounding their parent's illness

This was less frequently identified as a need which required a specific
service, although it was often mentioned as one of the aspects of work with
Anna at Stage 1. In Germany this was specified as being one of the tasks of the
SPFH worker. In Norway such a service does exist and there is a designated
worker in the adult mental health team with responsibilities towards the
families of patients who are parents. There is a similar project in Sweden
(Skerfving 1999). This worker would expect to talk to the children about their
parent's hospitalisation and help them to understand what was happening.
In the French specialist fostering scheme, the foster parent would have had
training and support in undertaking this work with the children. In the countries which had an expectation that the children would receive therapeutic
help from the child mental health services, this would be one aspect of the
help that was offered (unless, as might have been the case in England, the
therapy was limited to behaviour therapy for soiling). In England, the family
centre, which was one source of help for Anna, would have been able to offer
an exploration of her anxieties through play therapy, but it would be less
likely that a worker in a child care setting would have the knowledge to be
able to respond effectively to her need for information. This lack of knowledge about mental illness was likely to be a problem for all the countries
which relied on family support workers based on child welfare services to
meet this need, unless special training had been provided for the workers.

*Someone available for the child to learn to trust and talk to about fears, guilt,
confusion*

The general need for support outlined here overlaps with the need for
someone to explain what happened, but it implies and requires a longer term
commitment. It could be met in a variety of ways. The family support worker
was frequently expected to undertake this work, though the amount of time
available for family support varied from several times a week for several
hours (German) to a few visits from a social work student (England). In
Scotland the possibility of involving the school in supplying this kind of
support was promoted, and in the Scandinavian countries also, the school
and the school medical services were important in this respect. More than
any of the other needs of the child, meeting this need depended on the
worker concerned having time to build up trust, to develop a relationship
and be able to sustain it, and be available if Mary's illness recurred. This work
need not necessarily be undertaken by a trained worker in an agency, but an
unqualified worker would need supervision and some training. In Norway
and Sweden the service of volunteers called 'contact persons', who work
with children and parents who need extra informal support (Andersson
1999), might be able to offer this kind of sustained long-term support. In Italy
it would be part of the task of the Mental Health Centre worker to use her
knowledge of the community and the networks of the *medico di base* to look
for such support in the neighbourhood. Similarly in Greece, the community

was the likely source of such support, although there the shortage of social workers was such that they envisaged this mobilising of the community resources being undertaken by the priest. Providing support of this kind for a child does not fit easily into agency boundaries; children will talk to whom they choose. Anna needs to get her support 'from who she gets on with best' (Germany), and may only be able to accept it from that person.

Programmes where children can meet with other children

This request is not limited to 'other children who have a mentally ill parent', but is a general request for help in getting a social life and peer group support for the child. However, the special groups for children with a mentally ill parent are an important way of meeting this need, particularly for some children who may for various reasons find a more general group difficult to handle. Groups for children with a mentally ill parent were being run in Sweden, Denmark, Germany and Australia. The Swedish groups are described by Skerfving (1999) and the Australia groups by Rimington *et al.* (1999). A targeted group which might be available in England was a carers' group, where the basis of the group's formation would be the experience of being the carer for a parent with a disability. Other groups which could be useful were mentioned, such as after-school clubs, which could support Anna, and the groups run by family centres. In France, if the family were offered an AEMO order (*Action Educatif en Milieu Ouvert*—a package of support for the family, either offered on a voluntary basis or backed by a judicial order), as was suggested by the French child welfare group, a range of supportive interventions would be possible, including evening and weekend groups for children. However, apart from the specialist groups, there were not many suggestions of ways of meeting the children's need for social and peer group support, or much awareness of this need.

The Parents' Needs

The parents' needs dovetail with the children's needs but are not identical. Some are about family support in general, some are about their particular needs as parents.

Continuity of relationship with supportive worker

This may be one of the hardest needs for some countries to meet. It implies a continuity of worker in post, as well as an agency acceptance of the continuing need of the parent for support now and possibly in the long-term future. It is not only demanding of resources in terms of time, but is emotionally demanding for the worker. Any country which emphasised crisis work and was loath to intervene was unlikely to be able to provide this support. Countries like Italy, where professionals tend to stay in the same post and/or countries which prioritised preventive work were more likely to be able to respond. Countries which went on the principle that Mary should work with 'whoever she got on with best' (Italy and Northern Ireland) were more likely to be able to meet the need for continuity, even if their resources were not good in other respects. All countries emphasised the importance of a supportive relationship in improving communication and enabling the family to make use of the available resources. Well-resourced countries, such as the Scandinavian countries, Germany and Luxembourg, were best able to provide the workers. France was well structured for providing long-term support because of responsibility of the generic *assistante sociale du secteur* for a specific geographical population, regardless of the nature of their problem.

Reassurance about the quality of their parenting

Meeting this need depended on trust. Reassurance is not meaningful unless it comes from someone who is trusted. In some countries, the participants talked a great deal about trust, the need to establish trust and the difficulty of working with the family if this could not be done. For the parents, the location of the worker who gave the reassurance was not important. But for the professionals, meeting this need could raise considerable problems as to who should do it and who was qualified to know about parenting. This kind of support over parenting skills was never specifically mentioned by our groups, and the lack draws attention to the focus that the groups maintained on Mary as a mentally ill mother rather than Mary as a parent. The groups were very aware of her need as a mother to bond with her children, and of the distress it would cause her to be parted from them. They did not explicitly show awareness of the need for either parent to be reassured in their parenting role, although the caution voiced in some groups about 'taking over' too much might be an indirect expression of this. The Italian child welfare group talked about the need for the parents to acknowledge responsibility, but did not mention any need for reassurance.

Quality care for their children

Parents who know that there may be times when they are not able to care for their children, who think that their wider family cannot help out and who cannot afford to buy in help, are totally dependent on what the state can provide, either directly or through non-governmental agencies. This is true for any parent with a disability, but where the disability is a mental illness, there is the additional problem that, at the point when help is most urgently needed, it may be particularly difficult for the parents to articulate their wants and anxieties. Child placement services in this country are mainly set up with child protection cases in mind. Respite care exists, but it is limited and often geared to routine rather than unpredictable situations, and to disabled children rather than disabled parents. In England, the public image of residential care is still of a service for either bad parents or bad children. Foster care is less stigmatised, but it can raise great anxiety in parents whose children are fostered; fears that on the one hand the foster carers will be unsympathetic or even abusive to the child and, on the other, that foster parents will be perfect and make their own parenting seem inadequate. Parents who may at times have to rely on state care services for their children need to be able to trust not only their worker but also the agency. Their children are most likely to get good care if there is a good range of resources, with the possibility of choice. It was generally felt that there were not enough foster placements, especially for a group of three children, and that residential care might be necessary. However, residential care varied from small family group homes in Scandinavia to large rather institutional homes in Greece. The service that seemed most likely to meet the parents' need for good quality care was the French specialist fostering agency. In Denmark there was the possibility that respite foster care could be available on a permanent basis. Otherwise it was likely to be a matter of chance whether foster or residential care was available, and for a group of three siblings there might well be a difficult choice between foster care in separate households or residential care together.

Suitable place for children to visit parents in hospital

This was mentioned by some participants as a problem, but did not receive much attention. Here again is a need experienced by the parents in their parenting role, but not in their patient role. The provision of somewhere to meet was being discussed in Norway, but there was no mention of this elsewhere. The provision of space within a hospital setting depends on the motivation of the hospital-based professionals, who are farthest removed from the experience of the family, and likely to be more preoccupied by the mother's illness than by her role as a well person. This seemed to be the least met need, but it is important because it may have a major influence on the ability of the family to maintain contact between the ill parent and the children.

Parent support groups

Parent support groups were set up in Sweden as part of the project referred to previously. There were also groups in Australia. In Germany there was a group for the (adult) relatives of people with a mental illness, which was suggested as a support group for John, but this would not necessarily have looked at the parenting aspects of the well partner's role. In England Newpin and Pippin would offer support for these parents, but were not mentioned by our participants.

Understanding of mental illness in the community, including their own families

The last of the needs listed by parents is the most difficult to meet. The problem of community responses and family responses to mentally ill parents was hardly mentioned in the groups, but seemed to be addressed to some extent in Italy by the Mental Health Centres. The role of the Centres was described as including a brief to work with the community to decrease stereotyping about mental illness. The participants in the Italian adult mental health service team described how, when their Centre was first set up, they had had to work hard to make contact with other agencies in the community, and reach out to engage the *medico di base*. This had led to improved co-operation and the possibility of joint work in finding community support for people with mental illness. In Norway training was being developed for workers in nursery schools to help them to respond constructively and sympathetically where a child had a mentally ill parent, and to help them to recognise when mental illness might explain difficult or bizarre parental behaviour.

THE AVAILABILITY OF SERVICES

Some of the services described above may be provided at local level, and distribution may be patchy. Services might exist in close proximity that were not known to our participants, so the above survey does not give a complete picture of services anywhere, even at a regional level. Some services will be part of, or an aspect of, regional or national provision. General levels of provision are more likely to reflect national or regional levels of resourcing and be more widespread, and the broader thrust of policy may be centrally determined. Thus, while specific services like groups for children can develop as local initiatives, levels of funding and staffing for mental health and child welfare services, which enable time to be spent with family members, are likely to reflect central policy decisions and regional or national priorities. These funding and staffing levels determine what local developments can be afforded and supported. Major policy decisions, such as the targeting of prevention rather than protection, or decisions about mandatory reporting, are likely to be national. All these levels are involved in meeting the needs identified by the parents. In England we know that local initiatives have been aimed at improving co-operation and liaison between services, such as those described in Weir and Douglas (1999) and Reder *et al.* (2000). If such developments are taking place elsewhere, it may be just chance that nothing of that nature was known by our participants to be going on in the three boroughs that took part in the project. However, it seemed unlikely that developments needing extra resources as well as local initiative, such as children's groups, were happening, except where children were identified as young carers and therefore benefiting from resources for carers. In England, central government policy promotes preventive work but effectively requires child protection and work with the most severely mentally ill to be prioritised; the English groups felt pessimistic about the existence of services that could offer support for these families.

APPROACHES AND SERVICES

As we mentioned in Chapter 2, the resources of the countries taking part in the project varied, and in some places imagination and ingenuity could compensate for the lack of services. On the whole, the better resourced countries provided a wider range of services, and came nearer to meeting the needs listed above. Even so, we could not be sure that these services existed all over the country. With that in mind, we summarise the targeted services in the Scandinavian and continental countries for comparison with England.

The Scandinavian Countries

In Scandinavia, considerable resources are directed towards services for children and families. There is an extensive parent/infant psychotherapy service and if the health visitor is concerned about the family, parents with a small child or a baby can receive help. If Anna and her mother, father and baby Thomas had had some help, problems could well have been avoided. So many young families use this service that it is not stigmatising in terms of child protection, but it does indicate there is a parent/child problem. Scandinavia has mandatory reporting not only of child abuse but of concern about possible abuse, so when Mary was reluctant to seek help when the school was worried about Anna, this would have been acted upon and deterioration might have been prevented. In general, in the Scandinavian countries there are high levels of family support services, although less in Denmark, and there seemed to be a good range of state care with small family group homes and fostering services.

In Denmark there is a hospital-based unit which provides a treatment and support service for severely mentally ill women with infants and small children, and runs a video home training programme.

In Norway, in Stavanger, there is an initiative, which involves a community education programme targeting the schools. Young people and parents with significant mental health problems are offered once weekly therapy for up to two years. So far, there has been a considerable reduction in problems. Norway and Sweden also have a person in the adult mental health team who is responsible for the children of any patients who are parents.[1]

The Continental Countries

France, like Scandinavia, sees the children as the shared responsibility of the state with the family; the children are the next generation of citizens. This

---

1 Recently published research by Ruppert and Bågedahl-Strindlund reports on a longitudinal study of 75 children born to parapartum mentally ill mothers in Stockholm. The children's mental and physical health, academic achievement and family situation were reviewed while they were school age (6–16). The researchers found 'no difference in mental or physical health or in school achievement' between the children of mentally ill mothers and the control group. They note that this finding contradicted the findings of other studies and suggest that the better outcome might be related to the strengths of the Swedish education and welfare systems in providing support for the child and family. (Ruppert, S. and Bågedahl-Strindlund, M. (2001) Children of parapartum mentally ill mothers: a follow-up study. *Psychopathology* 1(34): 174–178).

contrasts with the English-speaking countries where individualism is pre-eminent and children are seen as the responsibility of the parents and family, so that when problems occur, parents are blamed and the state only intervenes if there is risk or danger to the child (Cooper *et al.* 1995).

France has mandatory child abuse reporting for professionals, but there is a possible leeway in the use of discretion to explore a situation. *Ecoles maternelles* (day nurseries) are widespread, so that child care is in place and is non-stigmatising, which gives a high level of monitoring of children without being threatening. Services in France are generally aware of the needs of children and when there are concerns, families and professionals can try to work together to improve the situation. If the parents or the child or professionals are concerned and feel that little progress is being made, any of them can request the involvement of the children's judge. The judge can call on a team of professionals who can assess the situation. Frequently, the children's judge and the child and family can arrive at an acceptable decision. Children are rarely removed permanently from their families, but when problems arise there are specialist foster families that can take the children and work with the parents until the situation has improved. If Anna, or Anna and Thomas, could have had access to such a placement, it could have been very helpful for the children and relieved the pressure on the parents, and the father might not have needed to disappear. Since the parents know that most children return home, there is much less anxiety in France about children being fostered or placed in residential care.

Italy, too, has extensive community services and the *medico di base* is actively involved with families. Child mental health is a neuro-psychiatric service. It is hospital based, but there are a large number of psychodynamic therapists in the community, and services are very aware of the need for individuals, adults and children to have a place to share their distress, their thoughts, their feelings and to receive help. Perhaps if the father, in our case, as well as the mother and Anna, had had help early on, many problems would have been avoided.

In contrast Luxembourg had plenty of resources but they seemed so used to families having sufficient money to buy the help they need, that services for poorer immigrant families or workers were limited. Admission to psychiatric hospital, if needed, was easily available. The child mental health service of the main hospital had been set up in the last five years, and one of their aims was to develop their role in offering consultancy to other workers.

Germany has an extensive range of family support services which are available across the population and are non-stigmatising. It is expected that young parents with small children need help, support and some education. We all have to learn to be parents. The principle of subsidiarity promotes active seeking of resources and makes it easier to access resources. The 'help conference' is likely to be called to put in place helping resources at an early stage before there are issues of child protection. The insurance basis of the health service extends to psychotherapeutic services for children, which is an extra resource and source of alternative help.

Greece has little in the way of resources but does have extensive family networks and a strong church presence. Whether this community support would have helped this family when the problems persisted over so many years is not clear. The mother's first unmarried pregnancy, the father's unemployment, violence and drinking, and mother's paranoid ideas might have distanced them from church and community. There was, however, the expectation and assumption that the local community and the priest would have been very concerned and supportive, and that they would have helped the family for the sake of the children who were clearly suffering. Anna might have been taken to stay with relatives for periods and then Thomas, also in the hope that this relieved pressure on mother and gave the children a more settled experience of being parented.

England

In England, there is the Sure Start Programme, which has been set up to offer support to young families in very deprived areas. It is open to all families in an area but is targeted at disadvantaged families. Newpin and Pippin also offer services and support to parents with young children. However, most of the English-speaking countries do not have many services for new young families and have little to offer families with a mentally ill parent. If child protection concerns arise, however, the UK now has a good service for investigation and assessment, the Quality Protects programme. This builds on the child protection system, but widens the focus to include children and families in need. The definition of 'in need' would include families with a mentally ill parent. Assessments are expected to be offered if the problems and difficulties are serious, but the question must then arise of the extent to which help is available. Sadly, this will vary depending on each locality (another postcode lottery). In the research, all the English boroughs made an assessment of need at Stage 2, but they had very little to offer.

CHILD MENTAL HEALTH SERVICES IN THE PARTNER COUNTRIES

In all the countries, child mental health services were potentially involved, but the extent of their involvement varied greatly. What they could offer varied: some services were very limited with long waiting lists, and others were reluctant to be involved if there were child protection or adult mental health problems. However, where members of this service did become involved, it was often very helpful. Their strengths include communicating with and understanding children, knowledge of child welfare legislation and knowledge of the adult mental health system. This meant that concerns about children could be verbalised and the legal frameworks be considered as well as the mental state of the adults.

Mental health services for children, families and young people evolved during the last century. In the UK, the first child mental health clinic, the

Emmanuel Miller clinic in the East End of London, started in 1927. It was staffed by a child psychiatrist, a psychiatric social worker and a psychologist, and it followed the pattern set up in the USA. The staff were all health service employees and the service was community based, offering help to troubled children and families in the locality. The service spread across the UK, remaining principally in the community. The psychiatrist provided links with physical health and adult mental health, the mind–body interface. The social worker was more concerned with environmental issues and seeing the parents while the psychiatrist assessed and often treated the child. The psychologist was more concerned with cognitive function, assessing children and young people and offering cognitive treatments and links with the schools.

During the 1970s, the service changed dramatically. The psychiatrists linked with hospitals, and began to specialise in different problems, such as eating disorders, child protection, learning difficulties, autism, in-patient services and adolescent services. As the social workers were employed by the local authorities, social case work disappeared as a result of changed priorities. The psychologists had also specialised as well as conducting an increasing amount of research. New disciplines emerged—child and adolescent psychotherapists, family therapists, clinical nurse specialists, art, music, drama and educational therapists, adult psychotherapists and counsellors to see parents.

As the requirements of the employing agencies, health, education and social services became more specific, the service has become fragmented. The multidisciplinary team—where the totality of the child in the family, in the community, body, mind, emotions, cognition and social contact, could be considered—has become a multidisciplinary network, made up of individual professionals who come together to work on particular cases rather than regularly working together.

These services have evolved very differently across Europe. In Scandinavian countries there are extensive community services plus hospital-based academic centres and there are school psychological services. In France the service is in part hospital based, but there are community clinics which are medico-psycho-paediatric. In Greece and Italy the service is part of the health and mental health service so that links with adult psychiatry are very strong. In Greece most services are located in hospital settings. In Italy there are neuropsychiatrists for the family so there are links with adult mental health and neurology. In Germany there are hospital-based academic clinics, private clinics (paid for by health insurance) and school psychological services. In Germany, as in Italy, there are many therapists who take on individual work with children or adults, which in Germany is insurance funded and in Italy is state funded. Northern Ireland and Ireland have very limited services outside the main centres but the joint boards/trusts mean that they have better links between services.

THE NETHERLANDS

One country which we approached to take part in the research, decided against participating. This was the Netherlands, and when we heard about their services, as part of our exploratory work, we could see that they might well feel less need to undertake such a project. We describe their services here because they already have in place structures and services which are in advance of any of the countries that took part in the project. The information given below is not based on the same practice-based exploration as the information about other countries, but though partial, it is sufficient to demonstrate that the Netherlands has both structures and services that offer new approaches.

The starting point is the structure of community mental health services, the RIAGG (Regional Institute for Community Mental Health; see Munday 1994; Van Doorm 1994; Van Mierlo 1994, 1995). This is a regionally based out-patient service which includes adult, child and adolescent mental health. There are also hospital-based adult mental health services with day hospital facilities and hospital-based child mental health services offering psychotherapy and in-patient treatment. The structure is still being developed, and the plan is for the RIAGGs and the hospital services to be integrated, and in some places this is already happening. As in many other countries, there are problems over waiting lists. There is some friction between the RIAGGs and the psychiatric hospitals, and between the RIAGGs and the child protection and judicial systems. The systems of the Netherlands, in other words, face the same resources problems as other countries and the same problems of boundaries. However, the RIAGGs have 'prevention workers', who co-ordinate projects from different teams. The examples given of the areas covered were: adolescent depression, child abuse prevention (for example, training for teachers), and services for children with a mentally ill parent. Some years ago, the prevention workers began to initiate, encourage and co-ordinate projects for children with a mentally ill parent. From this the KOPP organisations developed (KOPP stands for *Kinderen, Ouders, Psychiatrische Patiënte—*Children, Parents, Psychiatric Patients). The KOPP project workers come together in the National KOPPs Platform which was started in 1990 by prevention workers. The National Platform aims to develop projects, promote research, provide a centre for publicity and documentation, raise awareness of the problems for these families and promote research and the dissemination of ideas.

At a meeting with members of the KOPPs Platform, the following services were described:

- A crisis intervention response. A mental health worker from the 24-hour emergency service goes to the home to see the children and give them information about their parent's illness and explain what is happening. The worker must be the same person who handled the initial crisis. Sometimes there will be a joint visit by the adult mental health worker and a child/youth care worker within the RIAGG team. If the patient is admitted to hospital, it may be a hospital social worker.
- Very intensive family treatment. This combines preventive work and treatment. Workers go into the home for 16–18 hours a week for a maximum of 9 months. Mental health nurses from child psychiatric hospitals, with further training in social pedagogy, staff this service, and they have intensive support. They work with multi-problem families with a child or

young person up to the age of 18. The service is offered on a voluntary basis, but if necessary they use the threat of referral to the judge for children for a compulsory placement in order to get the family to co-operate.

- One project, a mother and baby unit, works in collaboration with the general hospital to offer a service for depressed or psychotic mothers who are not able to establish bonds with their infant, using video home treatment. There is a three-month follow-up with home visits. If the mother is unable to respond, they work with the father.

- Groups are run for different ages of children. Schools and the RIAGGs are informed about the groups, and can apply for children to attend. The criteria are that a child lacks support, lacks attention, has difficulty in expressing his or her feelings, has low self-esteem, feels over-responsible or feels guilty and ashamed about his or her parent's mental illness. The long-term aim of the group is to decrease the likelihood of children developing mental health problems at a later stage. The immediate objective is to help the children to find ways of explaining things to their peers, to find strategies for dealing with bullying and to have the support of meeting other children in the same situation. The groups run for a course of 8 to 10 weekly meetings with a follow-up after three months. The families are often difficult to contact and the workers visit the parents before and after the groups. There are explanatory audio cassettes for Turkish and Moroccan parents.

WAYS FORWARD

A striking feature in all the countries was that child welfare professionals often did not recognise adult mental illness, and adult mental health workers often did not recognise or think about the children. There are both training and structural changes that could, without major expenditure, ensure that:

- all professionals realise the need to be aware of child issues, child protection concerns and indications of adult mental health problems;
- when professionals are involved with such families, there should be an expectation within the planning and assessment framework that irrespective of who their designated client may be, all the professionals involved with a family talk to each other, share their understanding and plan, taking into account the concerns of their colleagues;
- the family as a whole is informed about sources of help.

These families whose problems span the boundaries of systems need particular skills, including consultative skills, to ensure that the differing systems do not act independently, unaware of each other's concerns. The involvement of a member of the primary care team, GP, practice nurse or health visitor as a co-ordinator of services for the family has great potential. This person could take responsibility for talking to family members and all the professional systems involved. Where possible, child mental health services should be involved.

The universal service which, in most countries, is least included in planning for these families, is education. In Norway and in Scotland there were links between schools and other services through special teachers, through regular consultation between social workers and teachers or through the involvement of a school medical service. These were all helpful in providing Anna with support and in communicating to both health and social welfare services that the family had problems. Forty years ago, addressing the conference on mental illness in the family and its effect on the child referred to in the previous chapter, Tizard pointed to the valuable contribution that schools could make. 'In discussions of factors affecting the mental health of children, may I express the hope that consideration should be given to the role of the school as a major socialising and stabilising influence on the child. Teachers in ordinary schools do their best for children; but they do not have your [the conference members'] knowledge of the problems of mental health and they need your help' (Tizard 1966: 10). This does not seem to have happened. In the experience of our English participants (and in most other countries), schools did not appear to be included in co-ordination or support.

Of course, for all countries to have access to all the resources allocated in some countries by governments or funded in a range of other ways, would be greatly advantageous, particularly the family support services, and the mother and baby units where the mother and baby Thomas or baby Jane could have been admitted together. This may seem unrealistic, but these services should be the priorities as and when funds become available. However, they take considerable funding, and there are smaller, cheaper initiatives that might be possible when the more costly are out of reach. These smaller initiatives are harder to prioritise, and depend to a considerable extent on local resources and the enthusiasm of individuals, but because of this they may be more achievable.

Chapter 14

Conclusions

Comparative research is easily associated with ranking or league tables, and indeed there is much research which does compare different countries on quantitative measures such as child poverty, mortality rates, etc. The purpose of this research was not to rank countries or create league tables. Rather it was intended to allow participants to reflect on their own policy and practice in the light of new knowledge about how colleagues in different systems approached the same problems. Inevitably the result is self-critical. We believe this to be positive. Paradoxically we believe that self-criticism and reflection are positive aspects of the English professional culture. Although they can sometimes lead to exhaustion and despair they also offer the possibility of change and development.

When we therefore focus on some of the difficulties of the English system it is in order to try to identify the causes of these problems and to point to what we see as the possible ways forward. We will also identify the aspects of the English system which are strengths or potential strengths, and suggest developments that would optimise these strengths.

We started this research with two propositions. The first was that children with a mentally ill parent are likely to have problems, and child protection research has shown that these problems can be very serious, even life threatening. Therefore, even though some children may experience no difficulties, as a group these children require attention. It is not contentious to suggest that some children with a mentally ill parent have difficulties; it is more contentious to suggest, as we do, that attention should be paid to all these children. The second proposition was that failures in communication and co-operation are important components of the problem, which again is a statement that would be generally accepted. Our approach was to look at other countries to see what they do in these situations and, from an analysis of their views, to attempt to understand better what alternatives there might be, and what lay behind the particular problems of co-operation experienced in this country.

INTRINSIC PROBLEMS

We found many different structures operating within different cultures, and there was no set pattern. There were, however, two consistent problems shared by all countries. Firstly, the difficulty of continuously 'seeing' the child; and, secondly, the problems of co-ordinating services. These we considered to be intrinsic problems, latent in the situation of the family. As discussed in Chapter 12, the painful reality of the children's situation is hard for the professionals to tolerate. The effect of the unmet needs of the professionals is a continuing and unavoidable obstacle to keeping the children's needs in focus within the context of the complex needs of the family. At the same time, family life is not co-terminous with the boundaries of agencies, and the needs of a family where there is a mentally ill parent cross agency boundaries, no matter how services are organised. The structures of health and welfare will always have difficulty in responding to the complexities of the live situation.

Faced with these intrinsic difficulties, the research group identified certain factors, listed in Chapter 7, which facilitated a good outcome for the family. These represent different ways of responding to and trying to counter the intrinsic problems described above. The factors listed in Chapter 7 are:

- the development of a 'whole family' approach by all agencies, supported by consultative use of child and adolescent mental health services;
- the development of a better knowledge base for child welfare professionals about mental health and for mental health professionals about child development;
- the development of greater professional awareness of the needs of families with a mentally ill parent and the children in these families;
- the development of links between universal services (primary health care and schools) and specialist services;
- the development both of formal links and regular meetings between health and social work agencies and informal inter-agency contacts.

The first two factors listed above relate particularly to the problem of keeping the child or children in mind, while caring for the ill parent. In the discussion groups, the roles of the different family members were easily lost sight of in the struggle to respond practically and therapeutically to the needs of the ill person. The parent was lost in the patient while the children and the father became aspects of the patient's problem. While the German group, which included service users, was able to hold the children's needs in mind, it was difficult for other groups. The groups that were most effective in this respect were those that demonstrated a systemic family approach in their discussions. The development of a 'whole family' approach by all agencies, supported by consultative use of child and adolescent mental health services, appeared to be the most successful way of responding. We are not suggesting that all services should be run by family therapists, but that all services need to work with the concept of the family as a whole, a family group made up of individuals with specific roles which they need to maintain.

The services that have most experience of working with individuals in the context of their families, and of keeping in mind the concept of the family as a group, are the child and adolescent mental health services. The professionals in these services also hold knowledge of both mental illness and child welfare. It is not possible (in most countries) to offer an extensive assessment service for children in families where there is a mentally ill parent. But it could be possible to offer consultation to workers in other services; to teachers, social workers or health visitors worried about a child, or about the functioning of a parent and to mental health professionals uncertain about the capabilities of a family or a child's need for information.

Working with the whole family, in the context of parental mental illness, requires a shared knowledge base. In order for child welfare professionals to feel confident in working with a mentally ill parent they need some knowledge of mental illness. Mental health professionals who take seriously the needs of the family as a whole need to know about child development and the emotional and social needs of children. Both groups need to understand the ways in which the family functions as a system. They need a shared knowledge base as well as their specialist expertise. There are bound to be problems for workers in any specialisation in knowing about areas outside their specialism, and the extent to which workers in mental health knew about child welfare and vice versa varied considerably. But a broad knowledge of the other field was necessary for all workers and demonstrably facilitated their work.

The other facilitating factors relate primarily to the problems of inter-agency co-operation. In order to offer services to families that may prevent problems, or prevent problems from escalating, it is necessary to be aware of their needs. Raising professional awareness of the needs of these families is the first and most important step in enabling agencies to co-operate. Professionals in the mental health services working with adults who may be parents are at the front line of this work. We saw that services that identified the parents among their adult patients were more able to respond preventively. This consciousness raising is also important for the primary health care services. They are often the first professionals to know about the illness, and they may (and in this country probably will) know about the rest of the family. Child welfare services have a role in reminding their colleagues of the needs of the patient as a parent and of the perspective of the children.

It was clear that where there were good links between, for example, GPs and mental health services, or maternal and child health services and social services, this greatly facilitated their work. Communication was easier in Italy when the mental health centres and the *medico di base* were used to working together and could collaborate in their response to a patient. Issues of confidentiality were less of a problem when, as in France, social workers and health visitors were part of the same team with regular meetings. In Scotland it could be seen how the school could be an active and effective partner in supporting a family where there were good contacts between the school medical service and the GP, and where the social services had an established contact with the school.

There were various systems of formal multidisciplinary and multi-agency meetings in operation, and these were seen as generally helpful and necessary. However, their functionality differed. There is an important difference between 'network' meetings, where staff from different agencies meet to discuss a particular case, and regular meetings of professionals where a range of cases are discussed by the same group of people. Informal meetings and discussions provide another communication system; consultation meetings can be either case based or related to the wider system in which the cases are located. Meetings that were 'case based'—that is, meetings that were called specifically to ensure co-operation between agencies over a particular case— were seen by the participants as necessary. However they were not felt to have the same long-term value as regular case discussion meetings that were usually attended by the same people. These regular meetings enabled workers to get to know each other and learn about the resources of other agencies. They enabled informal consultation at an early stage before problems had reached the point where a 'case based' meeting would be called. The meeting of health and social service agencies in Italy was such a meeting. At a less formal level, potentially extremely productive regular meetings developed as a result of the final group meetings of the project, at which the mental health and child welfare groups met to hear the research findings. In several countries, these groups decided to continue to hold regular meetings. The aims of these groups have varied in scope and ambition, but the focus has been on co-operation, on raising the awareness of other services and on multidisciplinary training.

Informal contacts were singled out as being important, out of all proportion to their status. Countries where informal contact was easy saw this as a clear advantage; countries where it was difficult were very aware of their disadvantage. Informal contacts were seen as complementary to formal meetings. If you had met informally, it was easier to ring up a colleague to discuss a nagging anxiety which might not quite merit a formal meeting, or to acknowledge lack of expertise. This is well summarised by Campbell writing about inter-agency networks in this context.

> 'The examination ... of case planning and review meetings suggested that they were simply "icing on the cake" of a good working relationship and did virtually nothing to compensate for poor interagency work at worker level'. (Campbell 1999: 205)

To summarise, we found that there was a range of ways in which services could work within their existing structures that would facilitate a good outcome for these families. Structures were important in making certain ways of working easier or more difficult. Resources were important, but the way that resources were used, and the expectations of the workers as to what was and was not possible and appropriate were equally, if not more, important.

PROBLEMS THAT DERIVE FROM THE SYSTEM

As we have indicated, this research raises wide issues about the functioning of health and welfare systems. Although it was not the primary purpose of the research to centre the comparison of systems on England, we believe that it is nevertheless legitimate for us, as practitioners and academics working in England, to focus our conclusions on the English system. We unashamedly set out to look at other systems so that they could act as 'mirrors' to our system and would allow us to better understand the English system and think about ways forward. Of course, our colleagues in other countries had a similar opportunity to consider their own systems in the light of others', and several of them will be publishing details of their systems. In addition the research report (Hetherington *et al.* 2000) focused on the implications for Europe as a whole.

English-speaking countries were strikingly alike in many respects, and out of the five English-speaking countries, England and Australia were the most alike and the most protocol driven. They were slow to intervene, risk avoiding, behavioural in their treatment approaches and pessimistic. This approach was rationalised, characterised and exacerbated by shortages of resources. In England the lack of resources has to be particularly important seen in the wider context of the high poverty levels. In 2000, the UK had the highest percentage of children living in poor households in the EU (Micklewright and Stewart 2000), and presumably a greater need than other EU countries to provide family support.

Our participants came from particular locations within their various countries, and there were probably places in their countries where services were worse, as there are probably places within England where services were less stretched than in the boroughs where our participants worked. We are not concerned with whether the English system is better or worse than others, but with understanding why it functions as it does, in order for change to be possible. We are concerned to point out for the benefit of English practitioners, that the problems they see in operating the English system are real, that some of them are shared with practitioners elsewhere in Europe, but that some of them are not, and that change might be possible.

It is also important to be aware that the structures of the universal services of health, education and child welfare in this country have considerable strengths. The primary care service creates a potentially extremely effective base line. In a multidisciplinary primary care team, a wide range of knowledge can be available and there are well-established links between the universal and the specialist services. The Scottish discussions of the role of the school health service as a link between other parts of the health service, and of the connections being built between social services and the schools, demonstrated a network of care that linked the education service to specialist systems. The child protection system ensures that there are structures connecting social services, education, health and primary health care, even if only on the basis of individual cases at a stage of crisis.

Problems were, however, faced by the English workers that seemed to be specific to our system and seemed to stem from the structure of the system, or from the way in which the English system is expected to work.

The English participants could not engage with the family because they had no resources to offer until there was a crisis. It was not possible to offer the sustained and long-term support to the mother that might enable her to accept help, and there was no one who could spend time with her. It was not possible to offer help to the children if contact could not be established with their mother. The need to establish risk led to an emphasis on the possible abuse of the children rather than their emotional needs. Help for the father either in looking after a new-born child, or in supporting an anxious and fragile partner, was not a possibility.

The child and adolescent mental health services were too under-resourced to provide any help, and they were not referred to as a possible source of consultation. And yet, as Etchegoyen (2000: 267) points out,

> 'child psychiatrists are ideally placed to provide a specialist service because of their dual training in adult and child psychiatry and their expertise in child development, parenting, and child risk assessment. Moreover, child psychiatrists and their teams are used to considering wider family interactions.'

The English participants lacked knowledge of each other's specialisms. They were very aware of this; thus using what knowledge they had became difficult, almost dangerous. Mental health workers were afraid to get involved in family assessment, and child welfare workers felt that they were unable to contribute unless there were child protection issues. This reinforced the other barriers between services.

Lack of resources prevented co-operation between services, because until the third stage only one service was involved—*either* health *or* welfare, but not both. Stanley and Penhale (1999) studied families with a mentally ill parent and children on the child protection register. They found that in 9 out of 13 cases no mental health worker was involved, in spite of the social workers' anxieties about the effect of the mother's mental illness on her parenting. Where both services were involved there was regular contact. The responses of the English professionals demonstrate how this can happen; if one service feels that a situation does not reach the threshold criteria of the other service, connections do not get made.

For our English participants, agency boundaries were rigid and not to be crossed. Mental health workers were unwilling to have an opinion on the parenting capabilities of the ill parent and her partner, while the child and family service workers drew the line at suggesting the level of mental health problem the mother might have. Rigid boundaries also led to problems over access to resources. If the relevant resources were in the budget of children and families services, it was very difficult for mental health services to use them, and mental health services did not have control of services suitable for children and families.

Both mental health and child welfare services, but particularly child welfare services, worked in a highly managed environment. The workers in the children and families teams were very time conscious and very aware of the need to work to specific timetables of assessment, to assess situations under specified headings and to follow the correct procedures. They had very little flexibility, and no time for informal contacts or meetings that were not strictly focused and urgent. This was less apparent in the mental health groups, but they were caught up in the same process when they needed to work together.

The sub-text was a shared uncertainty, particularly for the child welfare workers, over intervention in families. It was not only that the family was expected to cope without intervention because of a shortage of services. The family was not seen as *wanting* help. It was not expected that offers of help would be readily accepted, and intervention was not seen as a positive offer, but as a rather poor substitute for intra-familial support. The alternative of intervention in the community to develop support there was not discussed.

These difficulties are interconnected; rigid agency boundaries are not helped by a high level of specialisation, and may in turn contribute to the development of specialisation. A lack of confidence in offering help contributes to an emphasis on risk as the legitimate reason for intervention, which focuses attention on danger of abuse rather than distress. In the discussions of the English participants we saw these aspects of the structures contextualised by a pervasive pessimism about the ability of the system to help children and families. This was accompanied by an inability to command the resources necessary for preventive work, and thus the promotion of risk avoidance was the only realistic response.

We are not the first to identify the problems outlined above. The report on the Sieff Foundation Conference held in 1997, *Keeping Children in Mind*, referred to the need for everyone to 'think family' (p. 6) and for the need for services to be 'assertive and persistent in offering help' (p. 15). 'Boundaries are necessary, but they should be "soft" with the degrees of softening set at ministerial level' (p. 47). Training needs are identified by all researchers in this field. Since the Sieff Conference, several authors including Falkov (1998), Cleaver *et al.* (1999), Weir and Douglas (1999) and Reder *et al.* (2000) have pointed to the need for the same changes. We agree with the findings of a recent survey of 105 local authorities (Kearney *et al.* 2000) which recommends, *inter alia*, a review of training, inter-agency protocols, changes in commissioning arrangements and increased resources. In particular we agree with their recommendation that 'Child care training should include working with the family group as part of the curriculum for practitioners and first line managers...' (p. 53). However, these recommendations are all based on the current system being maintained, and we are sceptical that changes at the margins such as these will have the necessary effects on practice. The problem lies not in identifying changes that need to be made but in making them.

None of this is particularly controversial. After all most current training and policy would be aimed at instilling holistic thinking, child-focused practice and prevention. Yet there is no evidence to demonstrate that families involved with social services departments feel any more empowered or participatory. This means that there must be some driving force within our system which is so deeply ingrained that it forces practitioners to be defensive, crisis driven and to focus on the individual. The following discussion attempts to uncover some of these forces and to identify possible countervailing forces that could be used to improve the lives of families.

Reith (1998: 200), writing about mental health enquiries, considers the intractable problem of inter-agency co-operation:

> '... repeatedly liaison and interagency working are found to be less than satisfactory. This must lead us to question what inhibits the process. The frequency and complexity of the problem suggest there is no simple solution.'

The aim of using comparison is to try to understand more about the complexity of the problems and why the English professionals experienced them as they did.

APPLYING A COMPARATIVE ANALYSIS

In the introduction to Part I of this book, we discussed the complexity of learning from comparison, the circularity of the process, the experience of finding that there are many factors involved in the way that things work, and that functioning is multi-determined. In Part II and Part III we looked at some of the themes that we consider to be involved in the interplay between structures, culture, ideology and functioning. We considered in particular the relationship between the family and the state, the place of risk in state interventions and the ways in which the structures of services affect the delivery of services.

The methodology employed in the project was originally designed to enable a realistic account of the functioning of the child welfare system of another country. It soon became apparent that there were wider implications. Learning about the functioning of different child welfare systems and hearing the reflections of practitioners on their own systems compared to others led us to question why workers holding similar views and using similar theories should act differently. When we tried to disentangle the strands that determined their actions, it was clear that no one single factor was responsible. It could not be said that resources, laws, procedures or administrative structures could be held solely accountable for how things worked out in practice. Asking why this was so—why, for example, the law seemed at one point highly influential and at another point, fairly irrelevant—led to a consideration of the expectations that all concerned in child welfare might have about the system which they, as professionals, families, citizens and policy-makers, experienced. There was a chain that led from our first questions—what do you do, why do you do it—at ground level, to considerations at a very generalised and abstract level about the nature of the relationship between the state, the citizen and the family. There is an interplay between what people expect of their state, and what people think that their state expects of them. These expectations include a subjective, personal opinion—what I think the state should do—and a response which may be partly born of actual experience but which includes projections of internal responses to authority—what I imagine the state expects of me. Such expectations affect the professionals who deliver child welfare services and the policy-makers who design them just as much as the families who use them. They are determining factors in the actual ground level operation of child welfare services, affecting choices about the focus of resources, the implementation of laws and the organisation of administrative structures.

Thus the sub-text of a great deal of English social strategy is an unwillingness to intervene in the affairs of the citizen, and that includes the citizen as parent. It is very easy to evoke cries of 'the nanny state', always used as a pejorative phrase. In Chapter 9, different ways of regarding the state relationship to welfare services and citizenship were considered in the light of the research data. England (and the other English-speaking countries) appeared to be relatively antagonistic to state intervention and focused on the rights of the individual, in a way that frequently ran counter to the ideologies of professionals in health and welfare services. The workers were caught between theories of welfare that rested on the value of intervention and a culture that prioritised independence and was against intervention. Trying to 'rebalance' or 'integrate' family support and child protection essentially requires the reintroduction of prevention as a major policy aim, and the acceptance of early, preventive intervention. At present, this goes against the grain of the wider neo-liberal political philosophy of individualism and individual responsibility. In this context, promoting family support by changing laws, introducing new procedures or exhorting the professionals is unlikely to be effective.

This is the background against which change has to take place. Chapter 10, on risk, developed certain aspects of this theme. Early intervention is a necessary facet of preventive work, so the prioritisation of independence and self-help discourages the development of prevention. The identification and avoidance of risk becomes increasingly necessary, and the monitoring not only of families but also of workers becomes important. Resources then have to be diverted to monitoring and to the treatment of acute situations. Services develop in response to this, their expertise has to be targeted on the most dangerous situations and on assessment of risk. Managerial systems develop to ensure a quick response to dangerous situations, which strains resources in other respects.

Chapter 11 considers agency structures and their relationship to functioning as demonstrated in the responses of the professionals. The English (and English-speaking) experiences outlined there reflect the situation described in the previous paragraph, of the development of a culture of managerialism, and the effect this has on efforts to work constructively with other services. The divide at the top of the system between health and social welfare seemed to be important in institutionalising a rift between the services. This is in contrast to Ireland and Northern Ireland, where the joint Health and Social Welfare boards or trusts seem to facilitate co-operation. The moves to integrate heath and social services currently being developed in Hertfordshire and Camden are therefore encouraging. However, the development of specialisation may be just as much of a problem. Specialisation is encouraged by a focus on the 'heavy end' of problems, both in mental health and child welfare. It reinforces the separation between agencies that follows from the structural divide between health and welfare. Other countries have this divide, but do not have the same degree of specialisation, particularly in the social work field. Thus in France, where there is a similar split between a national mental health service and a local social service, the generic social worker who has a responsibility for all service users helps to connect the different agencies.

The culture of non-intervention that is the background to the functioning of health and welfare services in this country has many implications for responses to the needs of children. Our level of intervention in support of children is demonstrated in this case situation to be low in comparison to other European countries. If we had chosen a case scenario which focused on services for families where a child was proved to have suffered abuse, the picture might have been different; but because our case scenario focused on prevention, it showed the least well-resourced aspect of English services. A choice always has to be made about where to concentrate resources. The allocation of resources reflects priorities and judgements about where intervention is useful. The allocation of resources in this country suggests that there is a lack of confidence in prevention. It also reflects an expectation that the family should provide and that state intervention is not effective. Anna needs 'a good granny' and there is no suggestion that an alternative or supplementary formal provision might be helpful. Paradoxically, on the one hand there is pressure not to intervene in the family, and a high expectation of the ability of the family to cope, while, on the other hand, concentration on the individual, on risk and an unwillingness to intervene preventively make it extremely difficult to 'think family'. We expect a great deal of the family but at the same time we have a weak conceptualisation of the family as an entity.

Changes in thinking are necessary to enable operational changes to take place. If the problems we have outlined derive from assumptions about the undesirability of state intervention, change will depend on the development of a public consensus about the validity of state intervention to support the well-being of citizens. For state intervention to be valid, there needs to be confidence that professionals will act in the best interests of the public. This would provide a basis for prioritising prevention and early intervention rather than crisis intervention, and developing trust between users and professionals, and between professionals. It would facilitate the development of holistic thinking about families without losing sight of the child.

CONCLUSIONS

It is common ground in all social science research, and especially in qualitative research, that the views and beliefs of the researchers affect their findings. On a subject as value-laden as child welfare and the role of the state, our views are certain to be implicated in every aspect of the research process, starting from the methodology chosen, and culminating in the conclusions that we reach. It seems appropriate for us to state the philosophy on which our work and our conclusions are based, even at the risk of having our conclusions dismissed by those who do not share our views. Our responses to the comparative data we have collected are based, firstly, on the belief that the relationship between citizens and the state is such that citizens in difficulties have a right to turn to the state for help. Rights imply reciprocal responsibilities, so the citizen has responsibilities to the state; one of which is the responsibility to ask for help when help is needed. Rights are meaningless unless someone has a duty to respond to the right, so the state has a duty to offer help, and the delivery of state services should reflect this. Secondly, that the humanitarian and economic effects of social intervention are interdependent and cannot be separated. The state therefore has to be prepared to offer and value services focused on prevention that may appear to have a low economic return.

We think that in order to provide a basis for the improvements in functioning that are described earlier in this chapter, fundamental changes are needed. Yet in one country or another we could find examples of all these ways of functioning—they are not impossible, they are not even unusual. Nevertheless we would not want to be simplistic about this. Some changes and innovations are in principle relatively easy to institute, given the will and the resources. Other changes need fundamental shifts in managerial, professional and even national culture. Obviously this type of change is complex and requires much more substantial effort, with less chance of success. We are sceptical of 'checklist' policy just as we are sceptical of 'checklist' practice. In particular the development of trust and the belief in the value of social interventions are simply not amenable to quick-fix solutions. All these innovations will require action and changes in culture in several different domains—government, the professions and the population as a whole.

However, in saying this we do not despair of change. We are aware that, historically, there have indeed been massive and fast-moving changes in service delivery in England. In particular we are reminded of the change from professionalism to managerialism in the delivery and management of services in the UK. Although it had antecedents in the 1970s, this change took place over less than five years in the early 1980s, and permeated every facet of welfare and health intervention, in all the domains mentioned above. This change has led to a paradigm shift not only in the management of services, but even more importantly in the way practitioners think about their work. The changes have been described elsewhere (Exworthy and Halford 1999) but the important thing for our argument is that if these changes could occur in a direction with which we are uncomfortable, it may also be possible to establish change to facilitate the kind of values we are advocating. It is, however, important to go beyond the usual change agents of more training, research and policy developments.

Using comparison to try to understand the underlying rationale for the way our systems function has led us to look at the expectations concerning state intervention that are powerful determinants of practice. It is unlikely, we would say impossible, that practitioners can effect changes unless wider changes happen that can give an impetus to the developments that practitioners would desire. For example, changes in the specialist teaching on social work courses will not take place until the validation requirements of social work training courses change. The validation requirements will not change unless there is a central decision that a more generic curriculum is required. The researches that we have referred to earlier in this chapter, that urge changes in the way that we work with families with a mentally ill parent, are practice based, with input from both child and adult mental health, from primary care and from social work. The child guidance inter-clinic conference of 1966, addressed by Professor Tizard, was practice based. Our comparative researches have been practice based. There is a high level of agreement between the suggestions for change from all these sources. But the changes will not take place unless they are directed from the top and are part of a will to change the individualistic thrust of English welfare politics of the past 20 years. It may be that this is now beginning to happen, and the development of policies such as Sure Start and the Children and Young People's Unit give some grounds for optimism, but there is inconsistency between these initiatives and the wider emphasis on self-help and individual responsibility.

Practitioners can do a certain amount to make changes, as recent publications demonstrate. Weir and Douglas (1999) and Reder *et al.* (2000) have brought together information about projects that describe interesting and imaginative responses to the present situation, but the framework that would enable this work to be generalised is still lacking. Whether in the mental health field or the child welfare field, while the assessment of risk drives responses, and crisis is the normal point of intervention, a preventive service that would offer support to the families with whom we are concerned is a long way off. The welfare experience of families with a mentally ill parent provides a specific example demonstrating how English families in need of help can suffer from our reluctance to intervene and our fear of 'interfering'.

In comparing England with other countries, we saw English practitioners as informed by a similar ideology to their colleagues in other European countries and motivated by the same concerns. We saw them struggling with a situation which made it extremely difficult for them to carry out their work as they thought it should be carried out. They knew that they wanted change, but they felt powerless to achieve it. Both in mental health and child welfare, over the last quarter of the twentieth century, professionals have absorbed and adapted to substantial legislative, cultural, social and economic changes. They responded to directions from the centre, and showed themselves able to learn to work differently, even when this conflicted with some aspects of their professional ideology. The ideology of professionals would readily support a shift to preventive interventions if the framework of policy and the targeting of resources also supported this shift.

Other countries struggle with their own versions of the problems set out in the case vignette. One of our participants stated the situation in terms that were true for all of us.

> 'This case description gives a picture of a community that does not see the human being as having any worth. ... We should see from this story what we need to do in order not to have to deal with such a situation. It is not about how we should solve this particular problem. It is to see what we can do in order not to arrive at *having* such problems. Living in a community such as Greece, what can we suggest to this state, this government, *any* government, so that there are no longer cases such as John and Mary's.'

Professionals in the child health and child welfare services know what goes on at ground level, but the application of this knowledge in the development of policy continues to be problematic. The authors share the ambition of our Greek colleague in looking to contribute to a more general solution of the problem through an exploration of the links and connections between the experience of the individual family and the development of state responses to the needs of children.

Appendix

The Professions Represented in the Discussion Groups

Country	Adult mental health teams	Child welfare teams
Australia	Psychiatry, general medical practice, nursing, occupational therapy, social work, psychology, support work (music therapy)	Social work, child psychiatric nursing, psychology
Denmark	Psychiatry, social work, nursing, psychology	Child psychiatry, child psychiatric nursing, social work, psychology, social welfare medicine
France	Psychiatry, service management, nursing, social work	Midwifery, health visiting, paediatrics, child psychiatry, psychology, social work, family work (qualified)
Germany	Psychiatry, psychology, social work, service user	Social work, social pedagogy, child psychiatry, service user
Greece	Psychiatry, nursing	Social work, health visiting, child psychiatry
Ireland	Nursing, psychiatry, occupational therapy, social work	Social work, health visiting, paediatrics, child care
Italy	Occupational therapy, nursing, psychiatry, social work	Nursing, social work, child care, paediatrics
Luxembourg	Psychology, nursing, psychiatric nursing, social work	Child psychiatry, psychology, social work, child psychotherapy
Norway	Psychology, social work, general medicine, psychiatric nursing	Social work, psychology, health visiting, child psychiatry, student counselling
Sweden	Social work, psychiatry, nursing, psychology	Social work, family therapy, psychology

continued overleaf

The Professions Represented in the Discussion Groups (*continued*)

Country	Adult mental health teams	Child welfare teams
UK: England	Nursing, occupational therapy, social work, psychiatry	Social work, family work (unqualified)
N. Ireland	Nursing, psychiatry, social work, management	Social work, health visiting, nursing (child protection)
Scotland	Nursing, occupational therapy, psychology, psychiatry, social work	Paediatrics, health visiting, child psychiatry, educational psychology, educational development advice, social work

CHILD AND ADOLESCENT MENTAL HEALTH GROUPS

Ireland	Child psychiatry, social work
England	Child psychiatry, psychotherapy, social work, psychology, specialist teaching

GLOSSARY AND INDEX OF ACRONYMS

GLOSSARY

Accompagnement éducatif   Programme of home support (France).

Action Educatif en Milieu Ouvert   Order for support and supervision while a child remains within the family (France).

Aide Sociale à l'Enfance   Local authority specialist child and families service (France).

Animatori   Social worker (Italy).

Assistante sociale   Generically trained social worker (France and Luxembourg).

Assistante sociale du secteur   Generically trained social worker working for the local authority on a patch basis (France).

Assistenti sociali   Generically trained social worker (Italy).

Association Luxembourgeoise de Prévention des Sévices aux Enfants   The Luxembourg Association for the Prevention of Child Abuse.

Azienda per i Servizi Sanitari   Regional health service (Italy).

Centre d'Accueil Thérapeutique à Temps Partiel   Mental health out-patient treatment and support service (France).

Centre Hospitalier de Luxembourg   The central hospital in Luxembourg.

Centre-Medico-Psycho-Pédagogique   Child and family guidance clinic (France).

Centre-Medico-Sociale   Centre providing a general social work service and school medical and child health consultations (Luxembourg).

Centro di Salute Mentale   Mental health centre (Italy).

Circonscription d'Interventions Sanitaires et Sociales   Local authority multi-disciplinary team including the PMI, ASE and the generic social service (France).

Commission Départementale de l'Hospitalisation Psychiatrique   Local authority commission which hears appeals against compulsory admission to hospital (France).

Commission de Surveillance   Independent commission which is informed of orders for compulsory hospital admission and reviews them (Luxembourg).

Consultorio Familiare   Multidisciplinary health and social work team for maternal and child health and family support (Italy).

Distretto Sanitario   District health services (Italy).

Educateur Spécialisé   Social worker with training in residential and home-based family treatment (France).

Educatori   Social worker (Italy).

Erziehungskonferenz   'Help conference', meeting between workers in relevant agencies and the family to plan supportive intervention (Germany).

Giudice Tutelare   Judge in the guardianship court (Italy).

Gardai   Police (Ireland).

Hospitalisation du Demande d'un Tiers   Compulsory hospital admission on health grounds (France).

Hospitalisation d'Office   Compulsory hospital admission on public order grounds (France).

Jugendamt   Child and youth social services (Germany).

Kinderjugendhilfegesetz 1990   Children and Youth Service Act 1990 (Germany).

Kinderen, Ouders, Psychiatrisches Patiënte   Support programme for families with a mentally ill parent (Netherlands).

Land   Regional local government unit (Germany).

Médecin traitant   General practitioner (France).

Medico di base   General practitioner (Italy).

Mütterberatung   Maternal and child health service (voluntary organisation, Germany)

NeuroPsichiatria Infantile   Child mental health service (Italy).

Projet d'Action en Milieu Ouvert   Programme for support and supervision while a child remains within the family (Luxembourg).

Protection Maternelle et Infantile   Maternal and child health service (France).

Psichiatria Democratica   The Italian movement for the ending of large psychiatric hospitals and the introduction of care in the community for mentally ill patients.

Pouponnière   Residential nursery (France).

Puéricultrice   Maternal and child health nurse, health visitor (France).

Seelenot   Local organisation for children with a mentally ill parent (Germany).

Service Central d'Assistance Sociale   A child and family social work service undertaking assessments for the court and working with children on supervision orders (Luxembourg).

Service de Guidance de l'Enfance   Child and family guidance clinic (Luxembourg).

Service des tutelles   Service run by the welfare benefits offices for budgetary and financial support and supervision (France).

Service de Psychologie et d'Orientation Scolaire   School psychological service (Luxembourg).

Servizio Sociale di Base   Local authority social services department (Italy).

SozialPädagogische Familienhilfe   Intensive family support service (Germany).

SozialPsychiatrische Dienst   Local authority community mental health service (Germany).

Trattamento Sanitario Obbligatori   Compulsory hospitalisation order (Italy).

Tribunal de Grands Instances   High court (France).

Tribunal de la Jeunesse   Children's court (Luxembourg).

Wirtschaft- und Ordnungsamt   Local authority office which makes applications for compulsory hospital admission (Germany).

INDEX OF ACRONYMS

AEMO	*Action Educatif en Milieu Ouvert*
ALUPSE	*Association Luxembourgeoise de Prévention des Sévices aux Enfants*
ASE	*Aide Sociale à l'Enfance*
ASS	*Azienda per i Servizi Sanitari*
ASW	Approved Social Worker
EU	European Union
BVC	Child health care unit (Sweden)
CAMH	Child and Adolescent Mental Health (UK)
CAT	Crisis and Assessment Team (Australia)
CATTP	*Centre d'Accueil Thérapeutique á Temps Partiel*
CCSWS	Centre for Comparative Social Work Studies
CF	*Consultorio Familiare*
CISS	*Circonscription d'Interventions Sanitaires et Sociales*
CMHT	Community Mental Health Team (UK)
CMPP	*Centre-Medico-Psycho-Pédagogique*
CMS	*Centre-Medico-Sociale*
CPA	Child protection agency (Norway)
CSM	*Centro di Salute Mentale*
CSWB	County Social Welfare Board (Norway)
DoH	Department of Health (UK)
DPS	District Psychiatric Centre (Norway)
GP	General Practitioner
HDT	*Hospitalisation du Demande d'un Tiers*
HO	*Hospitalisation d'Office*
KJHG	*Kinderjugendhilfegesetz 1990*
KOPP	*Kinderen, Ouders, Psychiatrisches Patiënte*
MHO	Mental Health Officer (Scotland)
MST	Mobile Support and Treatment team (Australia)
NACRO	National Association for the Care and Resettlement of Offenders
NGO	Non-governmental Organisation
NPI	*NeuroPsichiatria Infantile*
NSPCC	National Society for the Prevention of Cruelty to Children
OPCS	Office of Population and Censuses and Surveys
PAMO	*Projet d'Action en Milieu Ouvert*
PMI	*Protection Maternelle et Infantile*
RIAGG	Regional Community Mental Health Service (Netherlands)
SCAS	*Service Central d'Assistance Sociale*
SPD	*SozialPsychiatrische Dienst*
SPFH	*SozialPädagogische Familienhilfe*
SPOS	*Service de Psychologie et d'Orientation Scolaire*
SSB	*Servizio Sociale di Base*
TSO	*Trattamento Sanitario Obbligatori*

REFERENCES

Abatzoglou, G., Athanassopoulou, E., Kamalakidou, S., Eleftheriou, E. & Zilikis, N. (2000) A network of psychiatric and social services for children: an account from Greece. *Social Work in Europe* **7** (3): 50–52.

Abosh, B. & Collins, A. (eds) (1996) *Mental Illness in the Family – Issues and Trends.* University of Toronto Press, Toronto.

Adamec, C. (1996) *How to Live with a Mentally Ill Person.* John Wiley, Chichester.

Alaszewski, A., Harrison, L. & Manthorpe, J. (1998) *Risk, Health and Welfare.* Open University Press, Buckingham.

Andersson, G. (1999) Involving key stakeholders in evaluations: a Swedish perspective. *Social Work in Europe* **6** (1): 1–7.

Anttonen, A. & Sipilä, J. (1996) European social care services: is it possible to identify models? *Journal of European Social Policy* **6**: 87–100.

Assimopoulos, H. (1998) 'Reform', developments and prevailing trends in mental health care in Greece. *Social Work in Europe* **5** (1): 41–48.

Atkinson, P. (1992) *Understanding Ethnographic Texts.* Sage, London.

Baistow, K. (2000) Cross-national research: what can we learn from inter-country comparisons? *Social Work in Europe* **7** (3): 8–13.

Baistow, K. & Hetherington, R. (1998) Parents' views of child welfare interventions: an Anglo-French comparison. *Children and Society* **12**: 124–133.

Baistow, K. & Wilford, G. (2000) Helping parents, protecting children: ideas from Germany. *Children and Society* **14**: 343–354.

Barankin, T. & Greenberg, M. (1996) The impact of parental affective disorders on families. In Abosh, B. & Collins, A. (eds) *Mental Illness in the Family – Issues and Trends.* University of Toronto Press, Toronto.

Barnes, J. & Stein, A. (2000). The effects of psychiatric and physical illness on child development. In Gelder, M.G., Lopes-Ibor, J.J. & Andreasen, N.C. (eds) *The New Oxford Textbook of Psychiatry.* Oxford University Press, Oxford.

Bateson, G. (1979) *Mind and Nature, a Necessary Unity.* Wildwood House, London.

Beck, U. (1992) *Risk Society: Towards a New Modernity.* Sage, London.

Bering Pruzan, V.L. (1997) Denmark: voluntary placements as a family support. In Gilbert, N. (ed.) *Combatting Child Abuse: International Perspectives and Trends.* Oxford University Press, Oxford.

Bernard, J. & Douglas, A. (1999) The size of the task facing professional agencies. In Weir, A. & Douglas, A. (eds) *Child Protection and Adult Mental Health. Conflict of Interest?* Butterworth-Heinemann, Oxford.

Bouamama, S. (1995) The paradox of the European social and political ties: 'nationalism' citizenship and identity ambiguity. In Martiniello, M. (ed.) *Migration, Citizenship and Ethno-National Identities in the European Union.* Avebury, Aldershot.

Bowlby, J. (1969) *Attachment and Loss, Vol. 1: Attachment.* Hogarth, London.

Bowlby, J. (1973) *Attachment and Loss, Vol. 2: Separation.* Hogarth, London.

Bradshaw, J., Ditch, J., Holmes, H. & Whiteford, P. (1993) *Support for Children: A Comparison of Arrangements in Fifteen Countries.* HMSO, London.

Butler, I. & Shaw, I. (eds) (1996) *A Case of Neglect? Children's Experience and the Sociology of Childhood.* Avebury, London.

Campbell, L. (1999) Collaboration: building interagency networks for practice partnerships. In Cowling, V. (ed.) *Children of Parents with Mental Illness.* The Australian Council for Educational Research Ltd, Melbourne.

Capek, K. (1937) *The War with the Newts.* Reprinted 1998, Penguin, London.

Capul, M. & Lemay, M. (1993) *De l'Education Spécialisé.* Edition Erés, Ramonville Saint-Agne.

Castells, M. (1977) *The Urban Question.* Edward Arnold, London.

Castles, F. (ed.) (1993) *Families of Nations.* Dartmouth, Aldershot.

Cesarani, D. & Fulbrook, M. (eds) (1996) *Citizenship, Nationality and Migration in Europe.* Routledge, London.

Chamberlayne, P., Bornat, J. & Wengraf, T. (eds) (2000) *The Turn to Biographical Methods in Social Science.* Routledge, London.

Child Psychotherapy Trust (1999) *Promoting Infant Mental Health: a framework for developing policies and services to ensure the healthy development of young children.* CPT, London.

Clasen, J. (ed.) (1999) *Comparative Social Policy. Concepts, Theories and Methods.* Blackwell, Oxford.

Cleaver, H., Wattam, C., Cawson, P. & Gordon, R. (1998) *Assessing Risk in Child Protection.* NSPCC, London.

Cleaver, H., Unell, I. & Aldgate, J. (1999) *Children's Needs – Parenting Capacity. The Impact of Parental Mental Illness, Problem Alcohol and Drug Abuse, and Domestic Violence on Children's Development.* The Stationery Office, London.

Colton, M.J. & Hellinckx (eds) (1993) *Child Care in the EC. A Country-specific Guide to Foster and Residential Care.* Arena, Aldershot.

Connor, A. (1999) Community based mental health services. In Ulas, M. & Connor, A. (eds) *Mental Health and Social Work.* Jessica Kingsley, London.

Cooper, A. (2000) The vanishing point of resemblance: comparative welfare as philosophical anthropology. In Chamberlayne, P., Bornat, J. & Wengraf, T. (eds) *The Turn to Biographical Methods in Social Science.* Routledge, London.

Cooper, A., Freund, V., Grevot, A., Hetherington, R, & Pitts, J. (1992) *The Social Work Role in Child Protection: an Anglo-French Comparison.* Centre for Comparative Social Work Studies, Brunel University, London.

Cooper, A., Hetherington, R., Baistow, K., Pitts, J. and Spriggs, A. (1995) *Positive Child Protection: A View from Abroad.* Russell House Publishing, Lyme Regis.

Cowling, V. (1999a) Finding answers, making changes: research and community project approaches. In Cowling, V. (ed.) *Children of Parents with Mental Illness*. The Australian Council for Educational Research Ltd, Melbourne.

Cowling, V. (ed.) (1999b) *Children of Parents with Mental Illness*. The Australian Council for Educational Research Ltd, Melbourne.

Dale, P., Davies, M., Morrison, T. & Waters, J. (1986) *Dangerous Families: Assessment and Treatment of Child Abuse*. Tavistock, London.

Dean, C. & Freeman, H. (eds) (1993) *Community Mental Health Care. International Perspectives on Making it Happen*. Gaskell, London.

Dearden, C. & Becker, S. (1998) *Young Carers in the UK*. Carers National Association, London.

Dearden, C. & Becker, S. (2000) *Growing up Caring: Vulnerability and transition to adulthood – young carers experiences*. The National Youth Agency, Leicester.

Department of Health (1995*) Messages from Research*. Stationery Office, London.

Department of Health (2000a*) Framework of Assessment of Children in Need and their Families*. Stationery Office, London.

Department of Health (2000b) *Working Together To Safeguard Children*. Stationery Office, London.

Department of Health (2001) *Reforming the Mental Health Act*. Stationery Office, London.

Diggins, M. (1999) Crossing over between services: the Lewisham experience. In Weir, A. & Douglas, A. (eds) *Child Protection and Adult Mental Health. Conflict of Interest?* Butterworth-Heinemann, Oxford.

Dingwall, R., Eekelaar, J. & Murray, T. (1995) (2nd edn) *The Protection of Children: State intervention and family life*. Avebury, Aldershot.

Donnelly, M. (1992) *The Politics of Mental Health in Italy*. Routledge, London.

Donzelot, J. (1980) *The Policing of Families*. Hutchinson, London.

Douglas, A. (1999) Building bridges: lessons for the future. In Weir, A. & Douglas, A. (eds) *Child Protection and Adult Mental Health. Conflict of Interest?* Butterworth-Heinemann, Oxford.

Duncan, S. (1991) *Self-Help Housing In European Perspective: Capital Accumulation And Social Context*. Centre for Urban and Regional Research, University of Sussex.

Duncan, S. & Reder, P. (2000) Children's experience of major psychiatric disorder in their parent: an overview. In Reder, P., McClure, M. & Jolley, A. (eds) *Family Matters: Interfaces between Child and Adult Mental Health*. Routledge, London.

Esping-Andersen, G. (1990) *The Three Worlds of Welfare Capitalism*. Polity Press, London.

Esping-Andersen, G. (1999) *Social Foundations of Postindustrial Economies*. Oxford University Press, Oxford.

Etchegoyen, A. (2000) Perinatal mental health: psychodynamic and psychiatric perspectives. In Reder, P., McClure, M. & Jolley, A. (eds) *Family Matters: Interfaces between Child and Adult Mental Health*. Routledge, London.

Exworthy, M. & Halford, S. (eds) (1999) *Professionals and the New Managerialism in the Public Sector.* Open University Press, Buckingham.

Falkov, A. (1996) *A Study of Working Together 'Part 8' Reports: Fatal Child Abuse and Parental Psychiatric Disorder.* Department of Health, London.

Falkov, A. (ed.) (1998) *Crossing Bridges. Training resources for working with mentally ill parents and their children. A Reader for managers, practitioners and trainers.* Department of Health and Pavilion Publishing, Brighton.

Farmer, E. & Owen, M. (1995) *Child Protection Practice: Private Risks and Public Remedies.* HMSO, London.

Foucault, M. (1967) *Madness and Civilization. A History of Insanity in the Age of Reason.* Tavistock Publications, London.

Fox Harding, L. (1996) *Family, State and Social Policy.* Macmillan, London.

Frank, J. (1994) *Couldn't Care More. A Study of Young Carers and their Needs.* Children's Society, London.

Frost, N., Johnson, L., Stein, M. & Wallis, L. (1996) *Negotiated Friendship – Home-Start and the Delivery of Family Support.* Home-Start, Leicester.

Gelder, M.G., Lopez-Ibor Jr. J.J. & Andreasen, N.C. (eds) (2000) *The New Oxford Textbook of Psychiatry.* Oxford University Press, Oxford.

Gilbert, N. (ed.) (1997) *Combatting Child Abuse: International Perspectives and Trends.* Oxford University Press, Oxford.

Goodwin, S. (1997) *Comparative Mental Health Policy: From Institutional To Community Care.* Sage, London.

Göpfert, M., Webster, J. & Seeman, M.V. (eds) (1996) *Parental Psychiatric Disorder: Distressed Parents and their Families.* Cambridge University Press, Cambridge.

Göpfert, M. & Mahoney, C. (2000) Participative research with users of mental health services who are parents. *Clinical Psychology Forum* **140** (June 2000).

Gough, I. (1979) *The Political Economy of the Welfare State.* Macmillan, London.

Green, R., Hyde, E., Katz, I., Mesie, J., Vincenti, O. & Worthing, D. (1997) *Long Term Problems … Short Term Solutions – Parents in Contact with Mental Health Services.* NSPCC, London.

Hacking, I. (1999) *The Social Construction of What?* Harvard University Press, Cambridge, Mass.

Hantrais, L. (1999) Comparing family policies in Europe. In Clasen, J. (ed.) *Comparative Social Policy. Concepts, Theories and Methods.* Blackwell, Oxford.

Hantrais, L. & Letablier, M.T. (1996) *Families and Family Policies in Europe.* Addison Wesley Longman, Harlow.

Hantrais, L. & Mangen, S. (eds) (1996) *Cross-national Research Methods in the Social Sciences.* Sage, London.

Henry, L.A. & Kumar, R.C. (1999) Risk assessments of infants born to parents with a mental health or a learning disability. In Weir, A. & Douglas, A. (eds) *Child Protection and Adult Mental Health. Conflict of Interest?* Butterworth-Heinemann, Oxford.

Herzog, T., Creed, F., Huyse, F.J., Malt, U.F., Lobo, A., Stein, B. & the European Consultation-Liaison Workgroup (1994) 'Psychosomatic medicine' in the general hospital. In Sensky, T., Katona, C. & Montgomery, S. (eds) *Psychiatry in Europe.* Gaskell, London.

Hessle, S. & Vinnerljung, B. (1999) *Child Welfare in Sweden – An Overview.* Stockholm University Department of Social Work, Stockholm.

Hetherington, R. (1996) The educational opportunities of cross-national comparison. *Social Work in Europe* **3** (1): 26–30.

Hetherington, R. (1998) Issues in European Child Protection Research. *European Journal of Social Work* **1** (1): 71–82.

Hetherington, R., Baistow, K., Johanson, J. & Mesie, J. (2000) *Professional Interventions for Mentally Ill Parents and their Children: Building a European Model. Final Report on the Icarus Project.* Centre for Comparative Social Work Studies, Brunel University, London.

Hetherington, R., Cooper, A. & Grevot, A. (1993) *The French System of Child Protection.* Centre for Comparative Social Work Studies, Brunel University, London.

Hetherington, R., Cooper, A., Smith, P. & Wilford, G. (1997) *Protecting Children: Messages from Europe.* Russell House Publishing, Lyme Regis.

Hetherington, R. & Smith, P. (1995) La Protezione del Bambino in Italia e in Inghilterra. *La Professione Sociale* **9**: 63–83.

Howe, G. (1998) *Getting into the System. Living with Serious Mental Illness.* Jessica Kingsley, London.

Ingerslev, H. (1999) Aspects of decision-making systems concerning compulsory child protection measures in the Netherlands, Denmark and Norway. *Social Work in Europe.* **6** (1): 30–40.

Jones, C. (1985) *Patterns of Social Policy: an Introduction to Comparative Analysis.* Tavistock, London.

Jones, K. (1972) *A History of the Mental Health Services.* Routledge and Kegan Paul, London.

Jones, K. (1988) *Experiences in Mental Health: Community Care and Social Policy.* Sage, London.

Jowell, R. (ed.) (1998) *British and European Social Attitudes: How Britain Differs.* Ashgate, Aldershot.

Katz, I. (1996) The sociology of children from minority ethnic communities – issues and methods. In Butler, I. & Shaw, I. (eds) *A Case of Neglect? Children's Experience and the Sociology of Childhood.* Avebury, London.

Katz, I. (1997) *Current Issues in Comprehensive Assessment.* NSPCC, London.

Katz, I. (1998) Is male circumcision morally defensible? In King, M. (ed.) *Moral Agendas for Children's Welfare.* Routledge, London.

Kearney, P., Levin, E. & Rosen, G. (2000) *Working with Families: Alcohol, Drug and Mental Health Problems.* NISW, London.

King, M. (ed.) (1998) *Moral Agendas for Children's Welfare.* Routledge, London.

Laot, F. (2000) Doctoral work in the social work field in Europe. *Social Work in Europe* **7** (2): 2–7.

Lier, L. (1997) The Copenhagen model of early preventive intervention aimed at high risk families. *Social Work in Europe* **4** (2): 15–18.

Lier, L., Gammeltoft, M. & Knudsen, I.J. (1995) Early mother–child relationship. The Copenhagen model of early preventive intervention towards mother–infant relationship disturbances. *Arctic Medical Research* **54**: (suppl.1): 15–23.

Lindsay, M., Potter, R.G. & Shepperd, A. (1999) Managing strategies for change in childcare and mental health services in Bath and North East Somerset. In Weir, A. & Douglas, A. (eds) *Child Protection and Adult Mental Health. Conflict of Interest?* Butterworth-Heinemann, Oxford.

Lobmayer, P. & Wilkinson, R. (2000) Income, inequality and mortality in 14 developed countries. *Sociology of Health and Illness* **22** (4): 410–414.

Mabbett, D. & Bolderson, H. (1999) Theories and methods in comparative social policy. In Clasen, J. (ed.) *Comparative Social Policy. Concepts, Theories and Methods.* Blackwell, Oxford.

MacIntyre, D. & Carr, A. (2000) Prevention of child sexual abuse: implications of programme evaluation research. *Child Abuse and Neglect* **9** (3): 183–199.

MacMillan, H., MacMillan, J., Offord, D.R., Griffith, L. & MacMillan, A. (1994) Primary prevention of child sexual abuse: a critical review. Part II. *Journal of Child Psychology and Psychiatry* **35** (5): 857–876.

Madge, N. (1994) *Children and Residential Care in Europe.* National Children's Bureau, London.

Makins, V. (1997) *The Invisible Children: Nipping Failure in the Bud.* The National Pyramid Trust, London.

Martiniello, M. (ed.) (1995) *Migration, Citizenship and Ethno-National Identities in the European Union.* Avebury, Aldershot.

Mayes, K., Diggins, M. & Falkov, A. (1998) *Crossing Bridges. Training Resources for Working with Mentally Ill Parents and their Children: Trainer.* Department of Health and Pavilion Press, Brighton.

Mendelson, E. (ed.) (1976) *W.H. Auden: Collected Poems.* Faber and Faber, London.

Meltzer, H., Gill, B., Pettigrew, M. & Hinds, K. (1995) *The Prevalence of Psychiatric Morbidity among Adults in Private Households.* HMSO, London.

Micklewright, J. & Stewart, K. (2000) *Is Child Welfare Converging in the European Union.* Innocenti Occasional Papers, No ESP 69: Unicef. International Child Development Centre, Florence.

Millar, J. & Warman, A. (1996) *Family Obligations in Europe.* Family Policy Studies Centre, London.

Ministry of Health (1962) *Hospital Plan for England and Wales. Cmnd. 1604.* HMSO, London.

Ministry of Health (1963) *Health and Welfare: the Development of Community Care. Cmnd. 1973.* HMSO, London.

Monkhouse, A. & Hetherington, R. (1997) Assessment and Allocation in England and France: who decides? *Social Work in Europe* **4** (1): 46–49.

Money-Kyrle, R. (1968) *Cognitive Development.* Institute of Psychoanalysis, Vol. 49. In Mettzer, D. (ed.) (1978) *Collected Papers of Roger Money-Kyrle.*

Munday, B. (ed.) (1994) *European Social Services.* European Institute of Social Services, University of Kent.

National Association for the Care and Rehabilitation of Offenders (NACRO) Mental Health Advisory Committee (1998) *Risks and Rights: Mentally Disturbed Offenders and Public Protection.* NACRO, London.

NAMH (1966) *Proceedings of the Twenty-second Child Guidance Inter-Clinic Conference, 1966.* National Association for Mental Health, London.

O'Hagan, K. (1993) *Emotional and Psychological Abuse of Children*. Open University Press, Buckingham.

Offe, C. (1996) *Modernity and the State*. Polity, Cambridge.

Office of Population and Censuses and Surveys (1996) *The Prevalence of Psychiatric Morbidity among Adults Living in Private Households*. HMSO, London.

Olsson Hort, S.E. (1997) Sweden: towards a deresidualisation of Swedish Child Welfare Policy and Practice? In Gilbert, N. (ed.) *Combatting Child Abuse: International Perspectives and Trends*. Oxford University Press, Oxford.

Øyen, E. (1990) Comparative research as a sociological strategy. In Øyen, E. (ed.) *Comparative Methodology, Theory and Practice in International Social Research*. Sage, London.

Øyen, E. (ed.) (1990) *Comparative Methodology, Theory and Practice in International Social Research*. Sage, London.

Packman, J., Randall, J. & Jaques, N. (1986) *Who Needs Care? Social Work Decisions about Children*. Blackwell, Oxford.

Parton, N. (1985) *The Politics of Child Abuse*. Macmillan, Basingstoke.

Parton, N. (1997) Child protection and family support: current debates and future prospects. In Parton, N. (ed.) *Child Protection and Family Support. Tensions, Contradictions and Possibilities*. Routledge, London.

Parton, N. (ed.) (1997) *Child Protection and Family Support. Tensions, Contradictions and Possibilities*. Routledge, London.

Parton, N. (1998) Risk, advanced liberalism and child welfare: the need to rediscover uncertainty, and ambiguity. *British Journal of Social Work* **28**: 5–27.

Parton, N., Thorpe, D. & Wattam, C. (1997) *Child Protection: Risk and the Moral Order*. Macmillan, London.

Perkins, R., Nadirshaw, Z., Copperman, J. & Andrews, C. (eds) (1996) *Women in Context: Good Practice in Mental Health Services for Women*. Mind, London.

Perkins, R. & Repper, J. (1998) *Dilemmas in Community Mental Health Practice. Choice or Control*. Radcliffe Medical Press, Abingdon.

Pino, P., Parrinir, A. & Savellini, S.G. (1993) Self determination for users in power relationships. In Dean, C. and Freeman, H. (eds) *Community Mental Health Care. International Perspectives on Making it Happen*. Gaskell, London.

Poole, R. (1996) General adult psychiatrists and their patients' children. In Göpfert, M., Webster, J. & Seeman, M.V. (eds) *Parental Psychiatric Disorder: Distressed Parents and their Families*. Cambridge University Press, Cambridge.

Pringle, K. (1998) *Children and Social Welfare in Europe*. Open University Press, Buckingham.

Ramon, S. (1996) *Mental Health in Europe*. Macmillan/Mind, Basingstoke.

Ramsay, R., Howard, M. & Kumar, C. (1998) Schizophrenia and the safety of infants: a report on a UK mother and baby service. *International Journal of Social Psychiatry* **44** (2): 127–134.

Reder, P., Duncan, S. & Gray, M. (1993) *Beyond Blame: Child Abuse Tragedies Revisited*. Routledge, London.

Reder, P. & Duncan, S. (1999) *Lost Innocence. A Follow-up Study of Fatal Child Abuse*. Routledge, London.

Reder, P., McClure, M. & Jolley, A. (eds) (2000) *Family Matters: Interfaces between Child and Adult Mental Health*. Routledge, London.

Reith, M. (1998) *Community Care Tragedies: a Practice Guide to Mental Health Inquiries*. Venture Press, Birmingham.

Renucci, J.-F. (1990) *Enfance délinquante et enfance en danger*. Editions du Centre National de la Recherche Scientifique, Paris.

Rimington, H., Forer, D., Walsh, B. & Sawyer, S. (1999) Paying attention to self: a peer support program for young people with parental mental health issues. In Cowling, V. (ed.) *Children of Parents with Mental Illness*. The Australian Council for Educational Research Ltd, Melbourne.

Rutter, M. & Quinton, D. (1984) Parental psychiatric disorder: effects on children. *Psychological Medicine* **14**: 853–880.

Ruxton, S. (1996) *Children in Europe*. NCH Action for Children, London.

Sainsbury, D. (1996) *Gender, Equality and Welfare States*. Cambridge University Press, Cambridge.

Savio, M. (1996) Community care and inter-professional relationships: Community psychiatric nursing in Britain and Italy. *Social Work in Europe* **3** (3): 1–11.

Sayce, L. (1996) Women with children. In Perkins, R., Nadirshaw, Z., Copperman, J. & Andrews, C. (eds) *Women in Context: Good Practice in Mental Health Services for Women*. Mind, London.

Sayce, L. (2000) *From Psychiatric Patient to Citizen. Overcoming Discrimination and Social Exclusion*. Macmillan, Basingstoke.

Schäfer, H. (1995) Legal notebook: the principle of subsidiarity. *Social Work in Europe*. **2** (3): 52–53.

Schwabe, M. (1999) The potential and limitations of the German 'Care Plan Discussion' in the helping process. *Social Work in Europe* **6** (2): 63–72.

Segal, S.P. (1989) Civil commitment standards and patient mix in England and Wales, Italy and the United States. *American Journal of Psychiatry* **146**: 327–344.

Sensky, T., Katona, C. & Montgomery, S. (eds) (1994) *Psychiatry in Europe*. Gaskell, London.

Sheehan, R., Pead-Erbrederis, C. & McLoughlin, A. (2000) *The Icarus Project*. Department of Social Work, Monash University, Victoria, Australia.

Sheppard, M. (1994) Maternal depression, child care and the social work role. *British Journal of Social Work* **24**: 33–51.

Sieff Foundation (1997) *Keeping Children in Mind. Balancing Children's Needs with Parents' Mental Health*. Michael Sieff Foundation, London.

Silverman, M. (1996) The revenge of civil society: state, nation and society in France. In Cesarani, D. & Fulbrook, M. (eds) *Citizenship, Nationality and Migration in Europe*. Routledge, London.

Skerfving, A. (1999) The Children's Project in Western Stockholm. *Social Work in Europe* **6** (1): 22–25.

Smith, P. (1995) Subsidiarity and the role of the social worker in Germany and England. *Social Work in Europe* **2** (3): 54–57.

Soydan, H. (1996) Using the vignette method in cross-cultural comparisons. In Hantrais, L. & Mangen, S. (eds) *Cross-national Research Methods in the Social Sciences*. Sage, London.

Soydan, H. & Stål, R. (1994) How to use the vignette technique in cross-cultural research. *Scandinavian Journal of Social Welfare* **3**: 75–80.

Stanley, N. & Penhale, B. (1999) The mental health problems of mothers experiencing the Child Protection System. Identifying needs and appropriate responses. *Child Abuse Review* **8**: 34–45.

Stroud, J. (1997) Mental disorder and the homicide of children: a review. *Social Work & Social Sciences Review* **6** (3): 149–162.

Stroud, J. (2000) European child homicide studies: quantitative studies and a preliminary report on complementary qualitative research approach. *Social Work in Europe* **7** (3): 31–37.

Stroud, J. & Pritchett, C. (2001) Child homicide, psychiatric disorder and dangerousness: a review and an empirical approach. *British Journal of Social Work* **31**: 249–269.

Taylor, P.J. & Gunn, J. (1999) Homicides by people with mental illness: myth and reality. *British Journal of Psychiatry* **174**: 9–14.

Taylor-Gooby, P. (1998) Commitment to the welfare state. In Jowell, R. (ed.) *British and European Social Attitudes: How Britain Differs*. Ashgate, Aldershot.

Therborn, G. (1993) The politics of childhood. The rights of children in modern times. In Castles, F. (ed.) *Families of Nations*. Dartmouth, Aldershot.

Thévenet, A. (1990) *L'Aide Sociale Aujourd'hui: après la décentralisation*. ESF éditeur, Paris.

Thoburn, J., Lewis, A. & Shemmings, D. (1995) *Paternalism or Partnership? Family Involvement in the Child Protection Process*. HMSO, London.

Tizard, J. (1966) Chairman's Address. In *Proceedings of the Twenty-second Child Guidance Inter-Clinic Conference, 1966*. National Association for Mental Health, London.

Trent, D. & Reed, C. (1994) *Promotion of Mental Health, Vol. 4*. Avebury, Aylesbury.

Trent, D. & Reed, C. (1995) *Promotion of Mental Health, Vol. 5*, Avebury, Aylesbury.

Tye, C. & Precey, G. (1999) Building bridges: the interface between adult mental health and child protection. *Child Abuse Review* **8**: 164–171.

Ulas, M. & Connor, A. (eds) (1999) *Mental Health and Social Work*. Jessica Kingsley, London.

Van Doorm, J. (1994) Mental health prevention in the Netherlands. In Trent, D. & Reed, C., *Promotion of Mental Health, Vol. 4*. Avebury, Aylesbury.

Van Mierlo, F. (1994) Implementing the prevention development projects. In Trent, D. & Reed, C., *Promotion of Mental Health, Vol. 4*. Avebury, Aylesbury.

Van Mierlo, F. (1995) Diffusion of the results of three prevention development projects. In Trent, D. & Reed, C., *Promotion of Mental Health, Vol. 5*, Avebury, Aylesbury.

Van Os, J., Galdos, P., Lewis, G., Bourgeois, M. & Mann, A. (1994) Schisms in European psychiatry. In Sensky, T., Katona, C. & Montgomery, S. (eds) *Psychiatry in Europe*. Gaskell, London.

Warde, A. (1987) *Industrial Restructuring, Local Politics and the Reproduction of Labour Power*. Lancaster Regionalism Group.

Wattam, C. & Woodward, C. (1996) 'And do I abuse my Children? ... No!' In *Childhood Matters: Report of the National Commission of Enquiry into the Prevention of Child Abuse, Vol. 2: Background Papers*: 43–148. HMSO, London.

Weightman, K. & Weightman, A. (1995) 'Never right, never wrong': child welfare and social work in England and Sweden. *Scandinavian Journal of Social Welfare* **4** (2): 75–84.

Weir, A. & Douglas, A. (eds) (1999) *Child Protection and Adult Mental Health. Conflict of Interest?* Butterworth-Heinemann, Oxford.

Whitney, L., Ruiz, P. & Langenbach, M. (1994) Detaining psychiatric patients. In Sensky, T., Katona, C. & Montgomery, S. (eds) *Psychiatry in Europe.* Gaskell, London.

Wilford, G. (1997) *Families Ask for Help: An Anglo-German Study of Parental Perceptions of Child Welfare and Child Protection Services.* Centre for Comparative Social Work Studies, Brunel University, London.

Willey, D. (2000) *Italians Demand Sex Crimes Crackdown.* BBC, London. (http://news.bbc.co.uk/hi/english/world/europe/newsid_891000/891411.stm)

Yin, R. (1994) *Case Study Research, Design and Methods.* Sage, London.

INDEX